# Monumental

Sara and John Lindsey Series in the Arts and Humanities

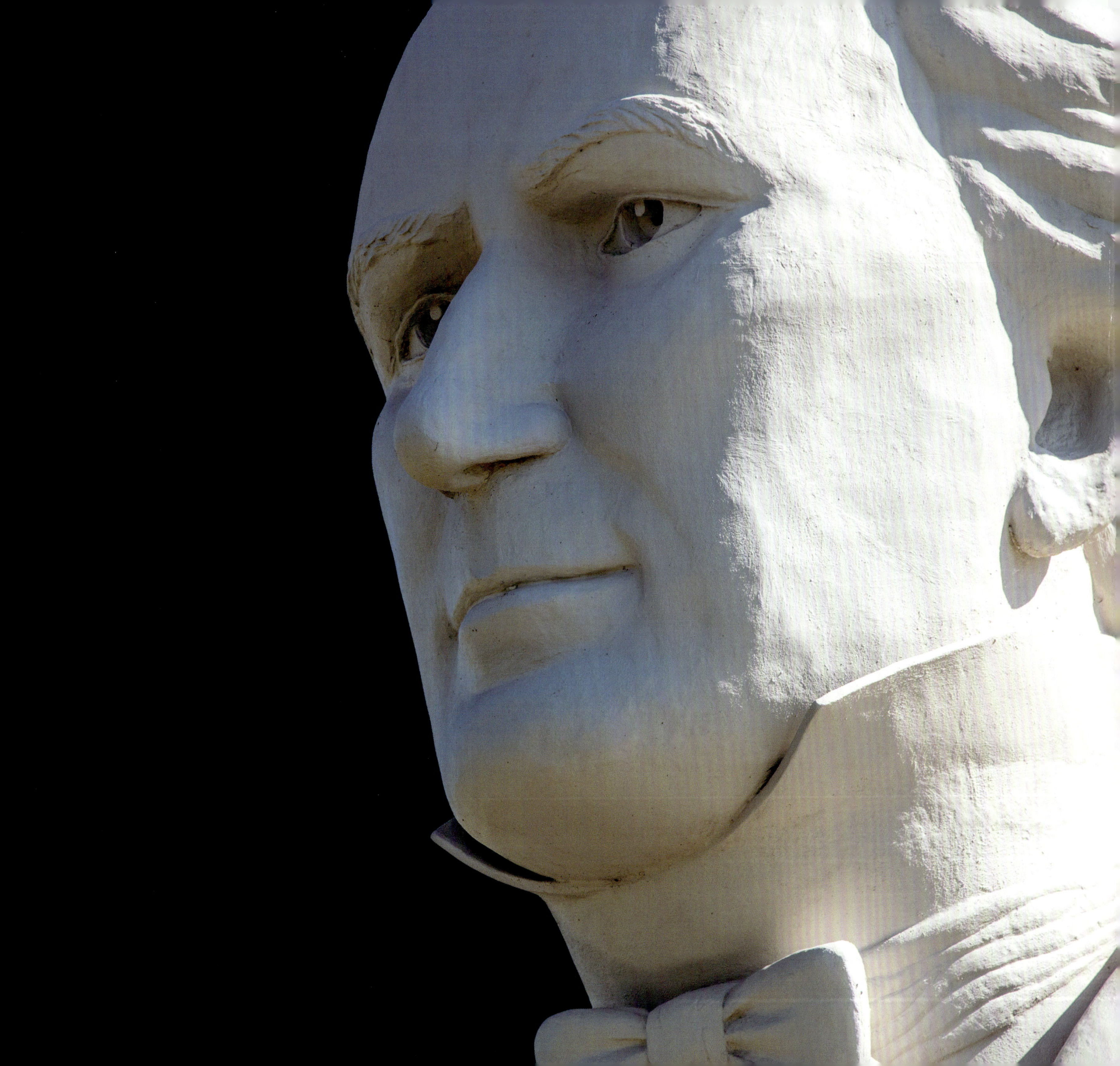

# Monumental

## The Art of David Adickes

Michael H. Henderson and Melissa L. Mednicov

*With a Photographic Essay by Rebecca Finley*

*Foreword by Ronald E. Shields*

TEXAS A&M UNIVERSITY PRESS    COLLEGE STATION

First edition

♾ This paper meets the requirements of ANSI/NISO Z39.48–1992 (Permanence of Paper).
Binding materials have been chosen for durability.
Manufactured in China through Martin Book Management

Library of Congress Control Number: 2024943730
Identifiers: LCCN: 2024943730 | ISBN 9781648432309 (cloth) |
ISBN 9781648432316 (ebook)
LC record available at https://lccn.loc.gov/2024943730

*Book Design by Kristie Lee*

# Contents

# Foreword

## A Welcoming David Adickes

Ronald E. Shields

Driving north on I-45 in the dark following a heavy storm, it is surprising to see the suburban sprawl and traffic drop away on both sides of the interstate ahead.

*Did we just see a moving neon cowboy waving, "Howdy?"*

*What could he be selling*?

A glance in the rearview mirror confirms the bright signage, but not the name of the store.

We turn our attention to the road ahead: a path forward into a new land and a new life, a journey toward a position at Sam Houston State University (SHSU), a university named to honor the first president of the Republic of Texas. Rain delays at the airport gave way to foggy driving conditions as we travel north. Leaving the outskirts of Houston, we trek through the Sam Houston National Forest on our way to Huntsville, located 75 miles away. The forest running north through southeast Texas has been known for generations as the Piney Woods. However, to honor Texas history, the forest around Huntsville and adjacent counties was designated the Sam Houston National Forest in 1936. Texans name things after Texas heroes.

We are alone for now, driving north into darkness pierced only by our headlights. Occasionally another pair greets us, moves quickly past, and continues south on the other side of the interstate. Opening the back windows, the car fills with the pungent aroma of freshly washed pine as we make our way through the shifting pollen-laden trees.

Following Google's directions that first night, we knew we were nearing our destination, our exit into Huntsville. Six miles ahead of us, a white object stands against the dark. Driving toward the object, it appears to move, following the interstate's contours through the rolling hills. Approaching, nearing, we pass the statue at 70 miles per hour. What looms strange from afar flashes by stranger still.

*What was that*?

Little did we know that we were passing the 67-foot-tall statue of Sam Houston called *A Tribute to Courage*, created by Huntsville native son, David Adickes. Rigid, formally dressed, sporting a walking stick and standing more than slightly ajar to my eye, we glimpse David Adickes's Sam Houston stepping out of the forest to greet us. We didn't realize it at the time, but earlier that night, we must have hurried past David Adickes's bronze statue of George H. W. Bush (called *Winds of Change*) located in Terminal C on our way to find the rental car. So, I guess you could say David Adickes's historical figures welcomed us to his Texas, twice in one night.

*A Tribute to Courage* resonates within the historical context of its physical placement on the edge of the Piney Woods. The Sam Houston National Forest is geographically as expansive as the career of Sam Houston, who served under General Andrew Jackson in the War of 1812, won election to the House of Representatives in 1823, and was elected governor of Tennessee in 1827. Although born in Virginia, Sam Houston advanced Texas independence from Mexico through his military leadership at the Battle of San Jacinto, an event leading to his election in 1836 as president of the newly established Republic of Texas. After serving a second term, he played a key role in the annexation of Texas by the United States in 1845. The following year he was elected to represent Texas in the US Senate. Leaving Washington, DC, in 1859, he returned to serve as the seventh governor of Texas, only to be forced out of office in 1861. He moved to Huntsville, built his steamboat house, and spent his days during the Civil War as the town's leading citizen. Sam Houston died in Huntsville in 1863 at seventy years of age and is buried in Oakwood Cemetery.

David Adickes created his *A Tribute to Courage* to commemorate Sam Houston's two hundredth birthday celebration on March 2, 1993. However, due to delays, the formal dedication of the monumental statue was moved to October 22, 1994. "Big Sam," as it is also known, was placed on a granite base purchased with funds provided through the sale of brick pavers, a civic-minded effort guided by the members of the Huntsville-Walker County Chamber of Commerce. The small park and visitor's center were soon added near the statue using local hotel occupancy tax revenue. A smaller version of "Big Sam" was later commissioned and placed on the Sam Houston State University campus near the university library. Quickly the statue took on a life of its own: *A Tribute to Courage* now serves as a visual shorthand for both town and gown, appearing on promotional materials for Huntsville and the university that bears the name of this Texas political hero. Sam Houston's historical legacy, and the statue that bears his likeness, continue to circulate in the popular imagination locally and beyond. David Adickes put these Texas memories and musings, literally and figuratively, on the map for many in the Piney Woods and beyond, particularly those eager to advance a useful and compelling civic image.

David Adickes, born in Huntsville in 1927, attended high school in a building only blocks from Sam Houston's tomb in the Oakwood Cemetery. He later graduated from Sam Houston Teachers College (now known as Sam Houston State University). During the final years of World War II, he traveled to study art and expand his artistic sensibilities, only to return to southeast Texas, specifically to the city of Houston and his birthplace, Huntsville.

I have had several opportunities to meet David Adickes in recent years. Through these interactions I've gained some personal insights into his body of work and his connections to Huntsville. I've also engaged with him to complete the acquisition of several of his early paintings for inclusion into the university's collection of Texas art. He was instrumental in helping secure studio space in town for our graduate students in art as social practice. Specifically, I refer to his willingness to allow the university to purchase the David Adickes's Art Foundation Museum Building, what was originally the historical high school building, located in the heart of Huntsville at 710 University Avenue. In 2009 he acquired his high school alma mater, an 80,000-square-foot structure, to rescue the deteriorating historical building from demolition and to display his personal work. An eager supporter of our academic plan to connect meaningfully with the local schools and communities, Adickes agreed to sell the building for university use. After significant renovations in 2020 and 2021, it now houses the SHSU natural history collections and provides space for programming in art education and art as social practice, including artist studios.

At the formal dedication of the SHSU Natural Science and Art Research Center on November 16, 2019, Adickes spoke of his family connections to the city, his years as a high school student, and his lifelong support of the regional art scene. After the ceremony, I invited the artist to meet me in my office to review plans for the use of the building going forward. I welcomed the opportunity to hear him talk more about his family connections to Huntsville, his current projects (he has several), future projects (he has several more), and his thoughts about

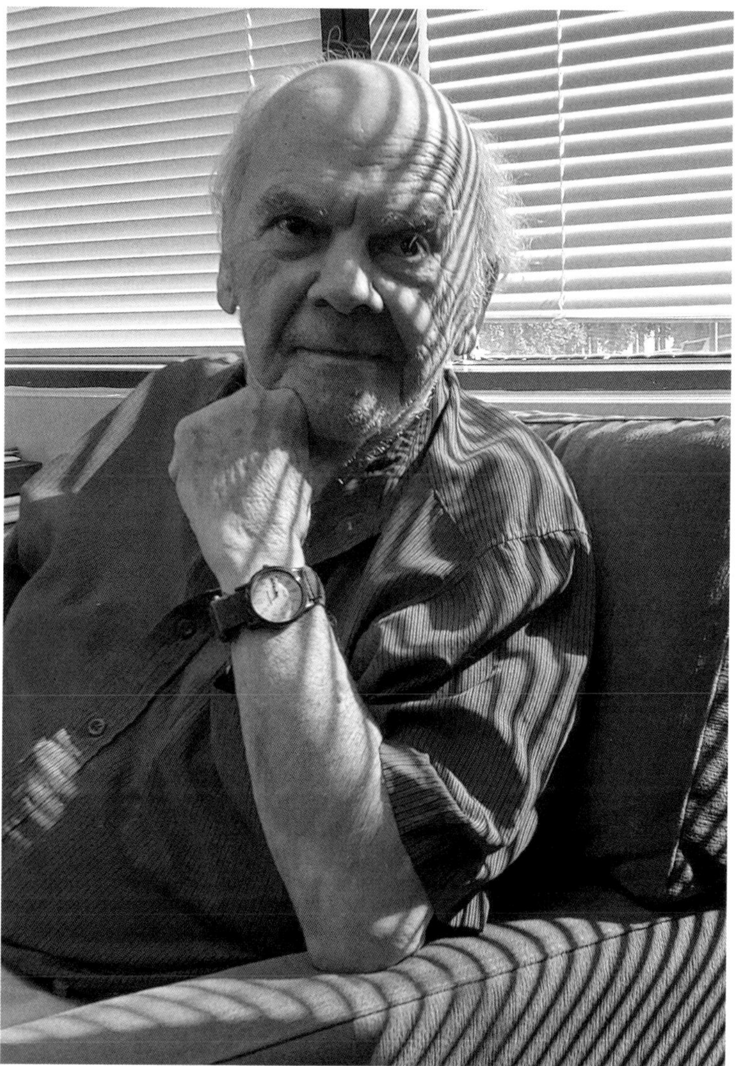

**Figure 0.1.** David Adickes. Credit: Ronald E. Shields.

the current regional art scene. At the end of our visit, I asked for a photo. He immediately shifted his chair, talked about how the light should fall across his face, and only half-jokingly suggested that, if I get it right, it should look cubist.

This volume, written and edited by Michael H. Henderson and Melissa L. Mednicov, with photographs by Rebecca Finley, extends that conversation. This volume is the first scholarly overview of David Adickes's work within the midcentury Houston art scene beginning with his earliest paintings and drawings and extending to his large-scale sculpture works created in more recent decades, such as *Virtuoso* (1983), *A Tribute to Courage* (1994), and his monumental series of "presidential heads" (2004). Consideration is also given to circulations and responses to his work on social media. The range of subjects within this edited volume, and the purposeful integration of images and scholarly voices, speaks to the range and reception of Adickes's work as well as to the historical moments in which they were created. To do so places his artistic practice in clearer context and helps to answer my naive response to Big Sam: *What was that*?

# Acknowledgments

## Michael H. Henderson and Melissa L. Mednicov

We would like to express our gratitude to David Adickes for his generous time, energy, enthusiasm, and support for the book. Additionally, we are grateful to Linda Wiley for her essential assistance.

We are grateful to William E. and Linda J. Reaves for their support and assistance with the project through many stages. Additionally, we are grateful to Sarah Foltz of Foltz Fine Art for her assistance and generosity with images and information. We are grateful to Kirby Mears for his generous assistance sharing stories about his father and mother. Additionally, we are thankful to Leila McConnell for sharing her recollections. We are grateful to Randy Tibbits for his support. We are also thankful for the support of Larry Martin.

We acknowledge the early transcription assistance by Yulissa Tijerina.

We would like to thank Dean Ronald E. Shields and the College of Arts & Media at Sam Houston State University for support of the project.

We are grateful to Sarah Greenmyer and the Interlibrary Loan Office staff at the Newton Gresham Library, Sam Houston State University, for their research support and assistance.

We are thankful to Thom Lemmons, anonymous peer reviewers, and the staff at the Texas A&M University Press.

We are grateful for the opportunity to collaborate with Rebecca Finley through a lively exchange of ideas, collaborative research, and her integral photographs used throughout the book.

We would both like to thank our families for their support and encouragement.

## Rebecca Finley

I would like to thank my dear friends and colleagues Michael Henderson and Dr. Melissa Mednicov for inviting me to collaborate on this project. Your support and trust in my work means everything to me. I am grateful for the support of Dean Ronald Shields and the College of Arts and Media at Sam Houston State University. Thank you to David Adickes for your time and jokes, as well as access to your life and work. I would also like to acknowledge my husband, Chad Watson, who is always in my corner and provides a sounding board for my ideas and an editorial eye for my images. Lastly, thank you to my family, Bill, Linda, Brian, Susannah, and Olivia Finley, for your patience, love, and encouragement.

# Monumental

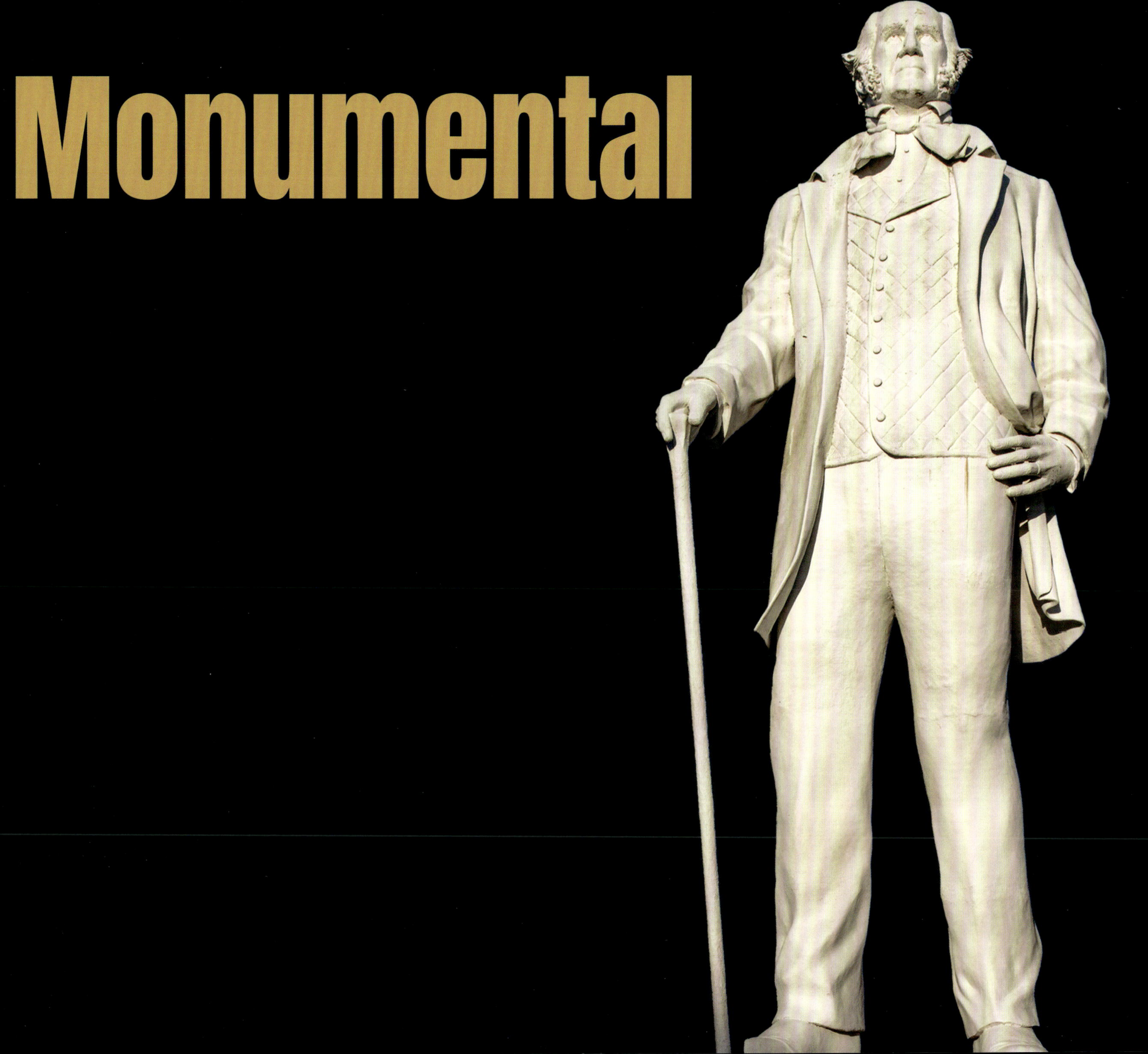

# Chapter 1

## Introduction

Michael H. Henderson and Melissa L. Mednicov

David Adickes has become well known in Texas, especially East Texas, since the monumental construction of his Sam Houston sculpture on Interstate 45 in Huntsville, Texas. The large, white concrete Sam Houston presides over the highway, a landmark for Huntsville and for those passing through to another city. At night, its illuminated presence guides and marks the highway. During daylight—and reasonable weather—the statue has many visitors eager to take family photos or selfies with the sculpture.

Like most people, the authors of this book first became acquainted with David Adickes's work through the Sam Houston sculpture that we would see on frequent commutes between Huntsville and Houston. Sam Houston State University also has a smaller version on the Huntsville campus. Adickes's sculptures and paintings proliferate in the Huntsville area, on campus, in the public library, and on street banners (for a time). In 2009, Adickes bought the old Huntsville High School building and renovated the auditorium and gymnasium as galleries. He exhibited his paintings there for about ten years before selling the building to the university. Through David Adickes's connections to the university and the city of Huntsville, we came to know the artist and the history of his work. We visited him several times at his studios in Houston in preparation for this book.

At the time of the writing of this book, David Adickes is a ninety-seven-year-old artist and has recently completed monumental sculptures of Sam Houston on horseback for a traffic circle in Baytown, Texas, and a giant five-ton bust of John F. Kennedy near the entrance to Bush Intercontinental Airport in Aldine, Texas. Adickes has been involved in the Houston art scene since its transformation from regional center to one influenced more by national and international art in the 1950s. Houston's art scene has been documented, but no other study has looked at Adickes's contribution to its expansion.

David Adickes was born with a spoonful of Texas history in his mouth. His ancestors were early settlers of Huntsville, Texas, where they lived and worked in the town that was home to Sam Houston. E. J. Adickes, David's great-grandfather, was postmaster of the town when Houston and his wife Margaret were residents. As a child, David Adickes grew up hearing stories that his great-grandfather lost his job as postmaster when he was fired by Sam Houston for refusing to deliver mail on Sunday. Houston mentions E. J. Adickes in several letters he wrote from Washington to his wife in Huntsville when he was a senator. In 1853, he writes about his dislike of postmaster Adickes and, in later letters, of the protests that occurred in Huntsville after Houston dismissed him. The letters imply that the dismissal came about because the two men were members of rival political parties.[1]

Sam Houston spent the last two years of his life in Huntsville. He was forced out of office as governor in 1861 when he refused to take an oath of loyalty to the Confederacy after Texas seceded from the Union against his wishes. Houston is buried in Oakwood cemetery in Huntsville, just a few yards away from the Adickes family plot where E. J. Adickes and several other members of the Adickes family are interred. In another part of the cemetery, not far away from these nineteenth-century gravesites, is a newer section known as the "Adickes Addition." This property was named in honor of one of David Adickes's uncles whose family donated the property to the cemetery. Before it became part of the cemetery, this property was the location of Sam Houston's last home, the "Steamboat House." Sam Houston died in the Steamboat House in 1863. In 1933, the house was purchased by a local businessman and donated to the Sam Houston Memorial Museum. It was moved to the museum grounds from its original location in the Adickes Addition in 1936 for the Texas Centennial Celebration. David Adickes was nine years old at the time, and he recalls watching the dismantled Steamboat House slowly pass by his elementary school as it was moved to Sam Houston Memorial Park.

Adickes's father was a civil engineer and a merchant who surveyed and laid out the streets of Huntsville. He later owned the music store in town, providing Adickes with access to records and record players that he took to high school so he and his classmates could learn the jitterbug. Adickes describes his mother as being the more creative one of his parents. The analytic nature of his father and the creativity of his mother were inherited in varying degrees by Adickes and his brothers. The two older brothers became pilots and engineers. David and his younger brother Fred were more creative but also had a seemingly innate aptitude for engineering. David combined his technical and creative abilities to produce monumental concrete sculptures. Fred was an inventor who worked for Mattel and designed several iconic toys in the 1970s, including Hot Wheels and Creepy Crawlers.[2]

The Huntsville High School building where Adickes graduated from in 1943 is one block away from the grave of Sam Houston. A ten-foot-tall granite monument depicting Sam Houston on horseback is located on the street side of the cemetery facing the high school. Students could see the monument through the classroom windows and would pass by it frequently. After graduating high school, Adickes went to Texas A&M to study engineering. He had been a Boy Scout and attained the rank of Eagle Scout. Adickes had a strong desire for service and desperately wanted to join the Air Force to become a pilot like his older brothers had done. In

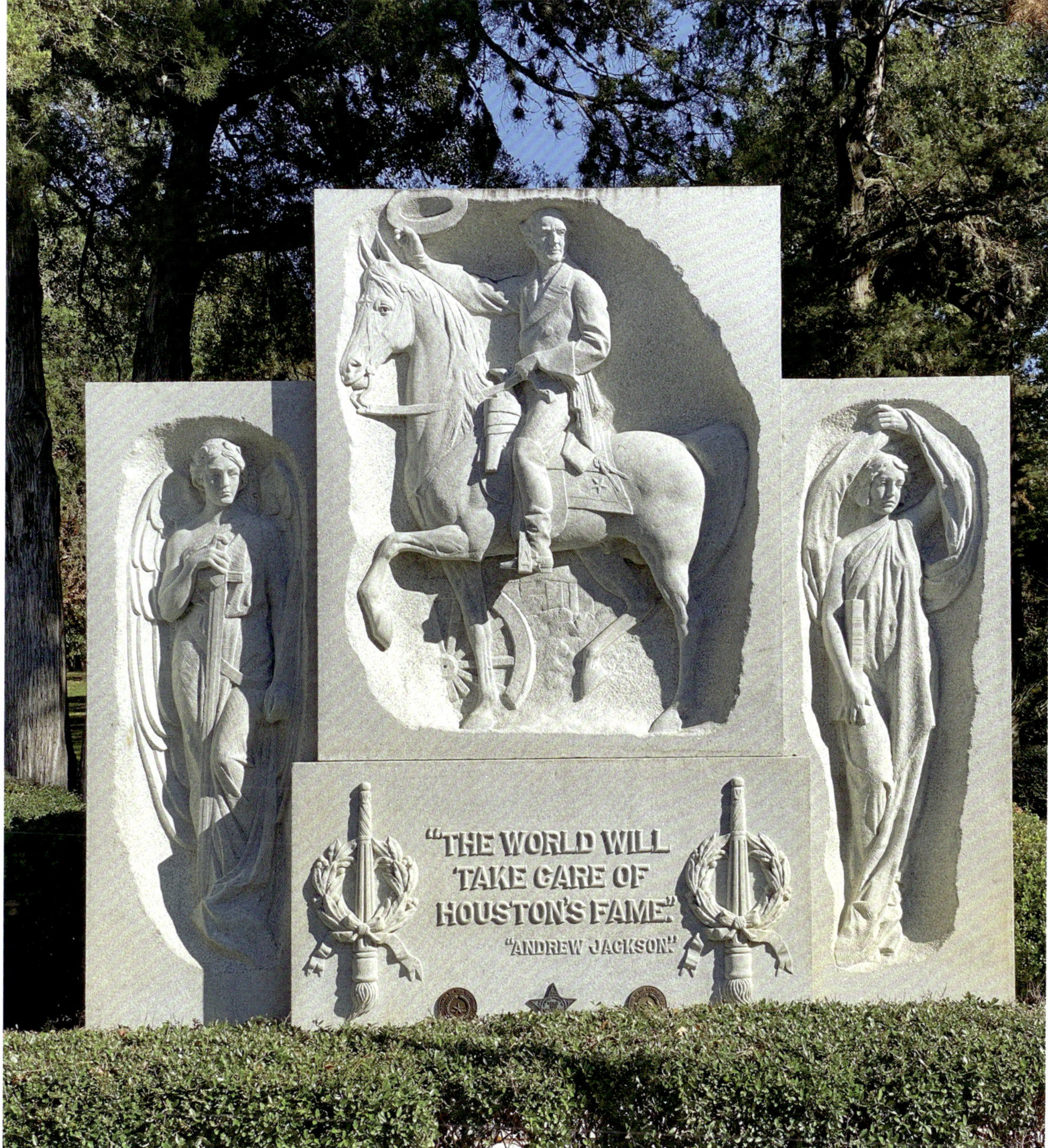


**Figure 1.1.** Pompeo Coppini, *General Sam Houston*, 1911, Oakwood Cemetery, Huntsville, Texas. Credit: Michael H. Henderson.

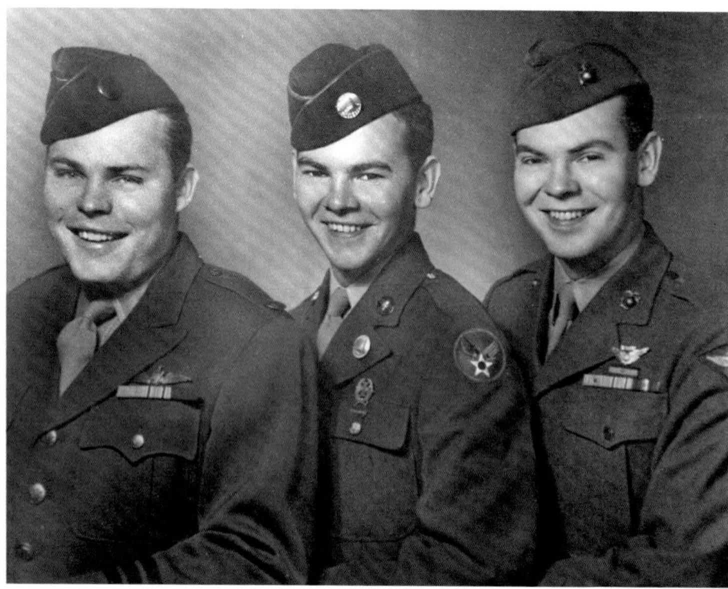

**Figure 1.2.** Three Adickes brothers in uniform. Credit: David Adickes.

1944, when he was seventeen and studying at A&M, Adickes planned to go to Houston to sign up for a pilot training program. He was slightly under the weight required to qualify for the program. To increase his weight, Adickes was encouraged to eat ten pounds of bananas, which he did the night before his appointment. The banana plan backfired and Adickes did not make it to the pilot program. Instead, he went to Louisiana State University and participated in a program to prepare him for the Army Air Corps. He wound up with a desk job in the army, and after the war ended in 1945, was given a position in Air Transport Command to transport supplies and troops between the United States and Europe.

Instead of war, Adickes witnessed the revival of Paris opening back up after German occupation. There was excitement in the air and the streets were filled with exhilarated young men and women. In one of the first demonstrations of an entrepreneurial bent, Adickes took advantage of his position and opportunities that arose traveling back and forth on the air transport. He bought cheap cigarettes in America and sold them in France where they were scarce, then used his profits to buy cheap French perfume to sell in America. He was nineteen years old with money in his pockets in Paris where he was excited and inspired by the bookstores, the art, and the vibrant street life.

After the service, Adickes returned to the United States to finish his undergraduate degree at Sam Houston State University (at that time Sam Houston State Teachers College). His brief experiences in Paris were life changing and had inspired him to become an artist. He took a few art classes at Sam Houston, but in order to get a degree as quickly as possible, he majored in physics. He graduated, and after a brief period at the Kansas City Art Institute he returned to Paris to study at the Atelier Fernand Léger on the GI Bill from 1948 to 1950. Adickes's experiences in Paris and his friendship with a fellow student, Herb Mears, had a lasting impact on the rest of his career. Adickes returned to the United States in 1950 and after brief stays in New York and Huntsville, moved to Houston. Once Adickes arrived in Houston, he quickly became part of the growing Houston art scene. The 1950s was a period of immense growth in art institutions in Houston: John and Dominique de Menil were established as patrons of the arts; the Contemporary Art Association (the organization that eventually became what is now the Contemporary Art Museum, Houston) was recently formed and organizing exhibitions; and galleries were just being established. One of the first art galleries in Houston, James Bute Gallery led by Ben DuBose (soon to then establish the DuBose Gallery), began the burgeoning gallery scene in the city. Adickes was instrumental in the formation of the DuBose Gallery. Adickes spent a brief period teaching at the University of Texas at Austin in the mid-1950s and then traveled the world before returning to Houston. While teaching at the University of Texas, he spent a summer in Tahiti, tracing the path of Gauguin. He realized he preferred traveling and art-making to teaching and decided to take two years to go around the world. He spent a year in Japan where he painted and exhibited his work, and then went to Barcelona and the south of France where he acquired a small studio. Between 1959 and 1964 Adickes spent part of each year in the south of France, returning to Houston to exhibit and live in the winter months.

David Adickes is an important figure for the development of modernism in Houston. He, along with Herb Mears, were part of what art historian Katie Robinson Edwards calls "School of Paris inheritors,"[3] bringing with them the French modernist strain to Houston. In Edwards's important book for Texas art history, *Midcentury Modern Art in Texas,* she describes Houston, in relation to another Texas modernist painter, Robert Preusser, as providing "a rapidly developing patronage system, and the state's first art museum. It is unsurprising that one of Texas's first fully abstract artists emerged from Houston."[4] Adickes is included in *Midcentury Modern Art in Texas* as part of "an abbreviated list of the modernist artists who emanated from Houston at midcentury."[5] Houston during the 1950s was the period in which aspects of what we today may recognize as the Houston art scene developed. As Edwards states, "During the 1950s, a decade in which its population doubled, Houston strove for world-class recognition in the arts."[6] As previously stated, many of the institutions that are familiar to Houstonians and visitors today were established, such as the presence of the de Menils (although the Menil Collection opens in 1987), the presence of the Museum of Fine Arts, Houston, and its support of Texas artists during this period, the Contemporary Arts Association (CCA, which later became the Contemporary Arts Museum Houston), and Houston galleries. The concept, too, of immense and quick growth in Houston is also familiar. Adickes's role in this growth and the development of modernism in Texas has been understudied. As Edwards writes:

> Adickes may be familiar to readers for his gargantuan statues of historical figures such as Sam Houston, the U.S. presidents, and the Beatles. Anecdotally and occasionally in print, his work is generally maligned by serious art critics. I am not convinced it should be written off, since his art captured something of the kitsch quality already inherent in School of Paris paintings and then amplified it in his later years, when postmodernism and irony reigned.[7]

Edwards suggests that many of the reasons that scholars and critics may have diminished Adickes's work and thus his role in Texas's art history are some of the very reasons he warrants further study.

Adickes has really had two careers in art. In his "first act," from the 1950s through the 1970s, he was known primarily for his paintings in the modern tradition of Picasso and Braque. He developed a vocabulary of images that he repeated in landscapes, still lifes, elongated portraits of women, and men representing philosophers, poets, or musicians, often mustachioed and sometimes with a bird perched atop the head. As noted by Edwards, the art world in the 1960s and '70s was moving in new directions, transformed by pop art, conceptual art, and minimalism. By the late '70s, Adickes's paintings seemed by many to be decorative, dated, and out of tune with the content-driven art that younger artists were making.

Adickes continued to paint, but beginning in the 1980s, it was his sculptural work that he became most known for. He states that he had long had a desire to make monumental sculptures. The subject matter for his first works were three-dimensional translations of the stylized, cubist figures from his paintings. Using concrete and steel, he translated these figures to an enormous scale and placed them outdoors in public sites where they were impossible to ignore. After being commissioned to create a bronze statue of President George H. W. Bush in 1990, Adickes expanded the subject matter of his sculptures to include historical figures and national heroes.

This book asserts the role Adickes had in the development of the Houston art scene and his continuing relevance and longevity. An interview with the artist tells the story of how a young artist from rural Texas studied with Fernand Léger in Paris, traveled the world, and came back to Texas to be the founder of a thriving art scene in Houston. His monumental works alter the landscape of Texas and at times, as in the case with his Sam Houston sculpture in Huntsville, alter our awareness of history. These sculptures, such as Sam Houston, the Beatles, and presidential portraits, present the opportunity to discuss the challenges of making public art and navigating its political, cultural, and bureaucratic restrictions. These sculptures, too, investigate the nature of "popular" art engaging with works that do not often receive critical attention. By looking at Adickes's career, we learn more about the development and history of the Texas art scene.

# Chapter 2

## Adickes in Houston at Midcentury

Melissa L. Mednicov

In the early 1950s, David Adickes painted a work of the Three Magi, *Three Wise Men* (1954), for the James Bute Gallery's window during the Christmas season[1] (figure 2.1). The painting, on loan from the artist for display, wishes viewers and, ostensibly, the Houstonian busily occupied with their holiday shopping, a "Merry Christmas" as one of the men holds a sign, "Bute's Wishes You a Merry Christmas." The painting acts as a holiday wish and, simultaneously, as an advertisement for the artist and the gallery, inviting the shopper walking by to make quite the holiday gift by purchasing a contemporary painting by a Houston-based artist. Among the artists represented by Ben DuBose at the James Bute Gallery, and later at the Ben DuBose Gallery, one of the first contemporary art galleries in the city, were David Adickes, Herb Mears, Leila McConnell, and Robert Preusser. Adickes's painting, with its European modernist influences, suggested to the shopper, walking past the Bute Gallery on the corner of McKinney and Lamar, a unique contemporary gallery experience in Houston in the 1950s, one that could be brought home through the purchase of an artwork.

During the 1950s and 1960s, Houston began to establish itself as an important part of the art networks of Texas, one with national and global connections. Texas-born artist David Adickes was an integral figure during this pivotal moment for Houston's art community, helping to shape the gallery system in Houston. During this period, he regularly showed in Houston and Texas Annuals, was exhibited both at the Museum of Fine Arts, Houston, and the Contemporary Arts Association (CAA, later to become the Contemporary Art Museum, Houston),[2] and encountered John de Menil. Adickes is a model of the successful midcentury working artist in Houston and one who is uniquely positioned to tell the story of Houston at midcentury. The midcentury period in Houston's art history continues to mark the contemporary art community in the city. Throughout

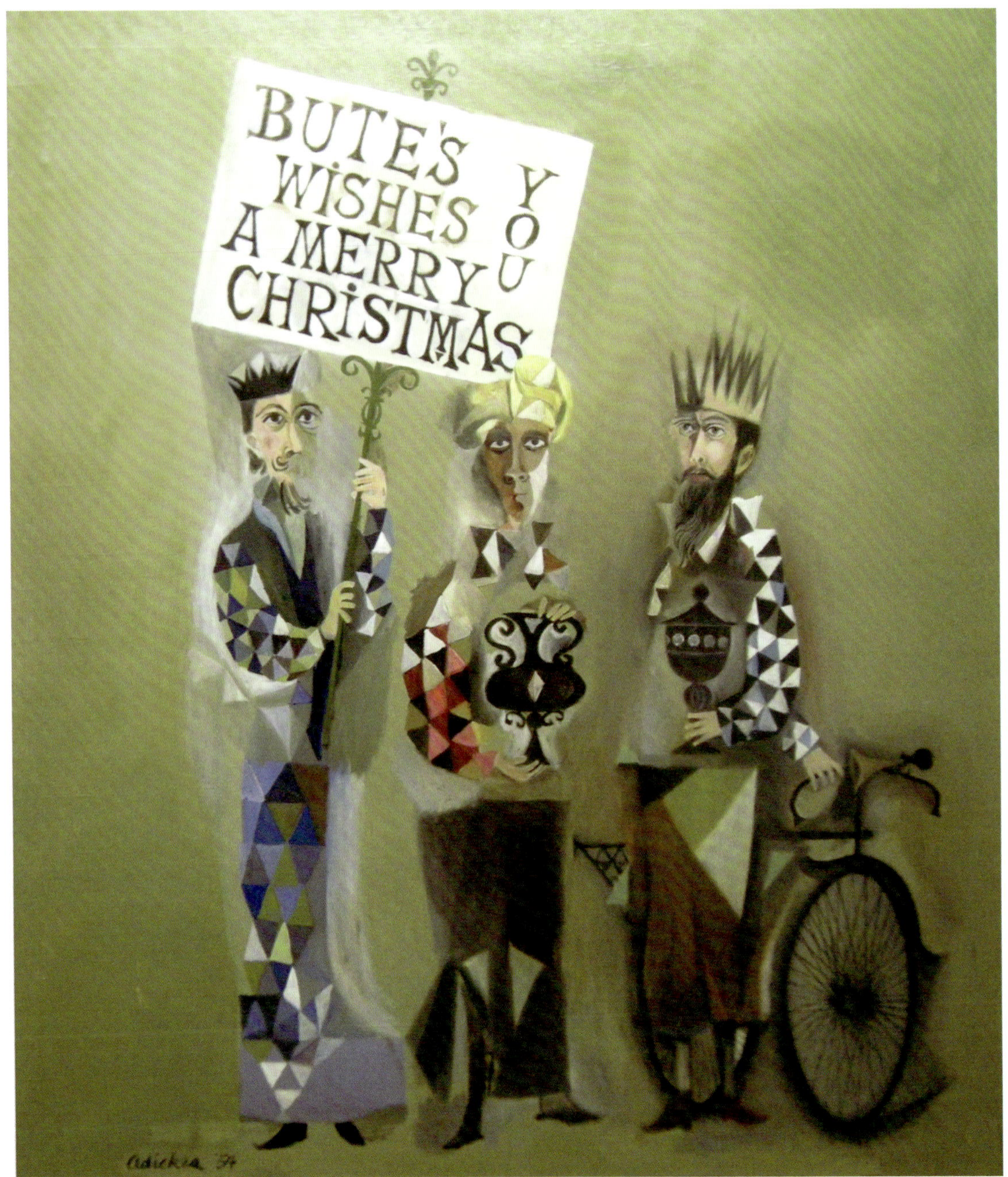


**Figure 2.1.** David Adickes, *Three Wise Men*, 1954, oil on canvas, 60 × 54 inches. Collection of David Adickes. Credit: David Adickes.

this period Adickes regularly traveled internationally, spending significant time in Japan and France (particularly in Antibes where he owned a home). Adickes's essential friendship with Houston artist and teacher Herb Mears influenced both artists' work. Their artistic friendship expands on the tradition of artistic networks, one that also continues in the contemporary Houston art scene. Additionally, Adickes had a close working relationship with Ben DuBose, who established one of the first contemporary galleries in Houston, further situating him within the burgeoning Houston art scene—with many aspects such as commercial galleries, the de Menils' importance to Houston, and the Art League of Houston—recognizable to Houston's contemporary art scene today.

Adickes, perhaps best known today in Texas for his monumental sculptures, was part of Houston modernist art networks. Looking more closely at Adickes's career in the 1950s and 1960s affords the opportunity to look at the intersections of regionalism, national and international modernism, and how a metropolitan city outside of preconceived ideas of "art centers" formed its own thriving gallery and museum system for artists locally and beyond. Adickes provides an example of a successful, entrepreneurial artist, showing his work in Houston both when he was in the city and not, and provides a template for understanding the working artist in Texas during the 1950s and early '60s.

Adickes's paintings from this time focus on a set of series, regularly revisiting subjects of still lifes, figures, and landscapes. A typical work of the period, *Three Men on a Beach* (1953), points toward the elongation of his figures of the period (figure 2.2). The work features three figures, each almost as high as the composition. The two figures on the left include more detail in their faces, with impossibly long torsos and arms. The figure on the right has his back toward the viewer. The figure on the left appears to be holding a clarinet or similar horn instrument. The piece, as Adickes has stated about his work during this period, is clearly influenced by European modernism of decades past. The group of figures, musician, and the appearance of the three on a type of road recall earlier moments of European modernism such as Pablo Picasso's circus performers or his references to harlequins. Adickes's attention to brushstroke throughout the painting recalls synthetic cubism along with the work's more muted palette. Both Adickes and Mears were influenced by their time in Paris, immersed in European modernism, and their time together at the Atelier Léger.

Fernand Léger began his painting academy in the 1920s, and after spending some time, particularly during World War II, in America, he returned to Paris in 1946 and taught at his academy.[3] After World War II, "Sometime around 1948, his school was officially recognized by the American authorities who dispensed G.I. Bill stipends, and for the next few years it was one of two or three principal destinations for a new generation of American artists looking for inspiration in Paris."[4] In a 1980 article, Léger's influence on Adickes was deemed "little" as "the school was in name only, and the French painter rarely attended outside of critiquing students' works twice a week."[5] Among those artists were David Adickes and Herb Mears. Other artists who studied at the atelier at various points include Louise Bourgeois, Robert Colescott, and Richard Stankiewicz.[6]

Another work by Adickes from the same year, *The Magicians of the Blue Angel*, follows a similar stylistic mode (figure 2.3). Three central figures, somewhat elongated, play while a fourth figure appears to be watching. Two outstretched arms reach

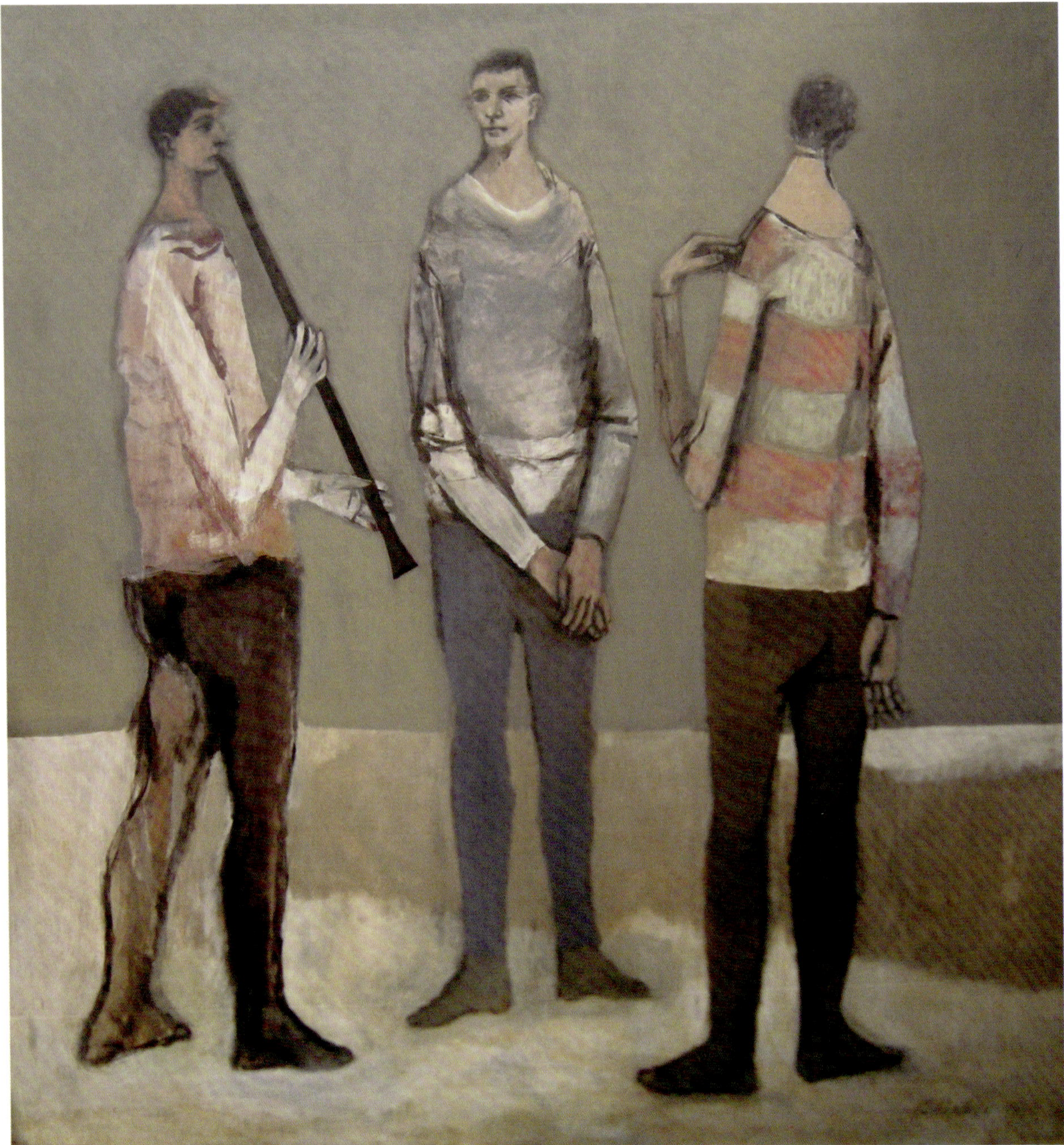

**Figure 2.2.** David Adickes, *Three Men on a Beach*, 1953, casein, 48 × 48 inches. Collection of David Adickes. Credit: David Adickes.

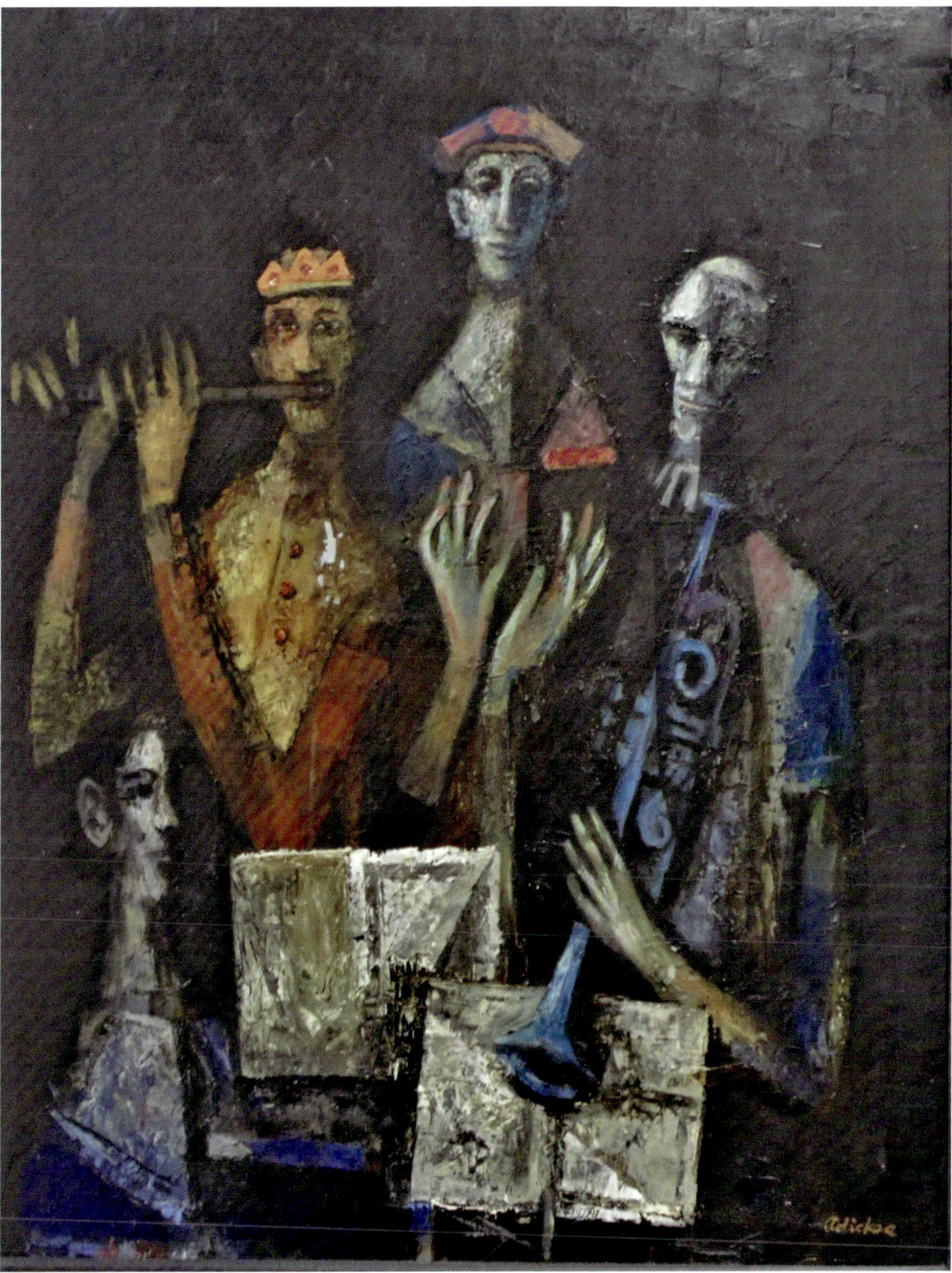

**Figure 2.3.** David Adickes, *The Magicians of the Blue Angel*, 1957, oil on board, 28 × 36 inches, Collection of David Adickes. Credit: David Adickes.

up; to whom those arms belong to is unclear. Suggestive of the title, this work contains more blue moments against a black background. Each figure contains features or aspects that elongate the body, a style that Adickes pursued for the rest of his career. Adickes emphasizes his brushwork, making his application particularly clear on the figures' faces and the backs of the music sheets.

Katie Robinson Edwards's *Midcentury Modern Art in Texas*, a foundational text about Texas modernism, focuses on a nexus of Texas artists asserting their regional and national importance. Edwards ties the growth of art in Texas to the state's growth, "Yet from the same Texas soil, modernist forms of painting and sculpture emerged. Not nearly as ostentatious as the oil boom and its attendant grandiosity, modernist art in Texas nonetheless retained an essential connection to the land, and thrived."[7] Edwards asserts how Houston's prosperity encouraged its growth in the arts, stating, "During the 1950s, a decade in which its population doubled, Houston strove for world-class recognition in the arts."[8] Edwards includes David Adickes and Herb Mears (among other artists regularly exhibited by Ben DuBose) in "an abbreviated list of the modernist artists who emanated from Houston at midcentury."[9] Adickes and Mears were friends, studied together in Paris at the Atelier Léger, and on Adickes's return to Houston (and Adickes's invitation to Mears to join him in the city) together briefly opened an art school, the Studio of Contemporary Art.[10] Adickes served in the Army Air Corps transport crew, flying back and forth to Paris, during World War II. After the war, he completed his degree in physics at what was then Sam Houston State Teachers College and, a few years later, then returned to Paris to study with Fernand Léger for two years. Edwards calls Adickes and Mears, "School of Paris inheritors."[11] This kind of criticism of Adickes and Mears was leveled by other Houston-based, abstract artists, such as Richard Stout's quotes from a 2014 interview appearing in Pete Gershon's *Collision: The Contemporary Art Scene in Houston, 1972–1985*: "'What I can say is when I arrived here,' said Stout in 2014, 'most of the other people operated from a stream of regionalist painting that developed and became richer, and a very strong influence of the school of Paris.'"[12] Gershon then elaborates on Stout's quote by stating, "He was talking about the decorative, usually figurative works of popular local artists like David Adickes and Herb Mears, who'd briefly opened an art school together in Houston in 1951 after meeting at the Atelier of Fernand Léger."[13] Mears and Adickes were continually influenced by their time in Paris and experiences with European modernism. Throughout the 1950s and '60s, Mears stayed in Houston teaching at various Houston institutions.[14] Adickes showed his work extensively in Houston and in Texas, while also regularly traveling abroad.[15] Gershon's *Collision*, an essential consideration of Houston's art scene with attention to the earlier years, but primarily focused on the 1970s and 1980s, includes Adickes among a group of male artists who "dominated Houston's art scene in 1950s and 1960s."[16] Both Edwards and Gershon place Adickes within a central moment in the development of Houston's art institutions and support and interest in modernist art.

Additionally, Edwards notes John de Menil purchased a work from Adickes's exhibition in Houston at the Shamrock Hotel, an event sponsored by the Art League of Houston in the spring of 1951.[17] William E. Reaves also cites this event as the first time Adickes exhibited work in Houston.[18] Adickes also notes that at the sale of contemporary art, held at the Shamrock Hotel's garage, the artist met Ben DuBose for the first time.[19] Ben DuBose ran the gallery space in the James Bute paint store, which was "one of the first commercial fine art galleries to handle contemporary art."[20] At this event, Adickes met DuBose and Houston art patrons such as Nina Cullinan.[21] At the Shamrock Hotel garage, among other collectors, John de Menil purchased a painting by Adickes.[22] John and Dominique de Menil, through their support of Houston artists and art spaces and in bringing international and nationally renowned scholars and artists to Houston, impacted the fabric of Houston then and today.[23] Today, Houston's Menil Collection, which opened in 1987, is a testament to their continued influence on the city.

Adickes regularly revisits familiar subjects in his paintings and sculptures. A. Cantey, in a 1962 James Bute–produced monograph of Adickes's work, states, "Like many cubists, Adickes has chosen the still-life as an endless thematic source."[24] In 1962, Adickes's artistic practice was still rooted in European modernism for its viewers (the James Bute exhibition additionally traveled to Dallas and Pasadena, California). Cantey opens the monograph with Adickes's local and international experiences: "Huntsville, Texas was his birthplace. He has lived in Paris, Barcelona and Houston; Tahiti, Kyoto and Antibes."[25] Cantey describes "the strange, mysterious elongated figures" of Adickes's work, starting in 1950, as "always those bizarre denizens of the Adickes world: the Adickes-men."[26] Edwards cites these visual motifs as: "Around 1950, those figures became elongated and mysterious—'Adickes men' became a recognizable trademark within his paintings."[27] Edwards's use of "trademark" is appropriate in a few ways. Adickes created a signature style in these paintings, a common motif in his still-life images and figures; he relied on this recognizability to create a market and kind of brand for his artwork. Similar to the James Bute Christmas painting, which served to advertise both Adickes and Houston's contemporary gallery, Adickes's style operated to continually remind the viewer one was unmistakably looking at an Adickes painting.

While Adickes was integral to the development of the Houston art scene, his work and position within Houston has not often been given sustained attention. Edwards describes Adickes and Mears, in *The Art of Texas*: "Houston artists David Adickes and Herb Mears both studied with Cubist painter and sculptor Fernand Léger in Paris before coming to Houston, effectively disseminating School of Paris ideals throughout Houston. They were colleagues and friends with the most expressionistic and avant-garde artists in the city, including Jack Boynton, Gene Charlton, Frank Dolejska, Dorothy Hood, Robert Preusser, Richard Stout, and Dick Wray, among others."[28] Edwards places Adickes, along with Mears, within the founding modernist Houston art network. Some of these artists have been given more recent scholarly attention. Additionally, Edwards positions the artists within a period of intense economic growth for the city and, in correlation to such growth, a period in which the city "strove for world-class recognition in the arts."[29] As Edwards notes elsewhere and as was included in the introduction about Adickes: "Anecdotally and occasionally in print, his work is generally maligned by serious art critics. I am not convinced it should be written off, since his art captured something of the kitsch quality already inherent in School of Paris paintings and then amplified it in his later years, when postmodernism and irony reigned."[30] As

Edwards alludes, Adickes's critical reception leaves a sparse trail; however, his work was regularly exhibited and sold during the 1950s and 1960s. Additionally, she names some of the reasons why Adickes's work, particularly his paintings, have not been discussed in recent years. Ann Holmes, in *Art in America*, described the 1963 art scene in Houston and included: "Ben DuBose at the James Bute gallery was featuring his star artist, the city's most financially successful David Adickes."[31] Adickes, a staple of the Texas art community, offers the opportunity to consider the formation of the Houston art scene, his place as a working artist within it, and his importance to it. The kitsch quality noted by Edwards may be marked by Adickes's entrepreneurial work ethic, promoting his own work in the 1950s and '60s, finding a way to sustain his artistic output, to fund his travel abroad to Japan and France, and, equally, to promote and support the Houston art scene through his investment in other artists and galleries. His work, influenced by his training in European modernism, as Edwards cites, takes that influence in a Texas direction—applying gestural brushwork and revisiting themes and subjects regularly then and more recently.

The Houston Annuals and Texas Generals were another important institutional element to Houston's and Texas' larger art community. Leila McConnell described how everyone would enter, and acceptance into the Annuals "was a great encouragement" for an artist.[32] Additionally, William E. Reaves described the Texas Generals as "a catalyst for incubating and expanding the postwar art community."[33] The three main Texas museums at this time, the Museum of Fine Arts, Houston, Dallas Museum of Art, and the Witte Museum (San Antonio) alternated and rotated hosting the Texas Annuals.[34] The Museum of Fine Arts, Houston (MFAH) showed an early commitment to exhibiting (and purchasing) Texas art in 1940 with the annual Texas General Exhibits.[35]

Adickes, early in his career, had a solo exhibition at the MFAH in 1951.[36] The circumstances of the show were unusual. Originally, Adickes had submitted work and won the purchase prize for the Houston Artists Annual in 1951. However, Adickes was disqualified from winning since he had not lived in Houston for a full year.[37] Instead, Adickes was then offered an exhibition due to the disqualification. Adickes described the exhibition as "a corridor show" and "a great success" due to a purchase by art patron Nina Cullinan.[38] The MFAH purchase prize (until it was discontinued) was one of many annual Texas-based juried and museum purchase exhibitions. In the early 1950s, Adickes regularly dominated these awards (as is seen in the chronology herein) throughout Texas in addition to regular exhibitions.[39]

The MFAH's commitment to Texas art shifted in the following decades as the museum attempted to mark its place within an international field. Alison de Lima Greene, curator at the MFAH, cites James Johnson Sweeney's directorship at the MFAH (1961–68) as fulfilling "the institution's goals of achieving international fame," and that he "came to Houston just as the city was once again assuming a new identity."[40] Sweeney ended the Houston annual exhibition and the annual exhibition of Texas painting and sculpture; Greene summarizes Houston's reaction: "The sense of abandonment felt by the local art community was immediate and long-lasting."[41] McConnell echoed this point, stating, when the annuals stopped, "things really changed" for Texas-based artists in the period.[42] The Contemporary Arts Association filled the MFAH's void even if the exhibition impetus was not on Texas. Greene notes in the same period of Sweeney's changes at the MFAH: Jermayne MacAgy worked with CAA for exhibitions, which also focused exhibitions of more international artists similar to the MFAH under Sweeney's leadership, yet "her treatment of the gallery space as an intellectual arena proved to be deeply influential on a number of Houston artists."[43]

The Museum of Modern Art's (MoMA) trajectory of European modernism, as integral to the traditional canon as was established by MoMA, was, according to Alison de Lima Greene, a model for Houston's adoption of modernism. Greene writes, "From the very beginning, MoMA was the muse of Modernism in Houston. Almost every major step that helped establish Modernism in Houston during this era can be traced to an example set by MoMA's staff and board."[44] While it can be argued that Houston was not completely marked by MoMA from the beginning, by the late 1960s, the Houston art institutions such as the MFAH no longer hosted the Texas and Houston Annual Exhibitions—a change within the Houston art scene that significantly changed the acceptance of those artists within the art establishment. An aspect of this is the shift, particularly among the major collectors of art in Houston, toward what was being collected and shown in New York City, and the canonization of abstraction via MoMA determined what was considered then contemporary art by those Houston collectors and exhibited in Houston's art institutions.[45] Adickes's work by the 1960s was decidedly made and marketed as opposed to what was celebrated in New York City at the time. Ben DuBose described Adickes's work in a 1962 James Bute River Oaks Gallery exhibition catalog: "A stiff reed in the high winds of contemporary currents, Adickes' new, sure compositions testify to a rather anchored place in American painting."[46] DuBose argues for Adickes's work as strong (as a reed) against the shifts (as temporary as the wind) of contemporary art. DuBose promoted a "stable" art and artist for a Houston collector to count on against the contemporary or avant-garde artist.

Later, in the 1980s, when Houston was being positioned as an art center by curators Barbara Rose and Susie Kalil in the exhibition *Fresh Paint: The Houston School* at the Museum of Fine Arts, Houston, Houston's art past was excavated. Kalil, in her exhibition catalog essay, "Dynamic Pioneers: A Brief History of Painting in Houston," describes Adickes and Mears as representative of Houston's 1950s art scene:

> Pervasive throughout the 1950s was a French salon style made popular by Houston artists David Adickes and Herb Mears, both of whom studied under the great French painter Fernand Léger. Their responses to Paris and the French Riviera produced finicky abstractions of bridges, villages, waterfronts, and ports as well as surreal compositions of elongated figures. Although many examples may be deemed flaccid decorations by today's standards, their Cézannesque interpretation was considered an appropriate style in those years.[47]

Kalil notes the European modernist connections within Adickes's and Mears's work and the appeal for their work in Houston in the 1950s, providing a bridge for those relatively new to art collecting who may be looking to grow an art collection with connections to established European modernist tropes and Houston artists. *Risque-Tout* (1953), a work in this mode, features three elongated seated figures seated with the beached boat (the Risque-Tout) behind them (figure 2.4).

Adickes's use of visible brushwork through form and color reiterates Kalil's reference of Cézanne. This is most evident in the foreground where patches of color such as white and grayish purple constitute the beach itself. The work, in the artist's collection, was purchased by the Contemporary Arts Museum Houston (at the time CAA) as a purchase prize, and when the museum shifted away from a collecting museum, Adickes was given the opportunity to purchase the work back.[48]

Furthermore, Kalil describes the challenges faced by artists in Houston during this period, citing the lack of serious collectors (John and Dominique de Menil were the exceptions).[49] One positive and major shift occurred in Houston for artists when gallerists such as Meredith Long and Ben DuBose committed to showing Houston contemporary artists and mounted regular exhibitions of such work. Kalil summarizes the pivotal actions of gallerists such as DuBose: "Whereas galleries had

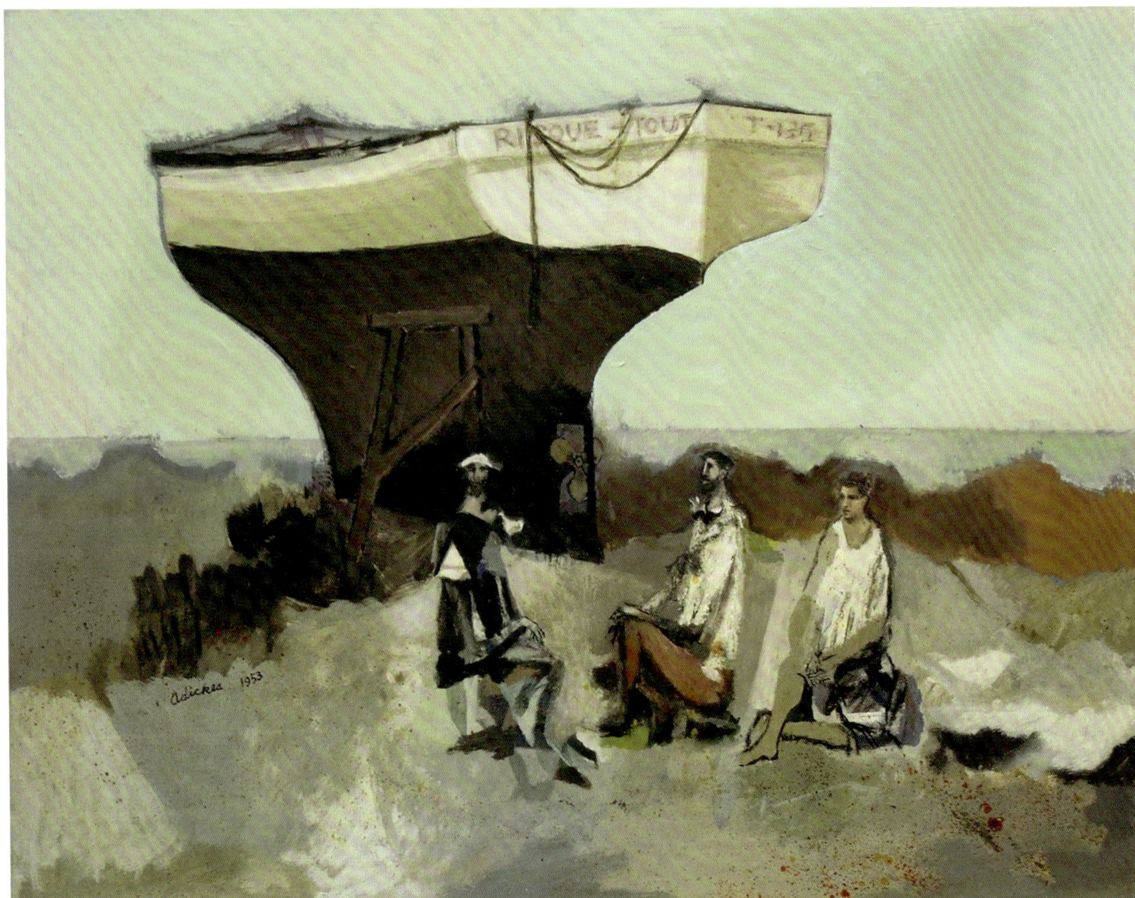

**Figure 2.4.** David Adickes, *Risque-Tout*, 1953, oil on board, 19 × 25 inches, Collection of David Adickes. Credit: David Adickes.

been content to display the robust life of the ranch and the usual reproductions of mixed masters, counting on gaudy frames to pull in customers, they had now become responsible for much of the growth in Houston."[50] Houston galleries provided an intervention—and opportunity—for the exhibition of contemporary artists in the city. Even so, Kalil argues the Houston audience for contemporary art by the 1960s was still difficult to find.[51]

Kalil places Adickes and Mears within the birth of the Ben DuBose gallery:

> The James Bute paint company had an art section with an exhibition space directed by Ben DuBose. In operation since the 1920s, it was one of the oldest galleries in Houston and carried the work of Adickes, Mears, and Gadbois in addition to that of Charles Schorre, Robert Weimerskirch, and Bill Condon. Both brilliant merchandisers, Long and DuBose stimulated people into buying local art at a time when most Houstonians were purchasing ornate objects for their homes. No longer satisfied to follow the lead of New York, the galleries chose to enlighten their audience by presenting and supporting the work of talented Houston artists.[52]

DuBose saw the potential in showing contemporary artists and selling work within a gallery space as part of the James Bute Paint Company.

As Kalil states in *The Color of Being/El Color del Ser: Dorothy Hood, 1918–2000*, about DuBose and Long: "More than simply exhibiting Houston artists, Long and DuBose helped to create a market. Art was coming to be thought of in Houston not just as something to hang on a wall, but as a force that could permeate and enrich important aspects of life."[53] Kalil asserts a palpable shift in Houston's art scene, one instigated, promoted, and sustained (in the early years) by the burgeoning gallery system along with concurrent Houston art institutions' establishment and growth in the period. Within the James Bute gallery space run by DuBose, Adickes stated, "Then Ben started bringing in artists. I was one of the very first. I think not the first, but of the professional artists in town, there weren't more than five or six."[54] Furthermore, upon Adickes's return from Japan, he

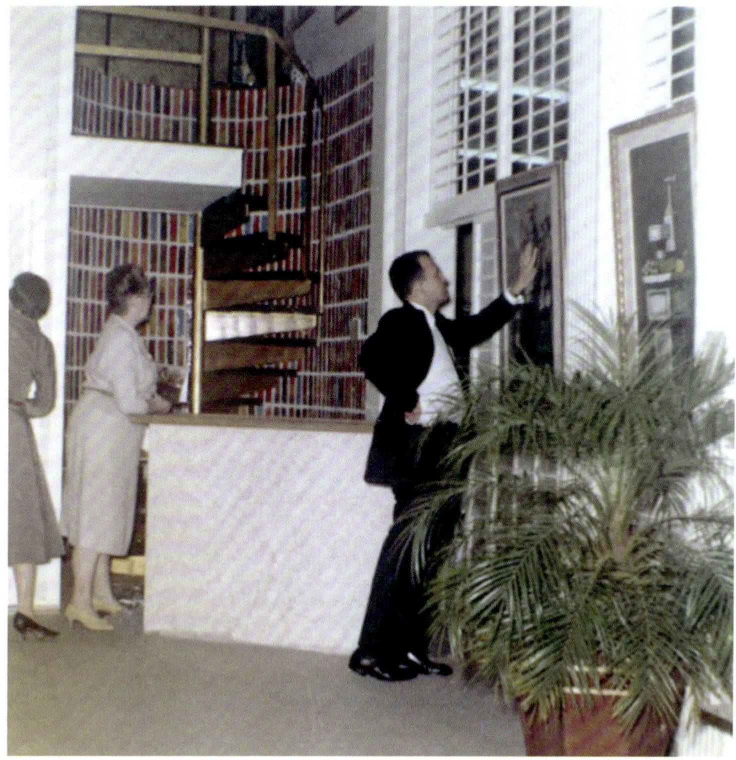

**Figure 2.5.** Photograph of Ben DuBose touching a painting by David Adickes at the James Bute Gallery, undated. Collection of David Adickes. Credit: David Adickes.

encouraged and helped to pay for Ben DuBose's new gallery on Kirby.[55] Adickes encouraged DuBose to leave the James Bute Gallery and to start his own gallery space, the Ben DuBose Gallery, which opened in May 1966, at 2950 Kirby.[56] Adickes found the vacant building that would become the Ben DuBose Gallery and covered two-thirds of the initial funding on behalf of DuBose.[57]

In one example of his entrepreneurial work ethic, Adickes sought out Houston area art collectors as investors for a planned trip. In Adickes's oral history with Sarah C. Reynolds, and in his interviews with Michael H. Henderson and me, he outlined his entrepreneurial approach to funding his regular trips to Europe in the 1950s. He described how he sold "shares in myself"[58] by offering people the opportunity to invest in his future work. He described his plan as: "outlined what I wanted to do: go to Europe, paint, bring back paintings and guarantee everyone who bought a $50 unit one painting and one copy of any lithos I did while I was there."[59] Through this process, he stayed in Europe for fourteen months. He would send boxes of works to Texas, and DuBose would host uncrating events in which the collectors would come and choose the works they wanted. The act of uncrating, the discovery of a new work one wanted, was an important aspect of the process—as an entrepreneurial act rooted in showmanship. Whatever was left behind would then be reboxed for the next collector to experience a sense of discovery.[60] He also continued to develop a market for his work, a beginning or continuation in collecting for the patron now invested in Adickes's career and, thus, likely to be interested in building their collection with his and other Houston artists' work.

Adickes helped to form the Houston modernist art scene alongside other Houston-based artists such as Mears, Leila McConnell, Robert Preusser, and Henri Gadbois. These artists are examples of working artists, with an interest in midcentury modernist abstraction, who regularly showed at the Ben DuBose Gallery during the 1950s and '60s. Stylistically, Mears shares formal characteristics with Adickes. Adickes and Mears met at the Atelier Léger in Paris (where Mears had already been studying for about a year),[61] and, on Adickes's encouragement and assistance, Mears moved to Houston, Texas, in 1951 to open an art school together, the Studio of Contemporary Arts.[62] Adickes rented the booth along with Mears (while Mears stayed in New York) for the Shamrock Hotel exhibition sale—both artists were introduced to the Houston art patron circle at the same time. After their short-lived art school ended, Mears stayed in Houston, regularly exhibiting in Houston and throughout Texas in the 1950s.[63] Mears had a substantial impact on Adickes's work. Campbell Geeslin, in a 1957 James Bute exhibition essay on Adickes, describes Adickes's Paris experiences with Mears: "especially Herbert Mears influenced him largely and the great city itself had its legendary impact."[64] Adickes is quoted in the same catalog stating, Mears "was the first talented person I met who was dead serious about being an artist."[65] In interviews for this publication, he stated:

> meeting one guy in particular from New York whose name was Herbert Mears, who was five or six years older than me and had been to all the art schools in Europe and knew a hell of a lot more about art than I did, became my best friend. And so, he taught me a lot. He taught me more than I learned in school.[66]

Ben DuBose first showed Mears's work in the James Bute gallery space in 1954.[67] Mears, in his conversation with Sarah C. Reynolds in 1995, published in *Houston Reflections: Art in the City, 1950s, 60s and 70s*, describes Ben DuBose as invested in Houston artists and selling work, stating:

> He was an extremely impulsive guy and there were occasions where you'd bring some work in and he'd get so excited he'd take it in the back and have them frame it right then! He'd call somebody in River Oaks and they'd come over and buy it that day. It was just really something. He'd never say, "Oh, that's a beautiful painting . . . I love that painting." He'd never say a damn thing, but he was crazy about selling work and manipulating customers, you know. He'd grab them by the arm and say, "Listen—if you don't take this you're going to regret it forever. This is a really important piece for you to have. This will change your life."[68]

Mears described DuBose as focused on working with Houston collectors to invest in local artists, believing in his artists' work, with a gallerist's push for sales. Furthermore, Mears cites DuBose's business flair, devoted to Houston artists, and creating a welcoming space for those artists. Mears, after his discussion of DuBose's salesmanship, states:

> He had studied psychology in college—not art—and so it was funny. He was marvelously successful and he really wasn't interested in the art scene in New York or Paris. He was interested in the people here in Houston, which was lovely for us. We were youngsters and all kind of broke—and he made it an interesting time. We routinely dropped in there to see what was going on and to have a chat; there were always people coming in there.[69]

DuBose used his background in psychology to promote and sell the work of Houston artists, supporting his gallery and the artists. His gallery space was successful and supportive—creating a place for artists to meet, as Mears's described.

Mears's *Promenade* (c. 1965) shares some European modalities with Adickes's work from the same period, they are part of a stylistic school (figure 2.6). The artist's son, Kirby Mears, described his father as a "Francophile"; returning again and again to France influenced his work.[70] The blue sky, marked by varying hues of blue and legible brushwork, creates immediate connections to Kalil's comments of "Cézannesque." The blue that pervades the sky, ground, trees, and people, owes a visual similarity to Pablo Picasso. The figures are somewhat elongated, but markedly different than men under Adickes's treatment. There is similarity of shared formal language between the artists—it is easy to see an ongoing artistic dialogue between the two. Another work by Mears, *Untitled, Village Port* (c. 1965) also participates in some characteristics between similar subjects in Adickes's work, again showing the influence of European modernism on both artists. The stacking of the village's buildings and visible, gestural brushwork throughout again creates a dialogue between the two artists. Brushwork and color become form for both artists, using vibrant color that repeats throughout the composition to direct the viewer's eye.

Mears's *Construction* (1960) was the Thirty-Fifth Annual Houston Artists Exhibition purchase prize winner at the Museum of Fine Arts, Houston, in 1960 (figure 2.7). The work departs somewhat from Mears's earlier shared artistic project with Adickes. The relatively large work (47 1/2 x 71 3/16 inches) continues to show the European modernist influence with its fragmentation of form, suggesting a landscape under

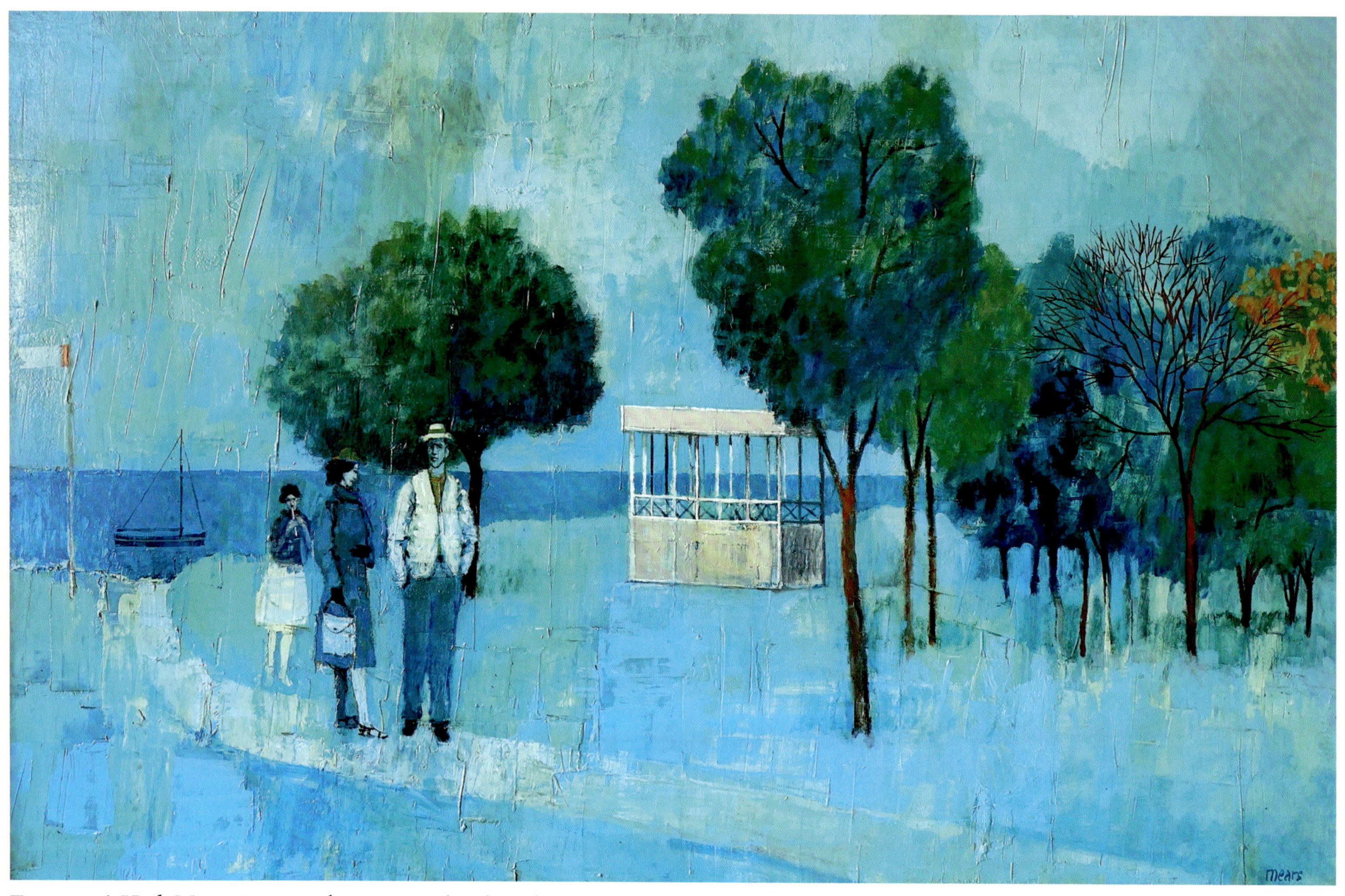


**Figure 2.6.** Herb Mears, *Promenade*, c. 1965, oil on board, 24 × 36 inches. Credit: Courtesy of Foltz Fine Art & The Estate of Herb Mears.

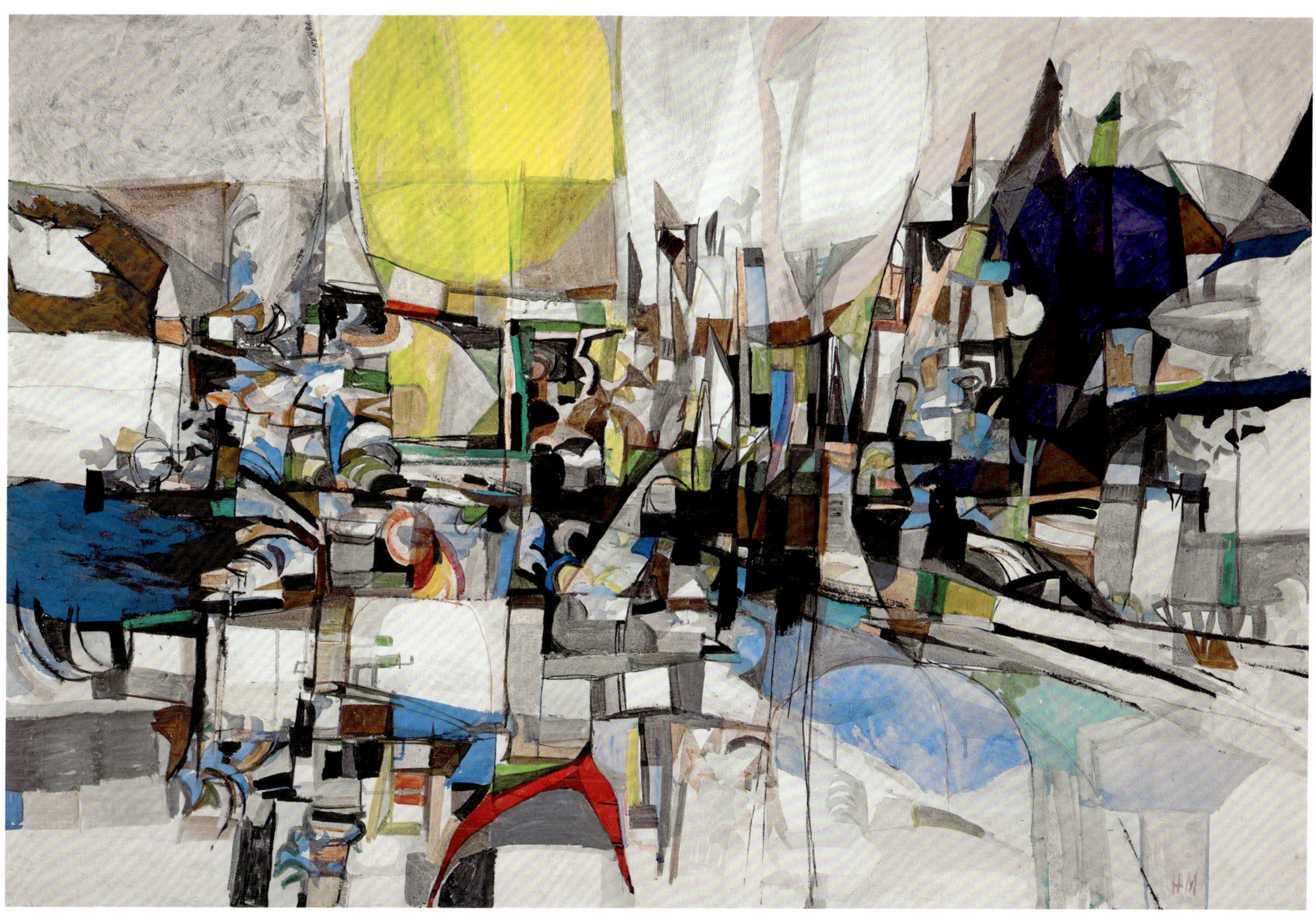

**Figure 2.7.** Herb Mears, *Construction,* 1960, acrylic polymer on Masonite, 47 1/2 × 71 3/16 inches. Credit: The Museum of Fine Arts, Houston, 35th Annual Houston Artists Exhibition, museum purchase prize, 1960, 60.10. Photo © The Museum of Fine Arts, Houston; photographer: Thomas R. DuBrock. Additional credit: Courtesy of Foltz Fine Art & The Estate of Herb Mears.

construction, yet not quite legible in its use of form. Gestural brushwork makes and denies form, such as in the right of the painting—where some gray suggests, yet does not complete, a bridge-like structure. The center of the painting is an abstracted cityscape, hinting yet never making whole a city's buildings. The centralized mass of gesture and color creates a congested middle register in the work. Suggestive in the bottom register is a reflective quality with some lighter applications of paint, although it is one that does not match the rest of the work.

Herb Mears, through his artwork and his artistic friendship with Adickes, contributed to the foundations of modernist Houston. In addition to what has been described, he taught at art institutions throughout the city such as the Contemporary Arts Museum; the Museum of Fine Arts, Houston; Rice University; and the University of Houston.[71] Mears exhibited regularly in the 1950s and '60s and taught artists. His wife, Ava Jean Mears, was integral to the establishment of the Contemporary Arts Museum, acting as the institution's secretary and, at times, documentarian.[72]

Additionally, Leila McConnell regularly exhibited her work with Ben DuBose and throughout Texas during the same period.[73] She described DuBose: "Ben was always bright and happy and full of life; this is the way he treated customers and he kept you going."[74] In an interview, she discussed her experiences at the gallery and Houston in the period as "a wonderful time."[75] She described the gallery openings as filled with people, artists, and collectors on DuBose's "lists." Additionally, she stated the gallery artists would bring in everything they painted to the gallery, they were then framed at the gallery, and would then be shown. Some works were hung while others were put on the floor in a stack to appeal to the different kinds of visitors and art buyers—some liked to see works hung on the wall while others liked to go through the stacked works and make their own discoveries.[76] By all accounts, including McConnell's remembrances as an artist represented by DuBose, the gallerist worked tirelessly to sell his artists' works to sustain the gallery and to support the artists during this successful period for the gallery.[77] McConnell's work is ethereal atmospheric abstractions, unsurprising as she calls many of her works "sky paintings." Her work *Drab Sky* (1966) manages the ethereal despite the drab of its title and the gloomy color palette (figure 2.8). A haze of brown and green form the horizon, or mountain, line and suggest a sky. Color becomes and mutates away from form developing into twilight.

Another artist shown by DuBose, Henri Gadbois, regularly showed in the same spaces.[78] Gadbois described DuBose as a "very influential, helpful person."[79] Additionally, Gadbois described DuBose's gallery as "probably one of the first commercial galleries in the city."[80] The artist further elaborated on the artist and gallerist relationship with DuBose and the impact of his gallery in the Houston art scene:

> In 1966 when Ben left Bute and formed his own gallery that was DuBose on Kirby Drive . . . most of us went, who were there with Ben. The Friday night openings at DuBose were very social . . . the place to go. I mean everybody sort of met there, and Ben did a good job selling. He loved sort of a messy gallery where you'd have to go through and find something that was already there. He never told you exactly what to paint, but he would give you hints, like, "People are painting their houses bold yellow, so . . . " Or he'd sort of chide you if you hadn't been painting.[81]

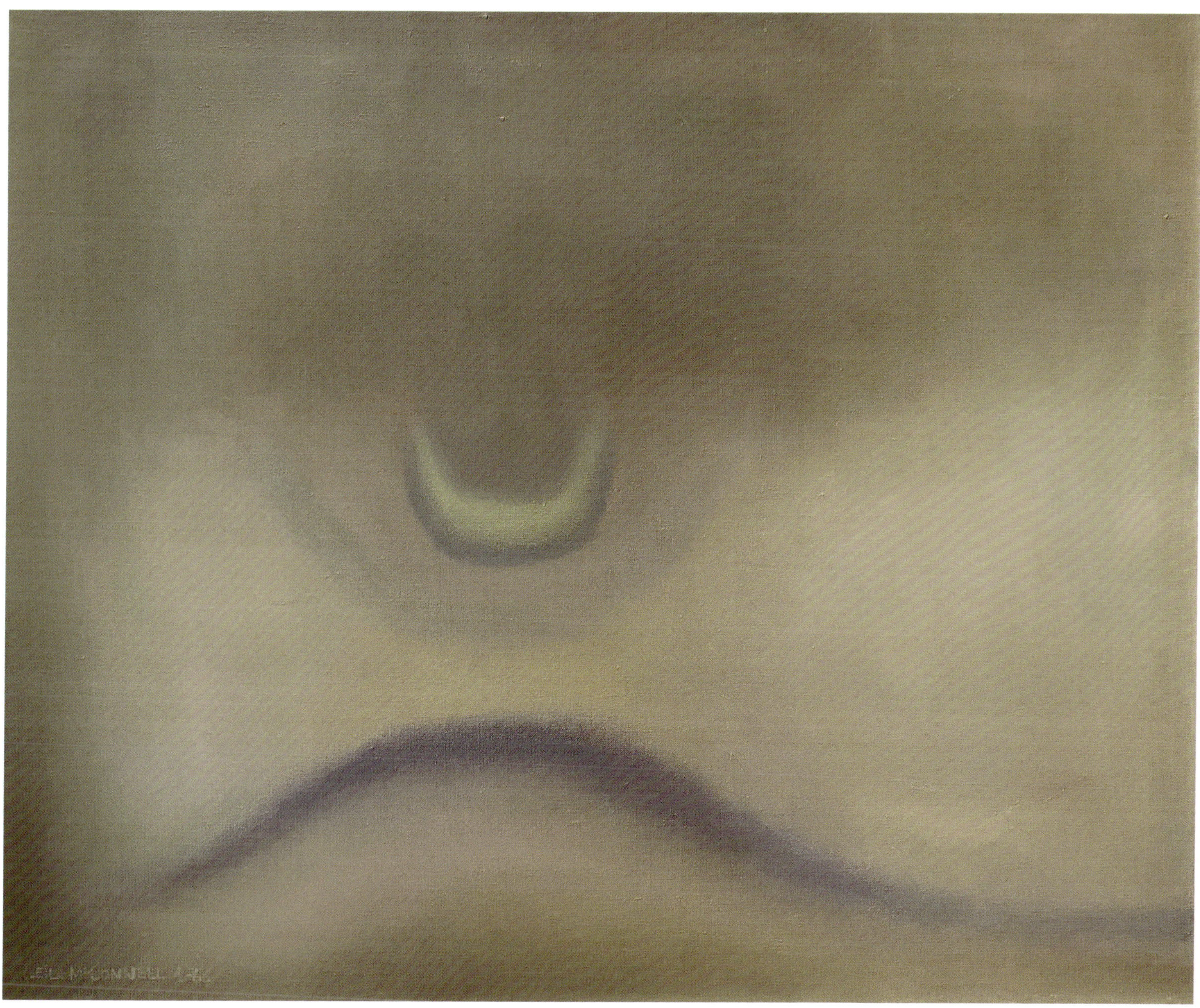

**Figure 2.8.** Leila McConnell, *Drab Sky*, 1966, oil on canvas, 24 × 30 inches. Credit: Courtesy of Foltz Fine Art & Leila McConnell.

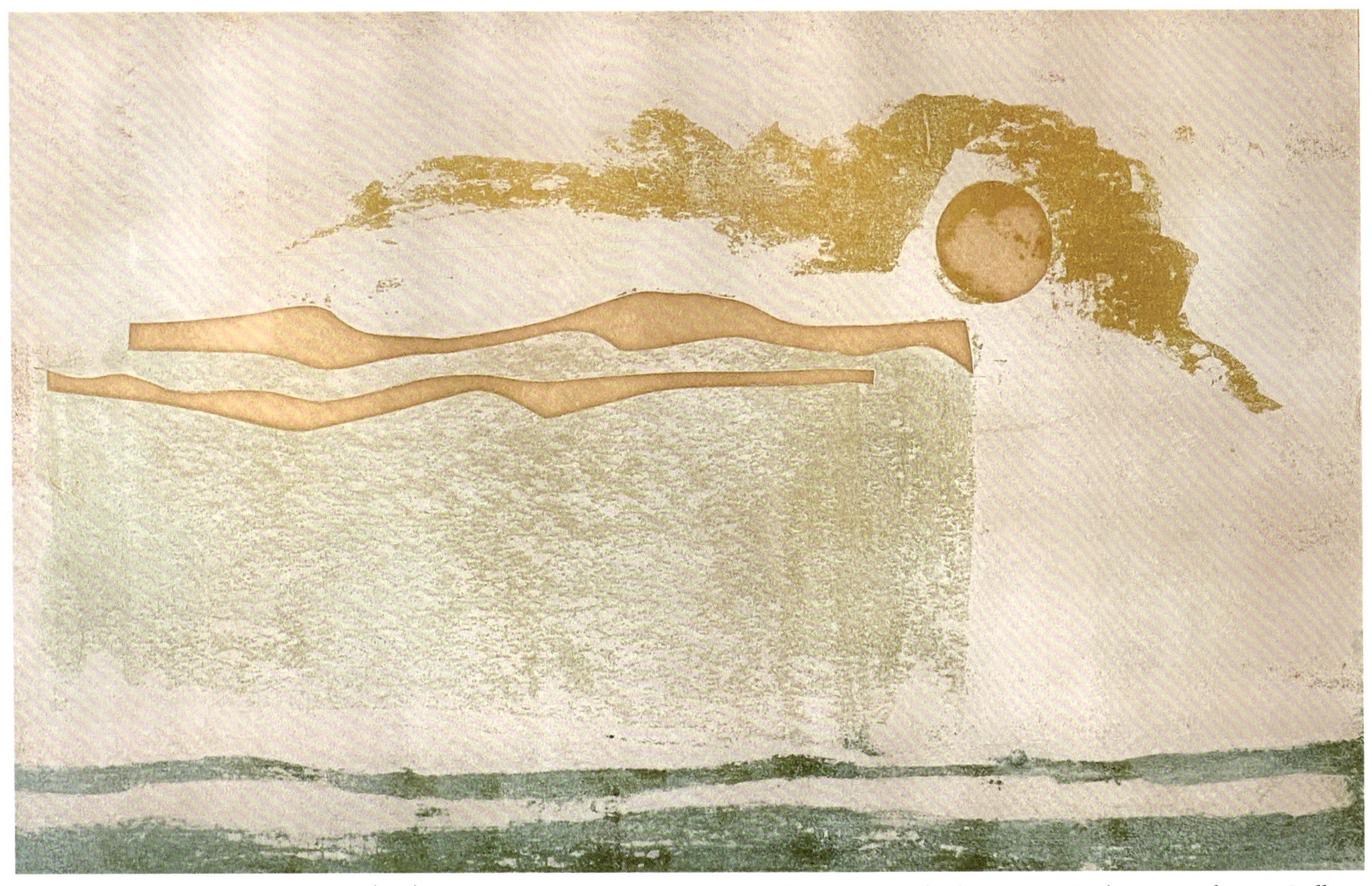

**Figure 2.9.** Henri Gadbois, *Whiteout* (2/7), 1958, lithograph, 10 × 16 inches. Credit: Courtesy of Foltz Fine Art & The Estate of Henri Gadbois.

Gadbois's description of the Friday night openings is matched by Adickes's telling, including of the other Houston galleries: "The openings themselves were on Fridays primarily, and were the social event of the week. That was where you saw and met everybody."[82] Art collector Larry Martin, who attended openings at the Ben DuBose Gallery, described the openings as "tremendous fun" and as a place "you wanted to go to because everyone was there."[83] DuBose's openings were fun and acted to gather and connect Houston's art community. McConnell described how the community was a group of artists who each pursued their own practice, not a "school" of artists necessarily, but one that was friendly.[84] A lithograph by Gadbois, *Whiteout* (2/7) from 1958 uses an economy of line and color to create an abstract landscape (figure 2.9). The title makes clear the abundance of negative space in its subject and composition, anchored by the yellow sun, a minimal circle, and lines suggestive of horizon and water.

Kermit Oliver, who exhibited at Ben DuBose Gallery in 1969, described why he chose to go with Ben DuBose as his gallery representation among the other galleries at the time:

> Ben was a person who placed great value in collecting . . . that was what makes art communities grow. He began to collect young artists and then let them grow. Some were recognized as some of the leading artists in the city and that was the compliment I had; it was also the intimidating aspect of being in that gallery.[85]

Oliver, who continues to be recognized as one of Texas' most important artists, describes how, with Ben DuBose in a central position, Houston galleries helped to create an art community. Oliver painted a work with Herb Mears as his subject, featuring Mears on a boat with a moon behind him. *Kissing the Moon*, places Mears both in the familiar and unfamiliar. The boat is on a beach, perhaps somewhere such as nearby Galveston. However, the sandy beach fills the foreground and its horizon like meets a sky-like void with a moon, appearing almost otherworldly. The only other object besides the boat is a shell in the foreground. Oliver's magical realism or realist surrealism is in full effect in the work. The majority of the work features the sky, boat, and beach. In a portrait of vivid clarity, Mears looks directly at the viewer from within a boat (figure 2.10).

According to Mears's son, Kirby Mears, his father was unaware of the painting until Ben DuBose called to tell him Oliver had delivered the work to the Ben DuBose Gallery. Mears promptly headed to the gallery to view and then purchase the work.[86] This kind of art community is one that often marked the Houston art experience up until recently, pre-pandemic.

By the late 1960s, Ben DuBose's gallery gained national press. In 1968 in *Art in America*, Eleanor Freed looked at Texas art in her essay "Texas Round Up." She writes that "not so long ago" galleries did not even exist in Texas: "Today a growing sophistication is beginning to take place along with the well-publicized escalation of population and prosperity."[87] Freed traces that shift within the gallery scene:

> Until quite recently, West and East Coast dealers set up shop in Texas hotel suites, peddling mediocrity along with masterpieces; but enough time has elapsed for a new, urbane, breed of collectors to have appeared on the scene. Now the cattle and Cadillac contingent rub elbows with young architects, scientists from the Space Agency and one of the most youthful, upward-and-outward-bound assemblages of art fanciers anywhere.[88]

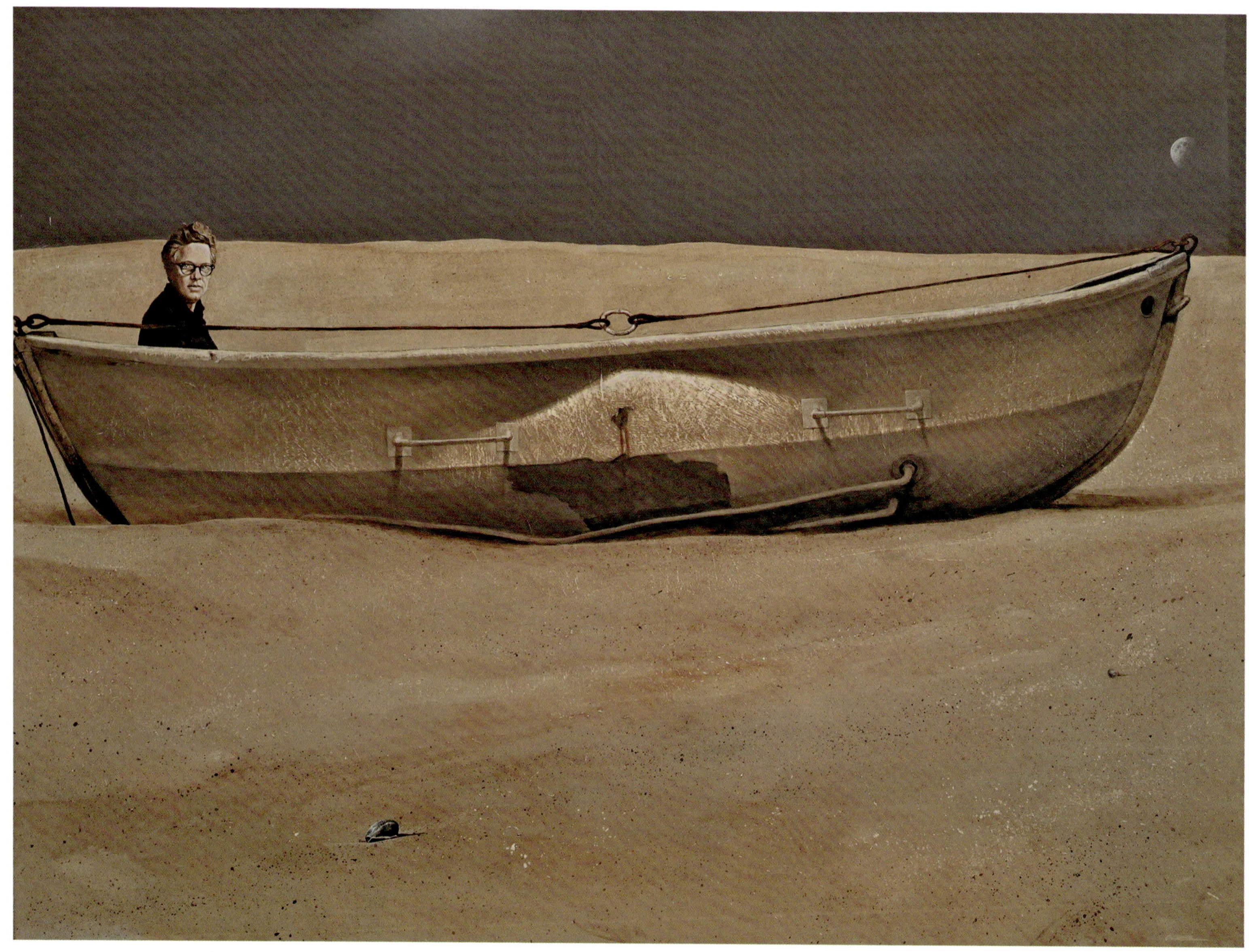

**Figure 2.10.** Kermit Oliver, *Kissing the Moon,* 38 inches wide × 32 1/2 inches high, acrylic on Masonite, date unknown. Credit: Courtesy of the Estate of Ava Jean Mears. Additional credit: Kermit Oliver.

Freed then provides a close look at various cities and galleries, starting with Houston and the DuBose Gallery. She places DuBose as first and established in Houston, "Ben DuBose has been at the game longer than anyone in Houston, fifteen years as manager of Bute's Galleries and for the past two years in extremely spacious quarters under his own name."[89] She lists some of the artists in his "stable," but leads with David Adickes: "In his stable one sees a fidelity rare in dealer-artist relationships; for example, David Adickes has had seventeen consecutive exhibitions with Du Bose."[90] Still, Freed notes at the end of her discussion of DuBose that he "has branched outside Texas."[91]

Robert Preusser, perhaps the best known of the Texas midcentury abstractionists, was instrumental in the formation of the midcentury Houston art scene. Scott Grant Barker and Jane Myers in *Intimate Modernism: Fort Worth Circle Artists in the 1940s*, cite Preusser as one artist essential to modernism in Texas, stating, "In fact, modernism in Texas art was not a development unique to any one painter or group of painters. Pockets of modernist work arose simultaneously in widely scattered areas of the state during the last half of the 1930s. Sometimes this work was the product of a single artist working alone, as in the case of Houston's Robert Preusser."[92] Edwards states he was "one of Texas' first fully abstract artists."[93] Preusser, along with Frank Dolejska, founded the Contemporary Arts Association in 1948.[94] Preusser was a painting prodigy mentored by Houston artist and teacher Ola McNeill Davidson, who drove him to Chicago at the age of seventeen to study with Lázló Moholy-Nagy.[95] The influence of the Bauhaus leader Moholy-Nagy on Preusser additionally had an impact on the Contemporary Arts Museum (CAM), Houston, when "the first exhibition organized by him and Dolejska in 1948 championed the Bauhaus ideal of integration."[96] The exhibition, in the mode of Bauhaus, included all forms of art, not just painting and sculpture.[97] Preusser resigned as codirector of the CAM in 1950.[98]

Houston, during this period, grew due to its status as a center for oil business, which supported the city's growth in population and as an art center. Edwards cites "three signal events symbolizing the city's national and international arts status":[99] the expansion by Mies van der Rohe of the Museum of Fine Arts, Houston (finished in 1958); the American Federation of the Arts convention (March 1957); and the Contemporary Arts Association exhibition *Totems Not Taboo: An Exhibition of Primitive Art*, curated by Jermayne MacAgy (who was supported by the de Menils) and held at the newly opened Cullinan Hall at the MFAH.[100] These events resonate with contemporary Houston, the MFAH's assertion of itself as an art center for Houston, including local (Houston and the larger state), national, and international art, particularly with the opening of the Kinder Building in 2020. Similarly, the de Menils' support of the city as an art center and their impact are continued in the contemporary city: the national and international artists brought into the Houston art landscape for exhibitions and discussions (such as Duchamp's talk, "The Creative Act," at the convention and the de Menils' further sponsorship of the American Federation of the Arts convention such as chartering a plane to bring conference visitors to other cities to view art[101]), the Contemporary Arts Association, and the important and pivotal presence of the de Menil family for art exhibitions and support in Houston. Additionally, MacAgy's exhibition influenced Texas artists.[102] In the same period, two more commercial art galleries opened, Meredith Long & Co. and New

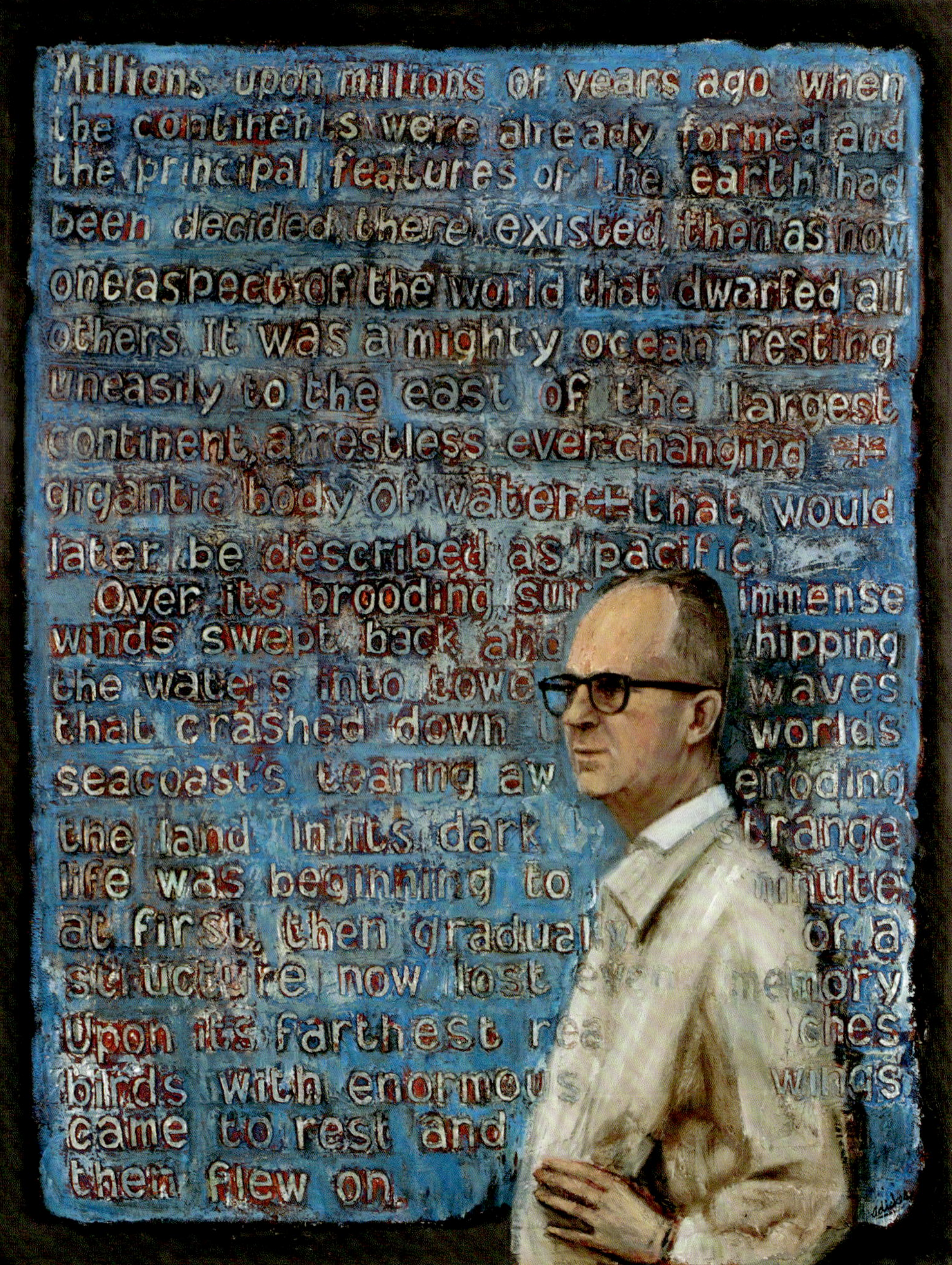


**Figure 2.11.** David Adickes, *Portrait of James A. Michener,* 1962. Carved gesso with oil paint and silver leaf on plywood on board. 48 3/4 × 37 9/16 inches. Courtesy of Blanton Museum of Art, University of Texas at Austin, Gift of Mari and James A. Michener, 1991. Additional credit: David Adickes.

Arts Gallery, in addition to the first established exhibition space for the Art League of Houston.[103]

An aspect that possibly separated Adickes from many discussions of modernism is his disavowal of contemporary art. In James A. Michener's essay, "Critique," in *Adickes*, the artist is quoted stating about "the contemporary statement . . . those preoccupations are for others who find in them the enrichment that I find only in a contemplation of all ages of time."[104] Adickes's statement repeats a familiar symbolism we saw with DuBose: Adickes's unchanging style as a "permanent" rather than shifting or changing with what he saw as contemporary shifts. Michener describes their meeting in a hotel in Tokyo and their friendship over the years in addition to Adickes's influence introducing him to some artists' work.[105]

Michener had a great impact on art in Texas through the Blanton Museum of Art at the University of Texas, Austin.[106] His collection of American art is rooted in his ideology as a collector (he also extensively collected and wrote about Japanese prints, later donated to the Honolulu Academy of the Arts, later the Honolulu Museum of Art[107]). Michener stated on the gift of his American art collection to the Blanton Museum of Art: "This collection was formed by a professional writer who felt that he ought to know what artists living in America during his lifetime were doing."[108] Upon meeting Adickes in Japan, he took an interest in the artist, contributing to the *Adickes* volume and collecting his work. Adickes painted *Portrait of James A. Michener* (1962) "as a gift of the painter to the writer"[109] (figure 2.11). The painting features the author in front of text from his popular 1959 book, *Hawaii*.

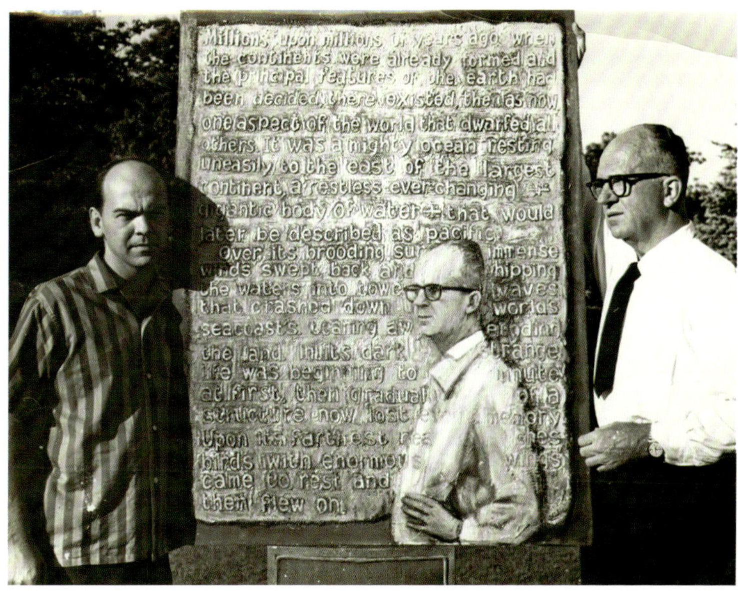


**Figure 2.12.** Photograph of David Adickes and James Michener with Adickes's portrait of Michener. Undated photograph. Collection of David Adickes. Credit: David Adickes.

The author, identified as A. N. in *The James A. Michener Collection: Twentieth Century American Painting*, describes the portrait as:

> The conception of the picture expresses well Adickes' concern for the elemental and central position of man in the universe. The text is taken from Michener's book *Hawaii*, and the technique of carving the letters out of a fast-drying base conveys an appearance of something archaic, monumental, and eternal. Adickes covered the letters with silver leaf and placed them on a background of blues suggesting the surface of the sea.[110]

The portrait entered the Blanton collection along with another work featuring Michener, *The Artist* (*Portrait of James Michener*), from 1964 and two other paintings typical of Adickes's series of still lifes and the elongated men, *Red Still Life* (1961) and *Three Blue Figures* (1965).[111] Works by other artists from the Michener collection show a vast and varying interest in American art from the Ashcan school to the 1960s, including William Glackens, Jo Baer, John Marin, Stuart Davis, Helen Frankenthaler, Ellsworth Kelly, Lee Lozano, and Richard Tuttle.[112]

By the late 1960s, Adickes's work, through its presence in the Michener collection, gained national notice. In 1969, David Adickes's artwork was featured in *Art in America*. Eleanor Freed's "Windfall for Texas" focused on the gift of the James A. Michener collection to the University of Texas. The brief essay featured David Adickes's portrait of his friend and patron, *Portrait of James Michener* (1962), alongside a Morris Louis painting, *Water-Shot* (1961).[113] Louis, assured in his status within the modernist canon by Clement Greenberg, is placed next to Adickes's portrait, with text behind the subject, of the popular author.

In the 1950s and 1960s, Adickes helped to create the Houston gallery scene that is still present today. He understood the economy of the gallery, focusing his work on what he had learned from European modernism and the taste of the Texas patrons. Art historian Louise Siddons, in her book *Centering Modernism: J. Jay McVicker and Postwar American Art*, describes how a focused study on an artist primarily based in Oklahoma, J. Jay McVicker, can elucidate how American artists, not just those in New York City or Los Angeles, understood and made modernism their own. She offers a framework for consideration here:

> Throughout this book, I suggest that McVicker (like many other midcentury modernists) was participating in historically significant international conversations that matter despite—and even because of—the extent to which they were marginalized by New York critics and more-recent historians. As historians, we are overdue to reconsider the modernisms being presented by artists across the country as culturally significant evidence of American modernity writ large, rather than as a series of isolated movements whose relevance was diluted by allegedly regional concerns.[114]

Siddons argues against coastalization while also, assuredly, asserting that one cannot place these artists back into a canon, stating, "At its heart, the structure of the canon has always been one of exclusion, both for its subjects and for its objects: those who cannot or do not speak *about* the canon are likewise denied the possibility of speaking *to* it."[115] Additionally, she states we can look to the reception of these artists (and Adickes, along with many of the artists otherwise briefly mentioned in this chapter). As we have seen, the focus of Texas-based critical reception reaffirms how the coastal canon of the avant-garde tautologically established and confirmed its status: "Looking at almost any regionally delimited survey of midcentury modernism, we can see both the effects and coastalization on critical and scholarly responses and the actual breadth of the American avant-garde."[116] There are moments within and without the canon throughout the careers of many Houston-based artists. As Siddons points out, questioning the credence given over to, for example, a New York City–based art critic allows us to question other ways in which an emphasis on only a few American cities as art centers marks and/or erases artists outside those art centers.

In 1967, Adickes opened Love Street Light Circus and Feel Good Machine in Houston, described by Adickes as "the hottest psychedelic club in town."[117] The nightclub, including live music and the space, "was a big room with giant mattresses and hundreds of colored pillows, and everyone would lie horizontal looking at the light show."[118] Additionally, Adickes described his inspiration as a visit to the Fillmore Auditorium in San Francisco. Upon his return to Texas:

> I bought an overhead projector and took it to my hometown of Huntsville. I showed it to a friend and we hung a sheet and experimented with making liquid projections. A dance class came over and started dancing behind it. It was a "happening."[119]

Somewhere between a multimedia installation with the live music and light experience, the club participated in the more psychedelic aspects of the late '60s. Many psychedelic bands, both local and national, played at the Love Street; including ZZ Top's first shows.[120] The club was successful during the summer of 1967; Adickes ended his involvement the following year.[121]

By the end of the 1960s, the Houston galleries and art institutions were a system, resembling the origins of the networks present in the city today. Adickes's career during the 1950s and '60s offers a view on a successful, working Texas artist. He helped to shape the Houston gallery scene with his reciprocal, supportive relationship with Ben DuBose. His friendship with Herb Mears provided an artistic community of reciprocal influence. His exhibition history during this window of his career showcases how Houston, and to some extent Texas as a whole, functioned as an art community for artists through his encounters, some brief and some sustained, with Ben DuBose, John de Menil, the Texas and Houston Annuals, Contemporary Arts Association, and Museum of Fine Arts, Houston, becoming part of the foundations of contemporary Houston's art institutions. His encounters with what are now well established Houston art institutions provide an example of a successful Texas midcentury artist.

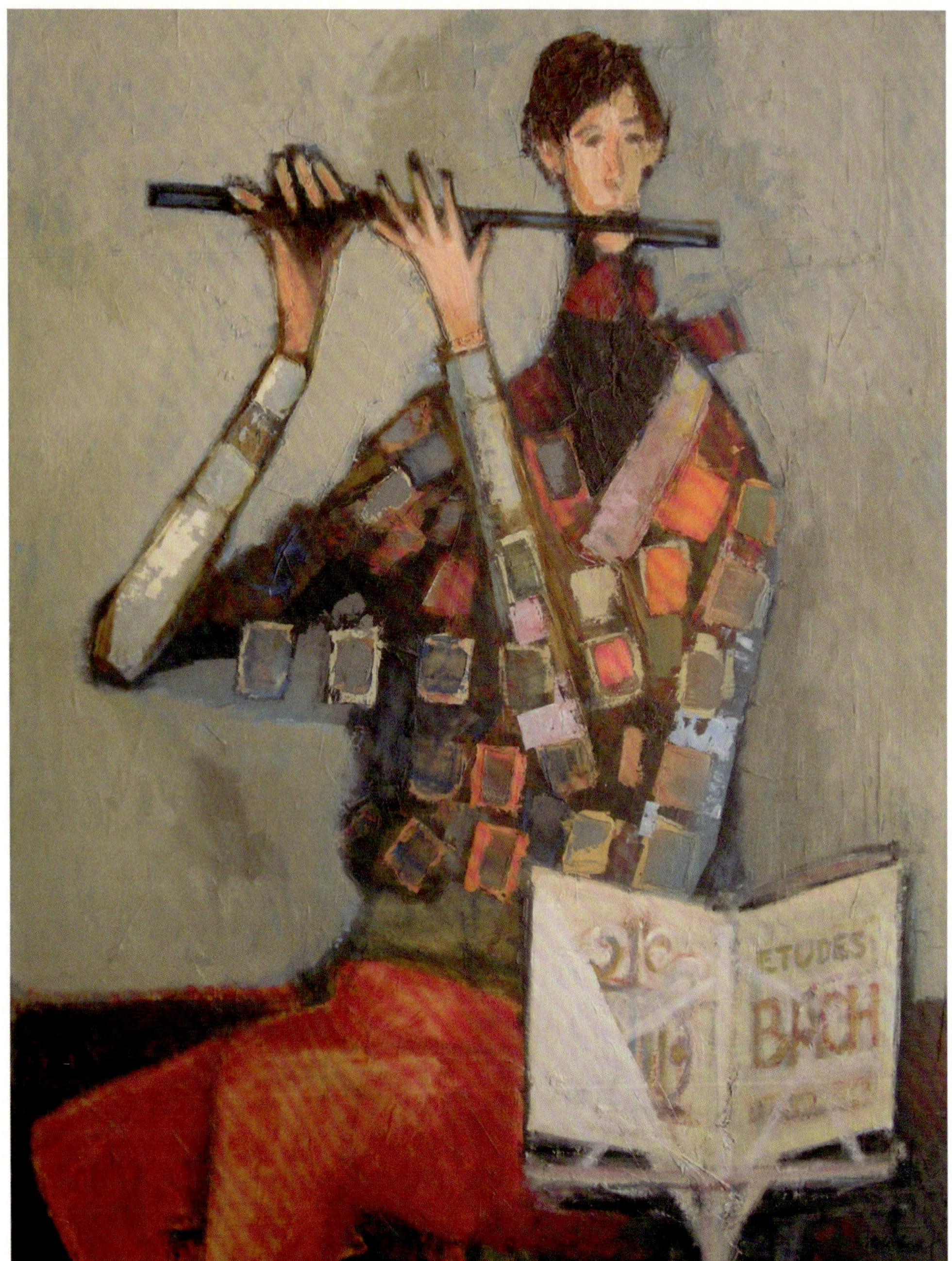


**Figure 3.1.** David Adickes, *Flutist Playing Bach*, 1960s, oil on canvas, 36 × 48 inches. Credit: David Adickes.

# Chapter 3

## David and Goliaths

### *History, Monumentality, and Kitsch in the Public Art of David Adickes*

Michael H. Henderson

In the 1970s, David Adickes was exhibiting his paintings throughout Texas and, for a while, had exhibits in New York at Wally Findlay Gallery. The New York exhibitions received brief notices in national art trade journals—single paragraph reviews in which one writer described Adickes's paintings as "Pop Impressionism."[1] The magazines that published these mini-reviews were filled at the time with images of abstract art (most of it minimalist, hard edged, and geometric), earth art, and pop art. The critical writing and essays that fill the pages surrounding these reviews is concerned with rethinking the idea of art, "de-defining" modernist ideas, and exploring new expanded definitions of what art could be. It is striking to think of Adickes's paintings in the context of these publications because his work remained firmly in the pre–World War II modernist tradition. One reviewer at the time seems to find a relief in Adickes's work, not only from the critical de-definition of art, but from the general turmoil of the time. The reviewer describes Adickes's works as:

> without fluctuating from a peculiarly personal vision of elongated youthful motionless people, unsmilingly happy, silently playing musical instruments, brightly looking without seeing anyone, people unaffected by cold or heat.
>
> Backgrounds of a single color put on gently by palette knife are a special factor in giving these large (and small) oils a serenity and feel of timelessness that are a haven to live with in these our times of metal beast and airborne terror.[2]

Adickes was forty-three in 1970, a successful mature artist who had introduced the school of Paris style of painting into the regionalist aesthetic of Texas art. His cubist paintings influenced by Braque and Picasso had been refreshing to Texans in the 1950s and '60s, but by the late 1970s a new generation of artists in Texas was catching up with the changes happening in the New York and international art world. Younger artists were making works that reflected the times, exploring the psyche and issues of identity, telling stories, and looking back to nature. Other artists of Adickes's generation were picking up where the abstract expressionists left off, emphasizing that a painting was an object and exploring new ways to use form and color.

In 1985, curators Susie Kalil and Barbara Rose set out to define the moment and a "Houston school" of painting in *Fresh Paint,* an exhibition they organized for the Museum of Fine Arts, Houston. The exhibition received international attention, was reviewed in the *New York Times,* and featured on the cover of *Art in America.* The curators included "56 paintings by 44 artists and designated them a fifth major regional school in America (alongside Chicago, Washington, D.C., Los Angeles, and San Francisco)."[3]

David Adickes, who had been a dominant figure in the Houston art scene in the 1950s and '60s was not included in the exhibition. As Melissa L. Mednicov states in chapter 2, Kalil, in the exhibition catalog essay, describes Adickes as popularizing a "French salon style" of "finicky abstractions of bridges, villages, waterfronts, and ports as well as surreal compositions of elongated figures. Although many examples may be deemed flaccid decorations by today's standards, their Cézannesque interpretation was considered an appropriate style in those years."[4]

Herb Mears, Leila McConnell, and Henri Gadbois were also excluded from the exhibition. Several artists of their generation were included, but those chosen were exploring trails blazed by the abstract expressionist movement, or making paintings that were personal and often narrative, and many of them considered painting an expression of something spiritual. These artists were making paintings that explored new visual territory and were different from what paintings had looked like before them. Adickes, in contrast, was making paintings that looked like art was "supposed" to look like because they looked like paintings that had been done before. Adickes's stylized figures and landscapes would remain in the school of Paris and not go on to the school of Houston.

*Flutist with Bach,* painted in 1964, typifies Adickes's style of elongated figures that include poets, musicians, philosophers, and artists. Rather than challenging formal conventions, exploring his psyche or Jungian archetypes, Adickes relies on his technical mastery of the brush and his intuitive understanding of color to make decorative paintings that are pleasing to look at. The elongation of the figure is reminiscent of Amedeo Modigliani, an Italian painter of the school of Paris. Adickes paints with a knife and a brush to apply layers of color that create depth and texture. The dominant warm oranges and reds in the painting are supported by small appearances of sky blue and a wide variety of neutral beiges and grays. The shirt of the musician is a playground for Adickes to explore the relations between these colors in rectangles that teeter toward abstraction and create a sense of rhythmic movement across and off the figure.

While he disavowed abstraction in a conversation published in Linda Wiley's *Making It Happen,*[5] Adickes was no stranger to it. In the late 1950s, Adickes spent a year in Japan and created a series of black-and-white sumi ink drawings that would influence his style of painting. While many of them appear nonobjective at first glance, they mostly all are loose

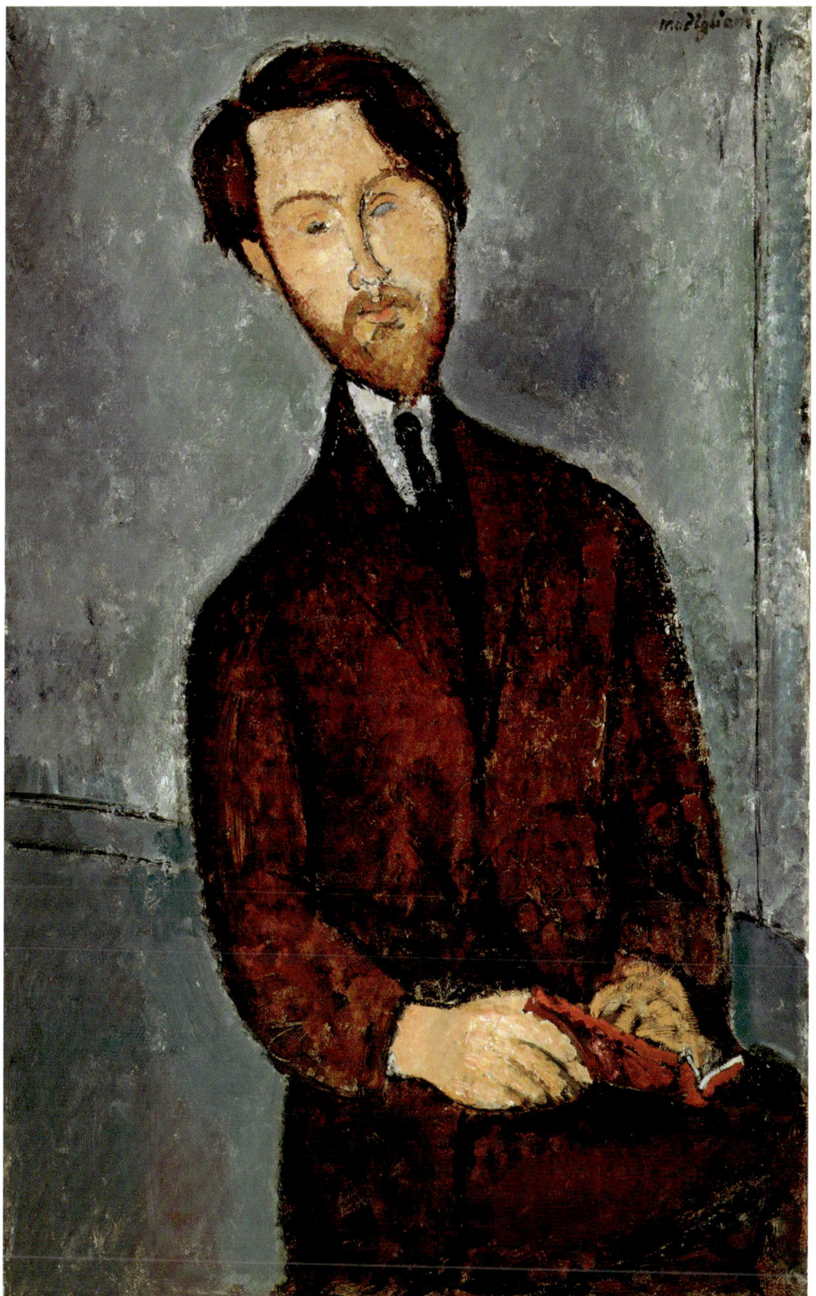


**Figure 3.2.** Amedeo Modigliani, *Leopold Zborowski*, c. 1916, oil on canvas, 45 3/4 × 28 3/4 inches. Courtesy of The Museum of Fine Arts Houston, John A. and Audrey Jones Beck Collection, gift of Audrey Jones Beck. 98.292 Photograph © The Museum of Fine Arts, Houston; Jud Haggard.

depictions of landscapes, still lifes, and figures. *Abacus* is a good example of what seems to be nonobjective image but is objectified by its title.

The sumi ink drawings prepared him for several oil paintings he made in black and white. *Storm Over Olive Grove* is another good example of how Adickes simplified an event and landscape and distilled it into an expressive abstraction.

Adickes's ink drawings, as well as many of his black-and-white watercolors and oil paintings from the 1950s and '60s, are stylistically related to work by John Hubley, an important animator of the time. Hubley was significant for developing a modern style of drawing used in animation that became known as the "UPA style."[6] The relationship can be seen in the still image from Hubley's animated film *The Tender Game* (1958) and Adickes's ink drawing *Night Riders* (1958). (*Night Riders* is a composition similar to an oil painting by Adickes, *Oriental Landscape.*)

*The Tender Game* is an animated short film that tells a love story set to a jazz score by Oscar Peterson and Ella Fitzgerald. In these drawings, both artists simplify forms into brushmarks and imply imagery by leaving things out. Hubley was a leader of a radical shift in animation design in the 1950s. Hubley and numerous other animators and designers

> conceived a bold visual style that was derived from the modern arts, assimilating and adapting principles of Cubism, Surrealism, and Expressionism into the realm of animation and in the process expanding and redefining the art form.[7]

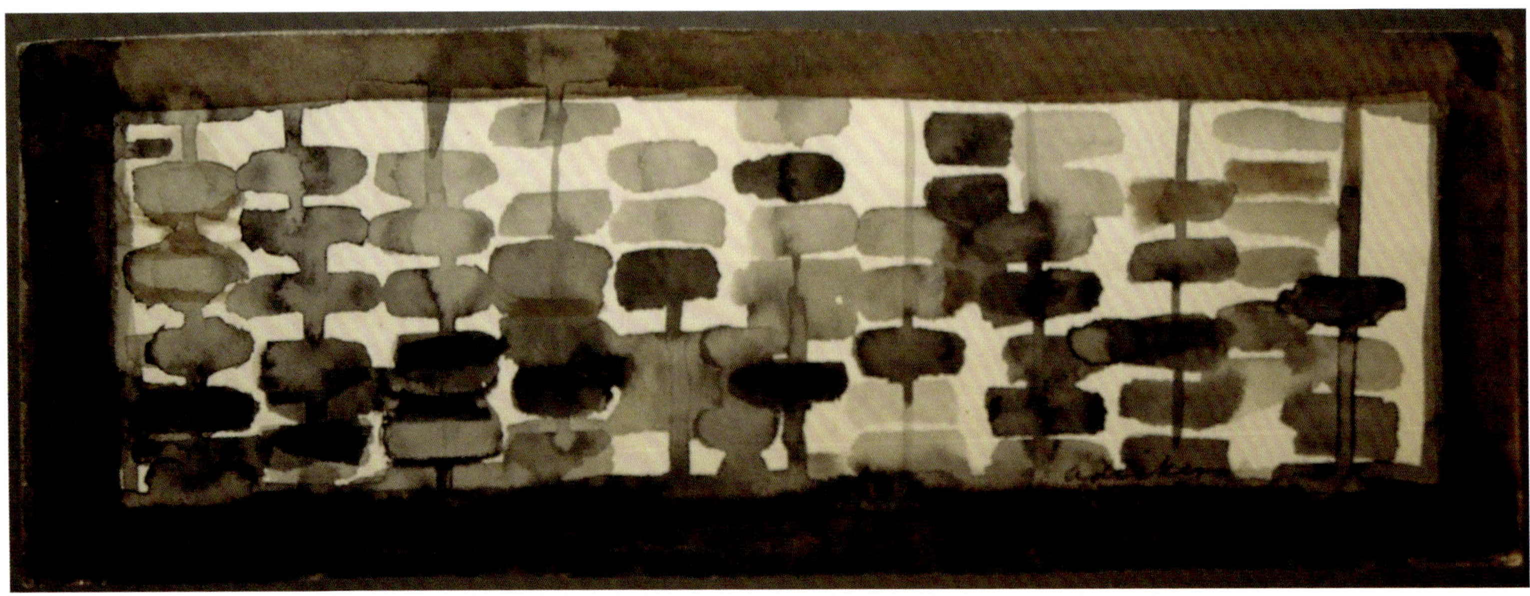

**Figure 3.3**. David Adickes, *Abacus*, 1958, sumi ink on paper, 4 1/2 × 11 1/4 inches. Credit: David Adickes.

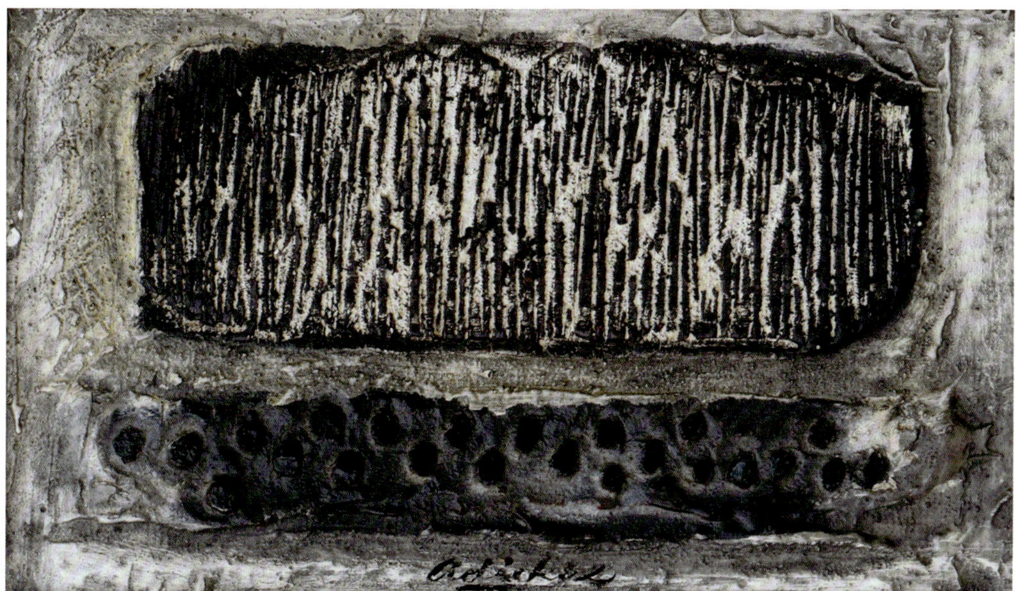

**Figure 3.4.** David Adickes, *Storm over Olive Grove*, 1960s, oil on board, 5 1/4 × 9 inches. Credit: David Adickes

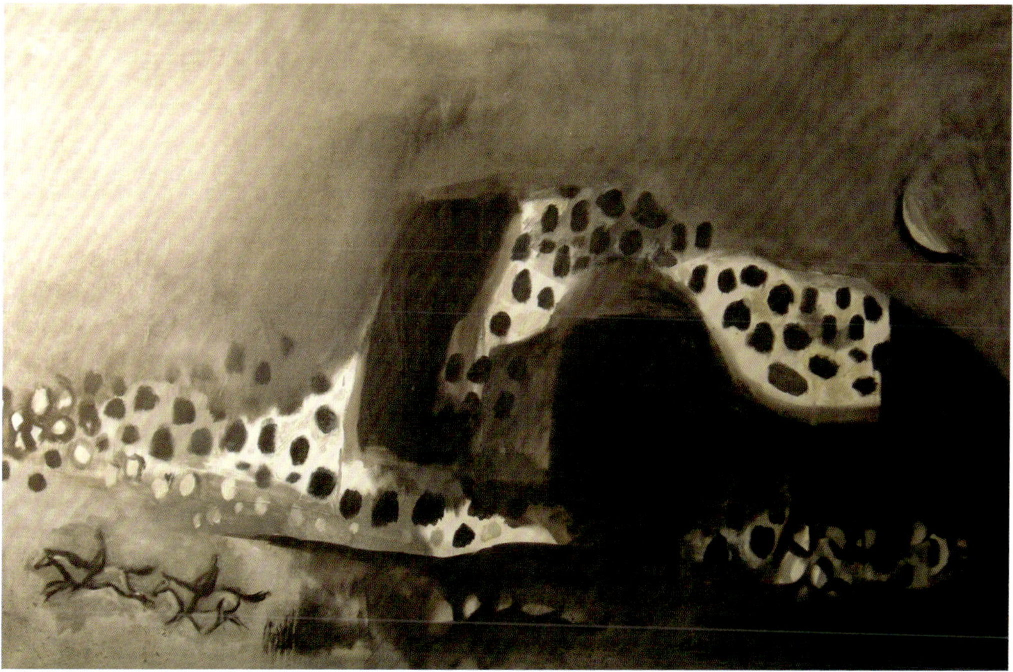

**Figure 3.5.** David Adickes, *Night Riders*, 1959, oil on canvas, 24 × 45 inches. Credit: David Adickes.

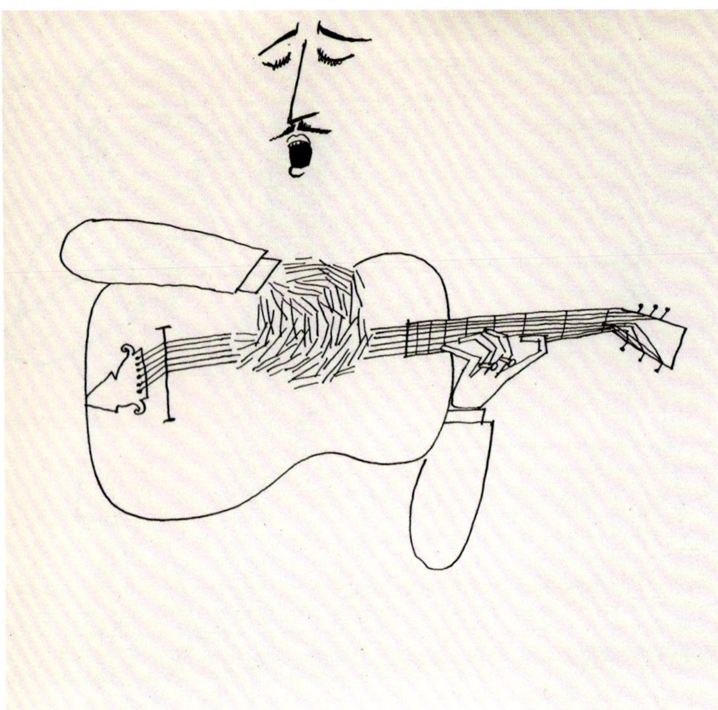

**Figure 3.6.** Saul Steinberg, *Singing Guitarist,* 1952–54, ink on paper, 11 1/4 x 14 1/4 inches. Credit: Private collection, © The Saul Steinberg Foundation / Artists Rights Society (ARS), New York.

These "Cartoon Modernists" were also influenced by jazz record album cover designers David Stone Martin and Jim Flora, and artists like Saul Steinberg.

It is not surprising that Adickes's paintings are stylistically related to mid-twentieth-century animation. Adickes and the animation artists shared influences and distilled the styles of modern art and embraced popular art. This embrace, demonstrated by Adickes's use of subjects such as owls, harlequins, matadors, and clichéd French cityscapes, is often mentioned and cannot be ignored. Clement Greenberg, the art critic of mid-twentieth-century American art, wrote that kitsch is an aspect of art that is made from

> the availability close at hand of a fully matured cultural tradition, whose discoveries, acquisitions, and perfected self-consciousness kitsch can take advantage of for its own ends. It borrows from it devices, tricks, stratagems, rules of thumb, themes, converts them into a system, and discards the rest.[8]

In the 1980s, two opportunities arose that would change the direction of David Adickes's career. Adickes had been making small bronze sculptures since the 1960s that were complements to his paintings. He had aspired to make larger sculptures since the early 1970s and wanted to move his work out of private spaces and into public spaces.[9] In 1975, Adickes presented a proposal to the city of Houston for a "16-foot abstract three-dimensional portrait of Sydney Lanier to be installed near Lanier High School."[10] The project proposal was developed and advanced but ultimately not realized due to changes in municipal administration and funding challenges. In 1982, Joe Russo, a Houston banker and real estate developer, asked Adickes to design a public sculpture for a plaza in front of an office tower he was building in downtown Houston. Russo was familiar with Adickes's work and owned several of his paintings. His building was to be located at the edge of the performing arts/theater district, and he wanted a sculpture that would represent the cultural arts.

*Virtuoso* is a thirty-six-foot-tall concrete sculpture located at Lyric Center in downtown Houston. It realizes in three-dimensions and on a grand scale the stylistic qualities of Adickes's paintings. A goateed male face similar to one of the

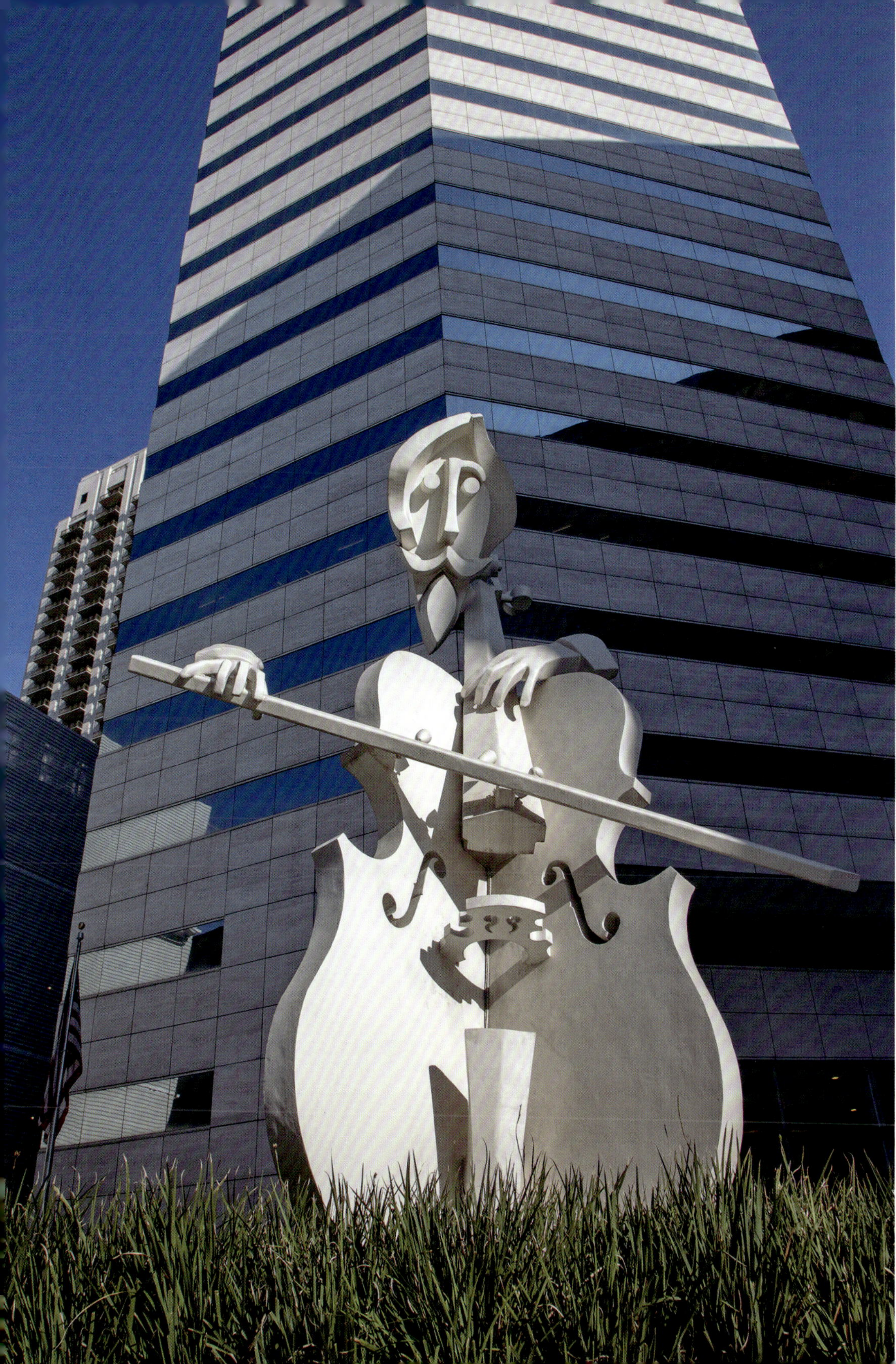

**Figure 3.7.** David Adickes, *Virtuoso*, 1982. Credit: Rebecca Finley.

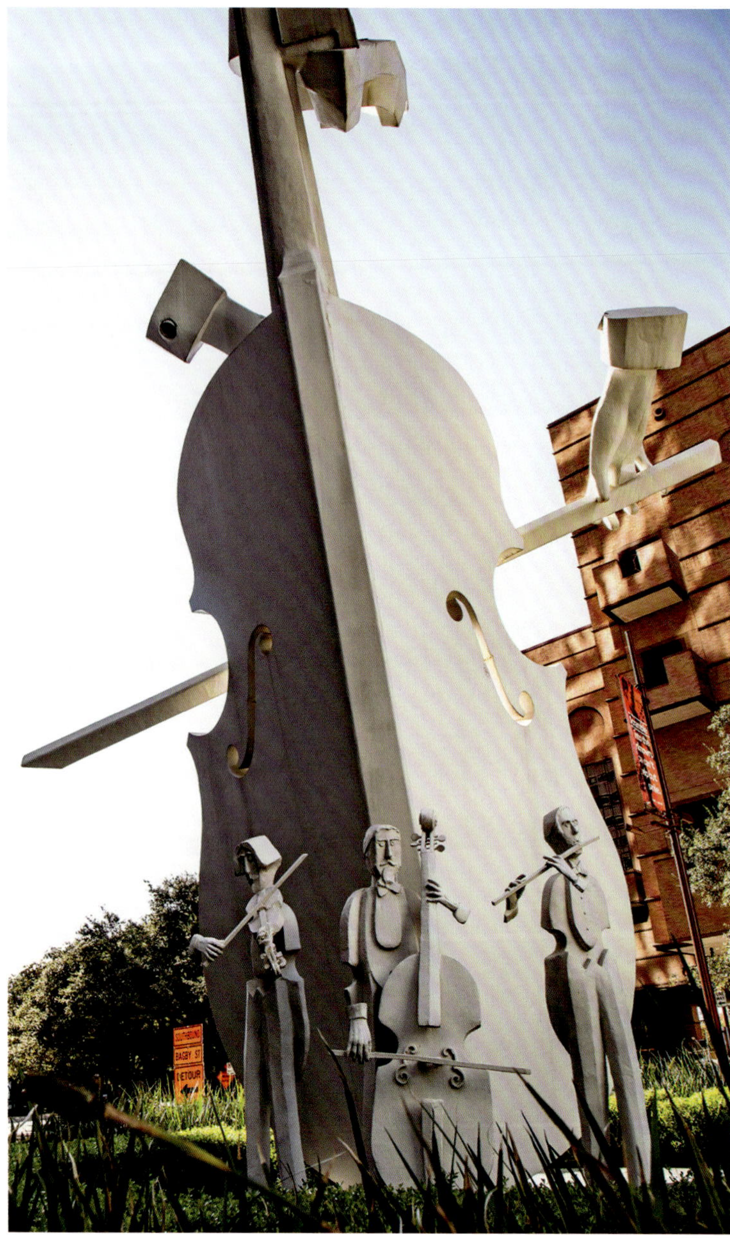

**Figure 3.8.** David Adickes, *Virtuoso*, 1982 (detail). Credit: Rebecca Finley.

men in Adickes's paintings floats in front of the neck of a giant cello. The only parts of the figure visible in the sculpture are the head and the two hands, one on the strings of the cello and one on the bow that crosses the body. The face of the man has simplified, stylized cubistic, and mask-like features. Without color and textural brushwork of Adickes's painted images, the smooth concrete renders the figure more cartoon-like. Behind the thirty-six-foot-tall cello are three life-sized figures of musicians playing the cello, a violin, and a flute. These figures have torsos and legs attached to their heads, and their coats echo the shape of the cello. They are absent arms, and, like the giant virtuoso behind them, their disembodied hands float in the air attached to the instruments they play. The violinist has the familiar shock of hair parted in the middle and the mask-like goateed face. The cellist's face has a similar blank expression. The flute player, however, purses his lips as he blows the instrument, and his eyes are more life-like and expressive than the others, they seem as if they might be fixed on something in the distance. This face is slightly more life-like than the other two characters, perhaps because the face is engaged with the musical instrument.

*Virtuoso* was installed in the public plaza in front of the Lyric Center in 1983 (see figure 4.65). Adickes incorporated two speakers into the sculpture that subtly played classical music and could be heard when viewers approached the sculpture. With this monumental sculpture, Adickes successfully freed himself from constraints of the gallery and the art world. *Virtuoso* was greeted with the same criticism that had been applied to his paintings, but Adickes would not hesitate. He unflinchingly proceeded to create more giant cartoon-like sculptures that had popular appeal, if not critical success. He embraced the kitsch-like quality that was suggested in some of his paintings by bringing it front and center in his early monumental sculptures, which included a six-foot-tall half peeled banana (see figure 4.72), a giant French telephone with the facial features of one of his male figures embedded in the device (see figure 4.33), and a twenty-six-foot-long *Stone Trumpet* (see figure 4.39).

Adickes was experimenting and exploring the technical challenges of large-scale concrete sculptures in these early works. He was "intrigued with the idea of producing oversized versions of objects from the early days of the Industrial Age. He admired the finely crafted details of the mechanical instruments of the time and imagined the impact of those details expanded to overpowering proportions."[11] Adickes had an old cornet that he acquired from a junk store that became the model for *Stone Trumpet* (sometimes called *Cornet*). In what would become a familiar modus operandi, he undertook the creation of the monumental musical instrument prior to having a dedicated site for the sculpture. While he was in the process of creating the work, Adickes arranged for the sculpture to be shown at the Louisiana World Exposition in 1984 at his own expense. The sculpture would be placed on a stage and serve as a backdrop to musical performances. After the conclusion of the Exposition, Adickes hoped to sell the sculpture to the city of New Orleans as a public work to represent the local music culture. The sale of the sculpture to New Orleans was not realized and, after the Exposition, the sculpture was returned to Adickes's studio where it was structurally redesigned and renovated. It eventually found a permanent home beside the Old Galveston Square Building in the Strand Historic District in Galveston.

The telephone sculpture titled *Big Alex* is a large box-like form that supports a fancy antique receiver in its cradle on top. The front of the large box has a face embedded in its flat surface, with the familiar features of a goateed man. On the phone sculpture, the facial features are simplified to the point of being blocky rectangles and cylinders, but the face is still recognizable as one of Adickes's men in the style of his paintings and *Virtuoso.* The back of the box was originally intended to have three telephone-booth-sized openings that would house functioning telephone booths. *Big Alex*, like the *Stone Trumpet*, was created without a specific site in mind. It was placed in front of the Grand Hotel in Houston for a short time but was returned to Adickes's studio and is, for the time being, parked on the roof of a small building in the Montrose neighborhood of Houston. The six-foot-tall banana sculpture that Adickes created around the same time was painted with red, white, and blue stars and stripes and titled *Star Spangled Banana* or *Star Spangled Bananer.* The banana is reminiscent of a favorite story that Adickes likes to tell; it starts with, "did I tell you about the time ten pounds of bananas saved my life?"[12] However, he states that the sculpture is not a reference to this personal experience but simply an expression of his humor and his fondness for puns.

*Virtuoso*, *Stone Trumpet*, *Big Alex*, and *The Star Spangled Banana* demonstrate Adickes's willingness to embrace and celebrate kitsch, to draw subject matter from popular culture, and the important relationship of his work to music. A later work from 2007, *The Beatles,* shares these themes. Formally, *The Beatles* refer back to the trio of musicians on the backside of *Virtuoso* and numerous paintings of three or four standing men.

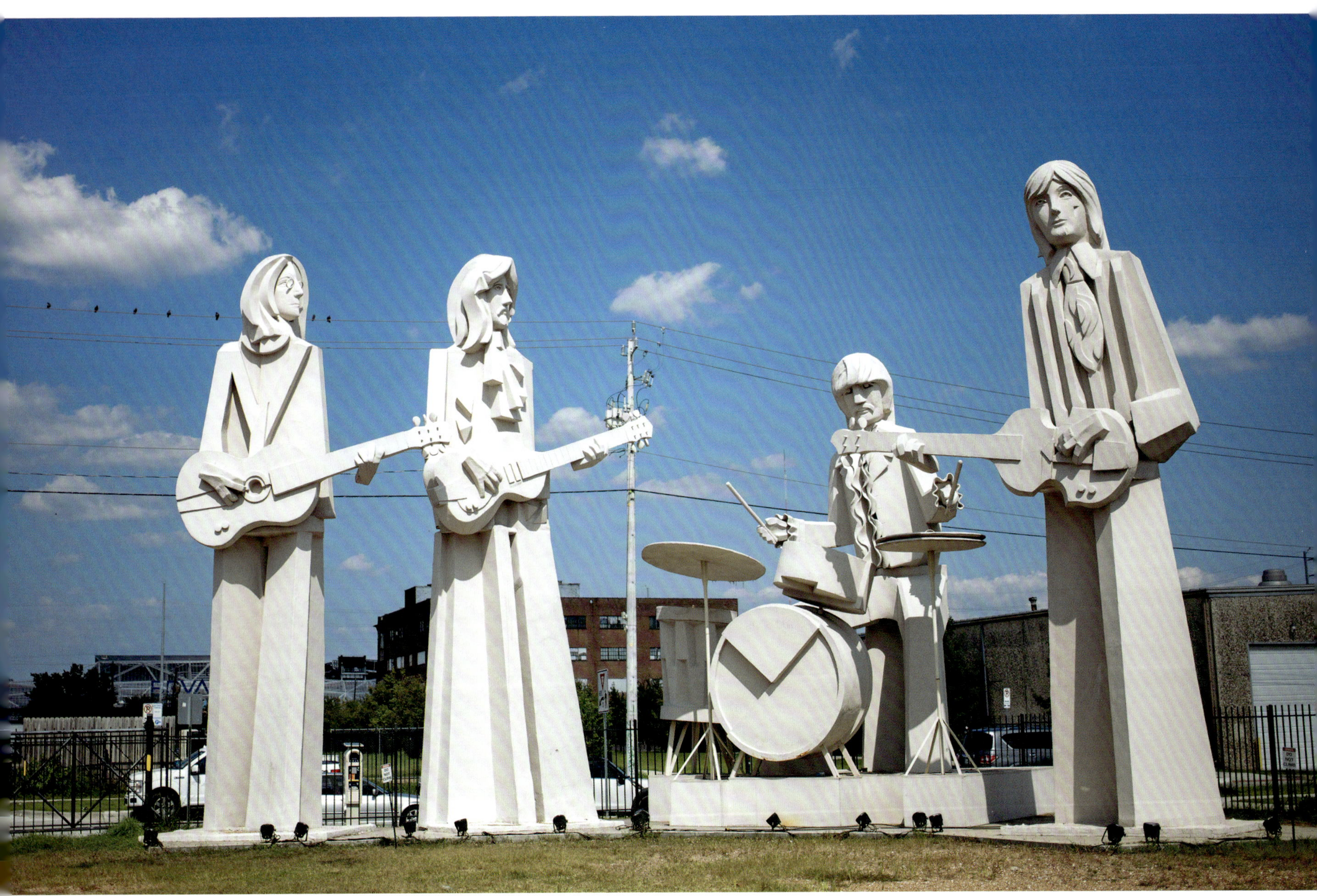

**Figure 3.9.** David Adickes, *The Beatles,* 2007. Credit: Rebecca Finley.

Adickes stated that his favorite compositions have three figures standing in a row and that he added the fourth seated drummer for the Beatles sculpture. The sculpture consists of the four Beatles rendered as thirty-six-foot-tall, elongated figures. Their forms, like the face of *Big Alex,* are abstracted and reduced to simple geometric blocky shapes topped with curvy locks of hair. The abstraction in the figures has more sharp edges and long straight lines than previous works. The few curved forms are limited to the hair and the musical instruments. The figures are at once expressive, cartoon-like, and evocative of an updated three-dimensional version of the animated Beatles in the film *Yellow Submarine.*

References to and images of music are pervasive in Adickes's paintings and sculptures. *The Beatles* is currently located in the outdoor area of a downtown brewery and pub that hosts live music and events. Adickes hopes another recent sculpture will be placed in a similar location. In 2014, Adickes created a thirty-five-foot-tall concrete sculpture of Charlie Chaplin with the intention of placing it outside a venue that shows films. Adickes said that he first saw the films of Chaplin in Paris in the 1950s where they were always playing in theaters, but he had never seen a Chaplin film in the United States. When he moved to his Nance Street studio in 2013, he planned to have Saturday morning screenings of Chaplin films and invite parents to bring their children. The studio quickly became too crowded to allow for this possibility, but the thirty-five-foot-tall figure stands in front of it, underneath the freeway, surrounded by presidents' heads and parts of presidents' heads. Adickes hopes to place Chaplin in a planned beer garden "theme park" that hosts musical events and film screenings.

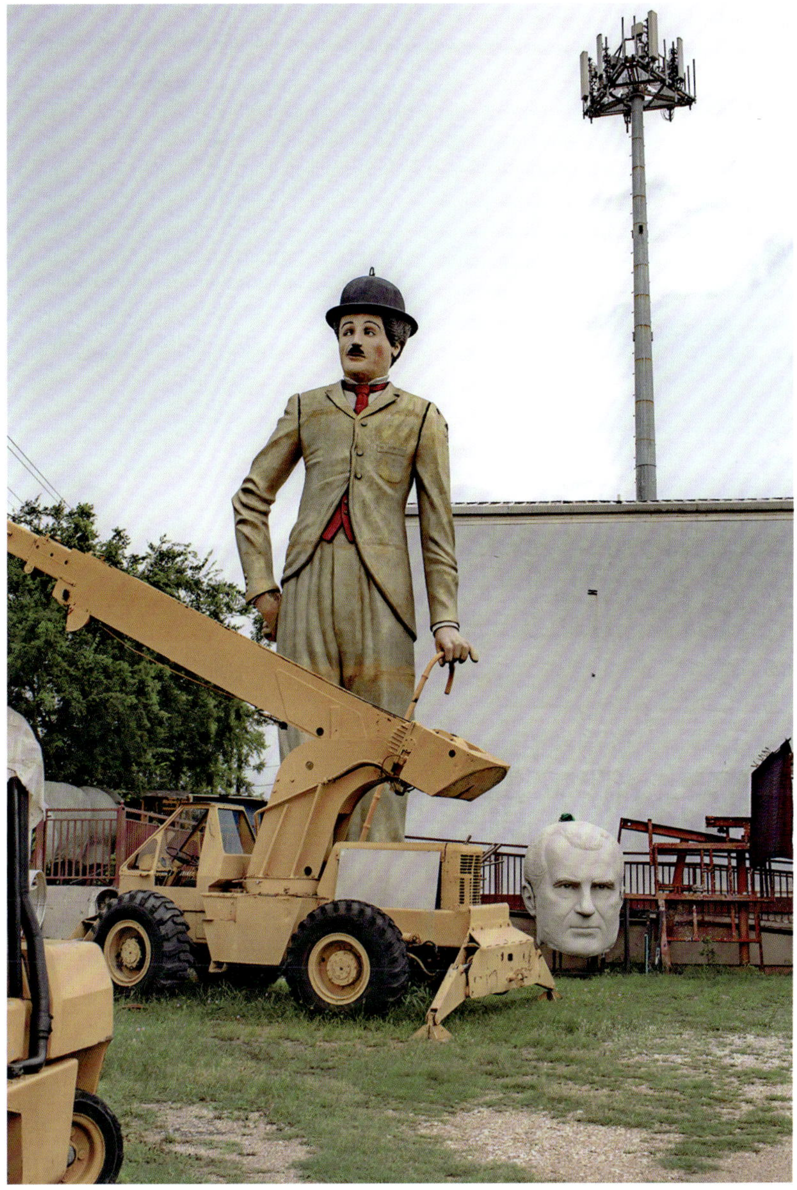

**Figure 3.10.** David Adickes, *Charlie Chaplin,* 2014.
Credit: Michael H. Henderson.

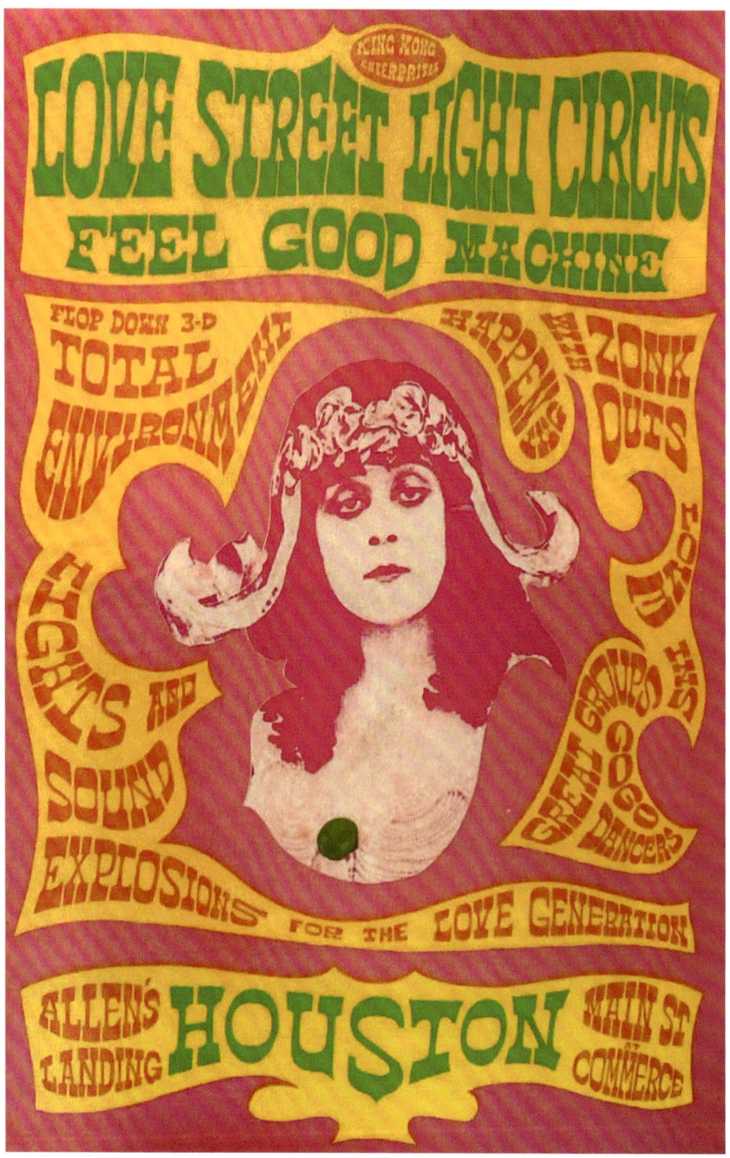


**Figure 3.11.** David Adickes, *Poster for Love Street Light Circus Feel Good Machine,* 1967. Credit: David Adickes.

Although Adickes claims no interest in pop art, his work often intersects with popular culture. His monumental sculptures with their musical and cultural references and engagement are manifestations of the same interests that led Adickes to open a nightclub in Houston in 1967.

At *The Love Street Light Circus and Feel Good Machine,* Adickes bought numerous projectors, hired dancers, and opened a club so that he could create his own psychedelic light shows to accompany musical performers. Over fifty years later, light shows are projected onto his sculpture of the Beatles at night during musical performances.

In 1980, Adickes's work was featured in the *Dick Tracy* comic strip that appeared in daily newspapers across the country. A storyline about a crooked art dealer trying to sell stolen paintings by Cézanne and Picasso includes images of Adickes's paintings on gallery walls. More recently, Karbach Brewing Company, a local Houston brewery, has christened two of their beers "Love Street" and "Light Circus" as an homage to Adickes's nightclub. The designs on the beer can labels are derived from Adickes's poster design for the nightclub. Another local brewery, Buffalo Bayou Brewing Company, included a silhouette of Adickes's statue of Sam Houston on the label of one of their beer cans. These examples are demonstrations of Adickes's work being embraced by and embedded in popular culture.

The opportunity for Adickes to create monumental sculptures came about because a real estate developer was familiar with Adickes's paintings. A second opportunity arose in the late 1980s when another man familiar with Adickes's paintings invited him to create a sculpture. This time the man was the

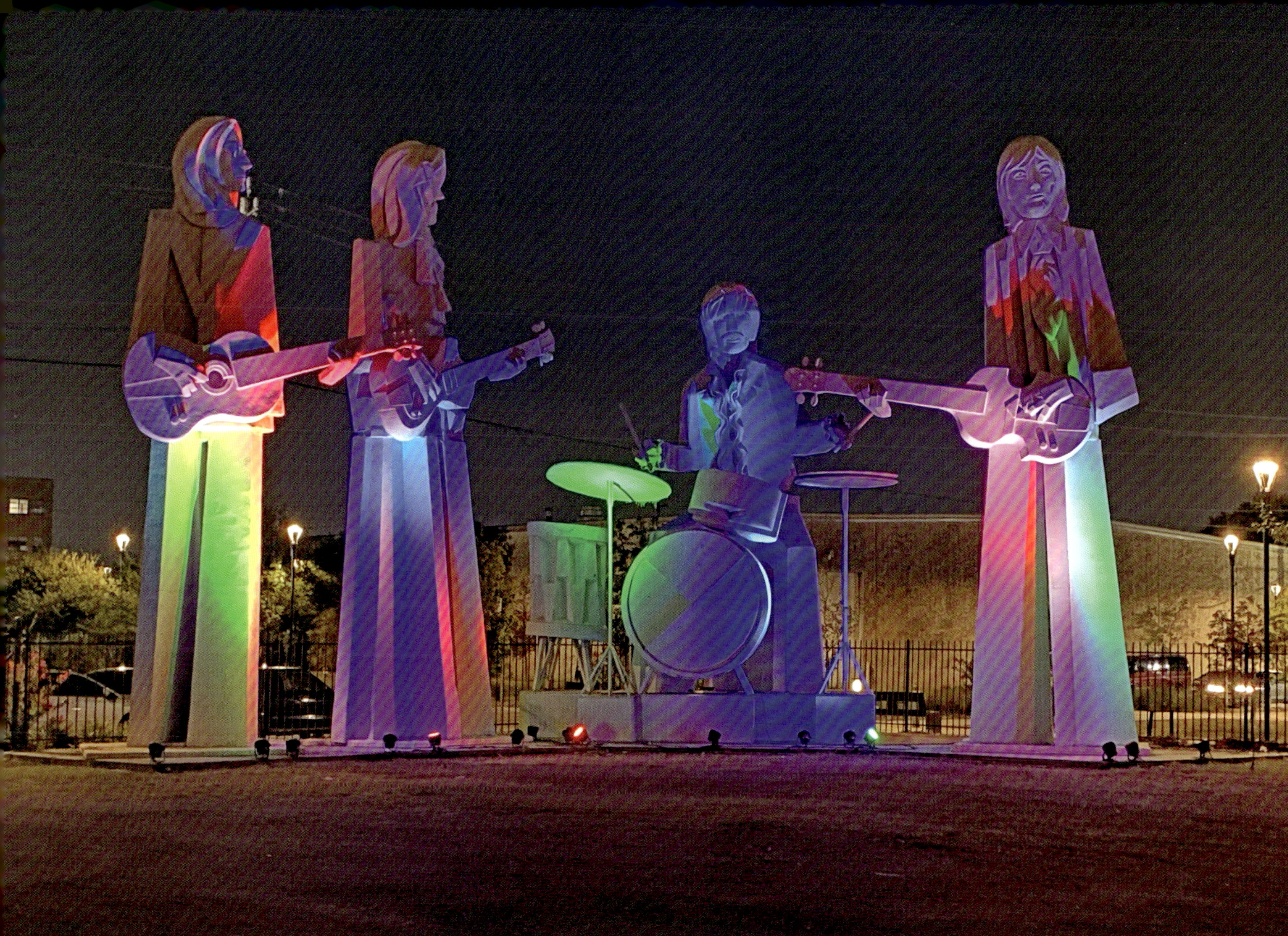

**Figure 3.12**. David Adickes, *The Beatles,* 2007. Credit: Michael H. Henderson.

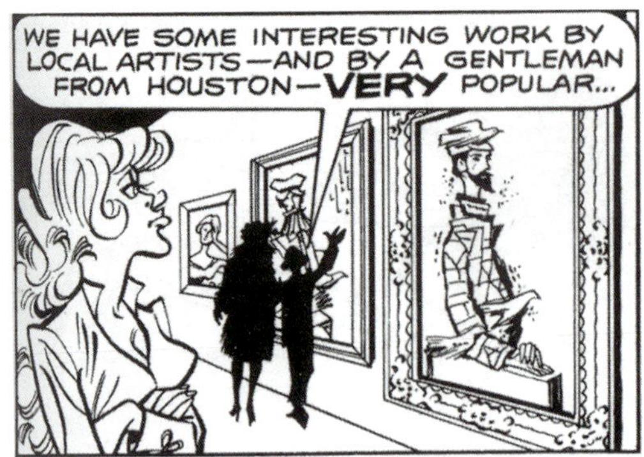


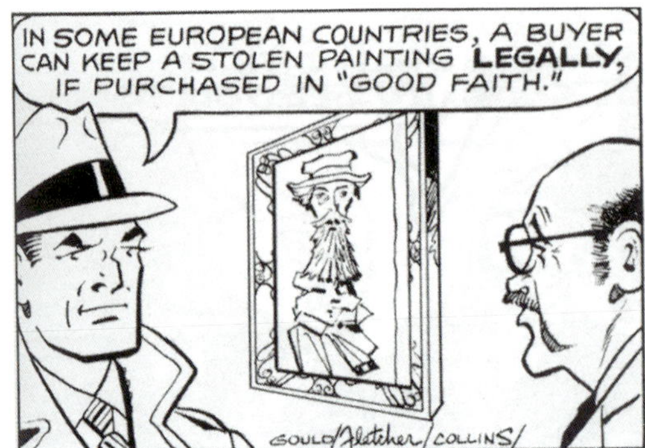


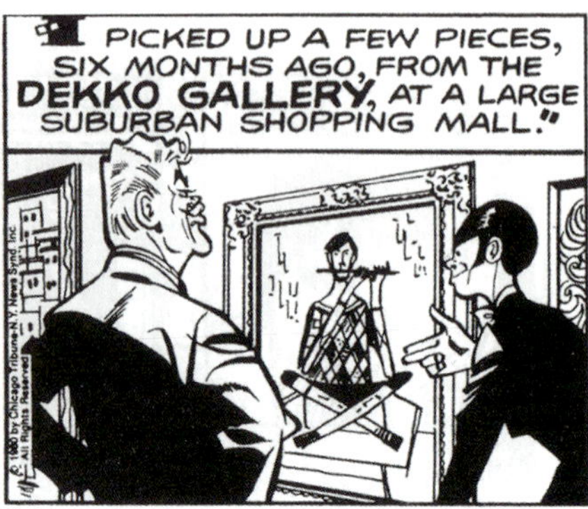


**Figure 3.13.** Rick Fletcher and Max Allan Collins, Dick Tracy comic panels, 1980. Credit: © 1980 Dick Tracy, reprinted with permission, TCA.

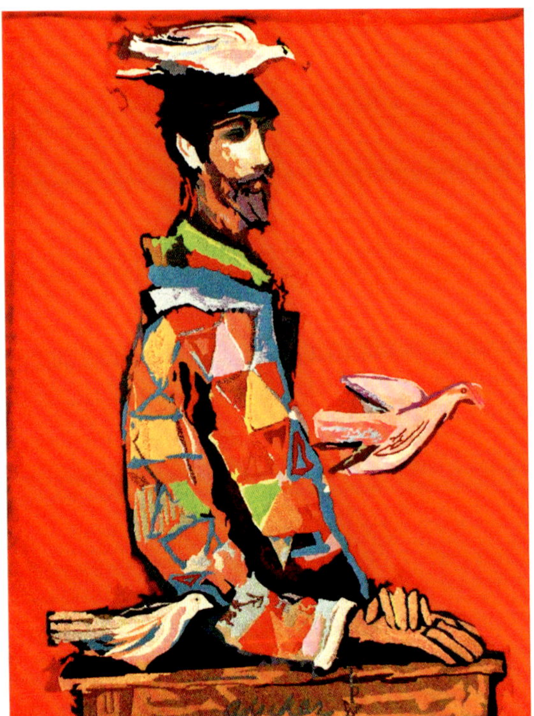

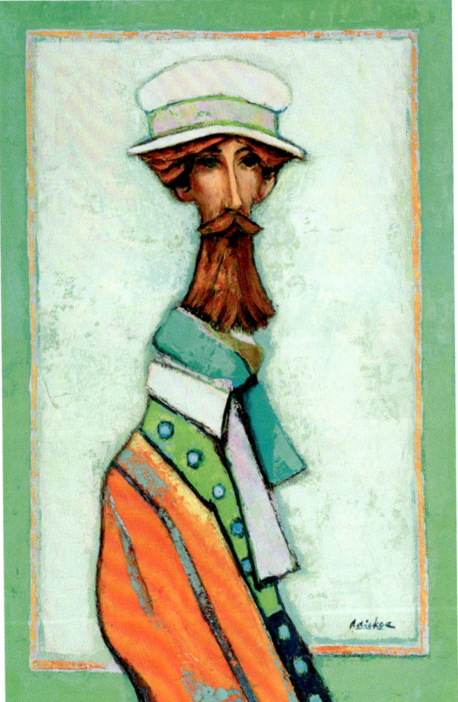


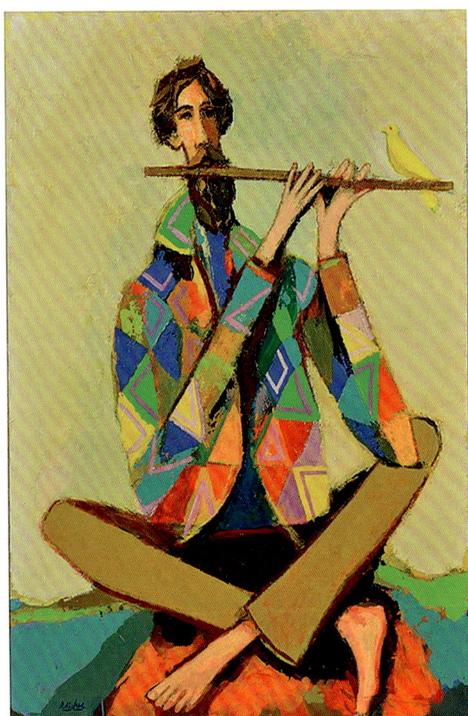

**Figure 3.14.** Three paintings by David Adickes from the 1970s. Credit: David Adickes.

president of the United States, and the opportunity would take Adickes's work in a different direction. George H. W. Bush had acquired one of Adickes's paintings when he visited an exhibition at DuBose Gallery in 1965; "Mr. Bush had met David in the gallery and had ended up with a painting of a group of trees by Adickes. Over the years George Bush forgot neither the gift nor its artist."[13] Years later, when Bush was vice president under Ronald Reagan, Adickes wrote to him and proposed creating a bronze bust. Bush remembered Adickes, whose painting now hung in the vice presidential residence. He was enthusiastic about the proposal, but attempts to schedule a sitting were repeatedly delayed until, by the time Adickes went to Washington to photograph Bush, he had become president.

After visiting Bush in the White House to photograph him for the sculpture, Adickes proposed to depict Bush as a full figure rather than a bust. He decided to pose Bush striding forward, into the wind, with his sleeves rolled up and his suit coat over his shoulder. The title of the sculpture, *Winds of Change,* would appear on the cover of the book in the statue's hand. Adickes chose the title and the pose in response to the fall of the Soviet Union and communism in Eastern Europe that took place during Bush's presidency. The statue was originally intended to be placed in the future presidential library of George H. W. Bush, and Adickes, fearing that the figure would be overwhelmed by architecture, decided to make the statue 30 percent larger than life size. Skills he had developed scaling up the large concrete sculptures *Virtuoso* and *Cornet* were applied to the statue of Bush, which would stand eight feet tall. The sculpture was finished in time to be unveiled at the 1992 Republican convention, which was held in Houston at the Astrodome. The sculpture did not go to the Bush Library; it is now owned by the city of Houston and greets travelers arriving at Terminal C in Bush Intercontinental Airport (see figure 4.8).

After *Winds of Change,* Adickes would make several more bronze sculptures of prominent people. He created a statue of famed cardiovascular surgeon Denton Cooley for the Texas Heart Institute in 2006. In 2011, he created *Standing Tall with Charlie Wilson* for the Charles Wilson V. A. Hospital in Lufkin, Texas, and, in 2013, a statue of Pat Summitt, the women's basketball coach, in Knoxville for the University of Tennessee. Each of these bronze statues stands eight feet tall. Adickes describes why he scaled the figures up in an interview about the Pat Summitt statue:

> "[The University] wanted it life-sized," Adickes said. "I had to convince them that, in my experience, a life-sized statue seen from afar looks diminished. In an interior [setting], life-sized looks O.K. But when it's outside, normally 120 percent to 150 percent is about where it should be. I think she's 144 percent of her real height."[14]

For many years, Adickes had dreamed of making a 280-foot-tall statue of a cowboy to be placed on the side of a Texas freeway. Even before *Virtuoso,* he created a model for the cowboy, which remains one of his dreams. In 1991, while Adickes was working on *Winds of Change,* he heard that the city of Huntsville had formed a committee to commemorate the two hundredth anniversary of Sam Houston's birth in 1993. Adickes attended a committee meeting and proposed creating a fifty- to sixty-foot-tall statue of Sam Houston for the celebration. The proposal, which was uninvited, was neither accepted nor rejected by the bicentennial committee. The committee, prior to Adickes's arrival, was considering projects like a commemorative cook-

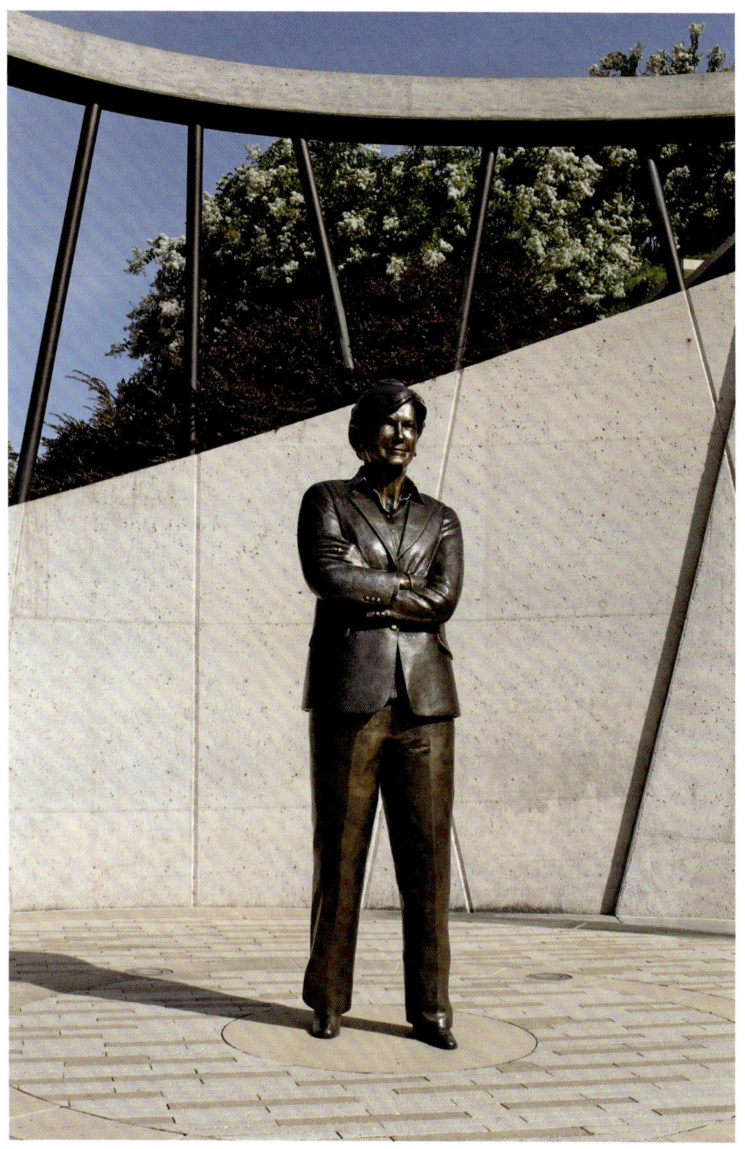

**Figure 3.15.** David Adickes, *Pat Summitt*, 2013.
Credit: Rebecca Finley.

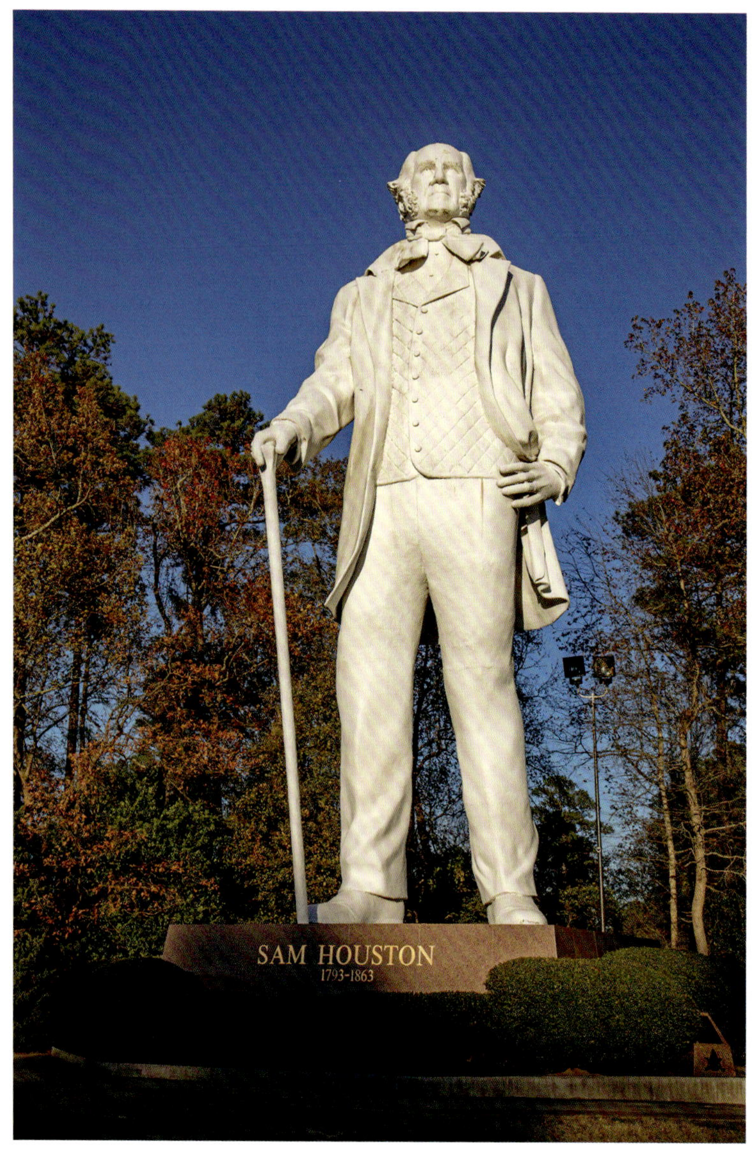


**Figure 3.16.** David Adickes, *A Tribute to Courage*, 1994.
Credit: Rebecca Finley.

book, a concert, commissioning Kenny Rogers to write a song, a poster, or naming a rose after Sam Houston.[15]

Without waiting for approval from the bewildered bicentennial committee, Adickes forged ahead, creating a life-sized plaster model of Sam Houston. He used the model to win support for the project from the president of Sam Houston State University, Dr. Martin Anisman, who provided Adickes with a construction site for the project. He notified the bicentennial committee that he would have the sculpture completed by March 2, 1993, Sam Houston's two hundredth birthday, and proceeded with his project. The statue was not completed in time for the bicentennial, but when it was near completion the following year, Adickes offered it as a gift to the city of Huntsville if they would pay only for the construction of a pedestal. There was opposition on the city council for using taxpayer funds for the pedestal, but eventually supporters who argued for the "immeasurable benefit to the local economy" prevailed, and the sculpture was placed in its location at the gateway to Huntsville.[16] Adickes chose a site just south of Huntsville on property adjacent to Interstate 45 where the freeway changes direction. Traveling north from Houston, the road turns to the northwest, and the placement of the statue on this spot makes it appear directly in front of northbound drivers for about six miles. At night, when it is illuminated, it appears as a speck of light up ahead that gradually grows into a giant white figure looming over traffic. Adickes located the desired property and discovered that it was owned by a friend who had been an Eagle Scout with Adickes in their youth and was happy to donate the land to the city for the statue.[17]

Although the materials and scale of the statue of Houston relate the work to the early monumental concrete sculptures, the style of *A Tribute to Courage* is similar to that of *Winds of Change*. To create the monumental figure, Adickes combined processes he had previously explored in concrete sculptures with those he used to create the bronze statue. The bronze sculpture of Bush and the concrete sculpture of Houston are much more realistic and less stylized and abstracted than the musicians in his other sculptures. The process he developed in the creation of the earlier concrete sculptures involved constructing shapes from metal lath and carved Styrofoam and then coating the forms with concrete. The results were simplified and more geometric and cartoon-like than the style he needed to represent the Texas heroes. The bronze casting of Bush and the life-sized model of Sam Houston were both created in plaster, which allowed Adickes to carve finer details into the sculptures. To enlarge his plaster model of Sam Houston to a monumental sixty-seven-foot-tall figure, Adickes used a combination of the techniques, applying concrete to constructed forms and adding and subtracting from the surface to create detail in the clothing. Adickes wanted more realistic detail in the head so Houston would be recognizable, "Instead of building a frame and attaching a metal lath and concrete, the head [of Houston] was to be constructed from the outside in. This part of the statue would be cast like bronze—by building a rubber mold and pouring thin layers of concrete into it."[18]

Adickes's career path as a sculptor has some parallels to that of Elisabet Ney, who created statues of Texas historical figures and important "men of the world" in the late nineteenth and early twentieth centuries. Ney was a thirty-eight-year-old artist who had sculpted "numerous well-known personalities, among them statesmen, scientists, and artists"[19] when she left her native Germany in 1871 and settled in Texas.[20] She had been a prominent sculptor in Germany before she built her studio in Austin, which now houses the Elisabet Ney Museum. In 1892, Ney was commissioned to create statues of Sam Houston and Stephen F. Austin for the Texas pavilion at the World's Fair in Chicago: "The exposition, which would prove the most expensive and elaborate of the nineteenth century's many world's fairs, was designed to showcase the achievements in art and industry of the United States as a whole as well as of the individual states."[21] When debating the advantages of participating in the fair, a Fort Worth businessman predicted that it would mean "a million more people in six years and $200,000 increase in the wealth brought into our state."[22] After raising money to construct a pavilion, "The Women's World's Fair Exhibit Association of Texas (also referred to as the State Board of Lady Managers)"[23] sought sculptors to create statues of Sam Houston and Stephen F. Austin. Prominent sculptors such as Augustus Saint-Gaudens were beyond the budget. Ney, who had previously created a bust of Texas governor Oran Roberts, and had exhibited her sculpture at the second World's Fair in Paris in 1867,[24] was selected with the recommendation of Governor Roberts, and because Ney offered "her time, skill and ability, free of charge, as an evidence of her desire to assist the ladies of Texas in [their] great work."[25]

Ney's depiction of Sam Houston is unlike Adickes's: "Although most Texans thought of Houston as an elder statesman, by costuming him in buckskin rather than in the fancy capes, frock coats, and leopard vests for which he was well known in his later years, Ney clearly underscored her purpose of representing him as vigorous and still youthful man of forty."[26] Ney hoped that dressing him in buckskin would signify Houston as a pioneer, and "an example of the individual,

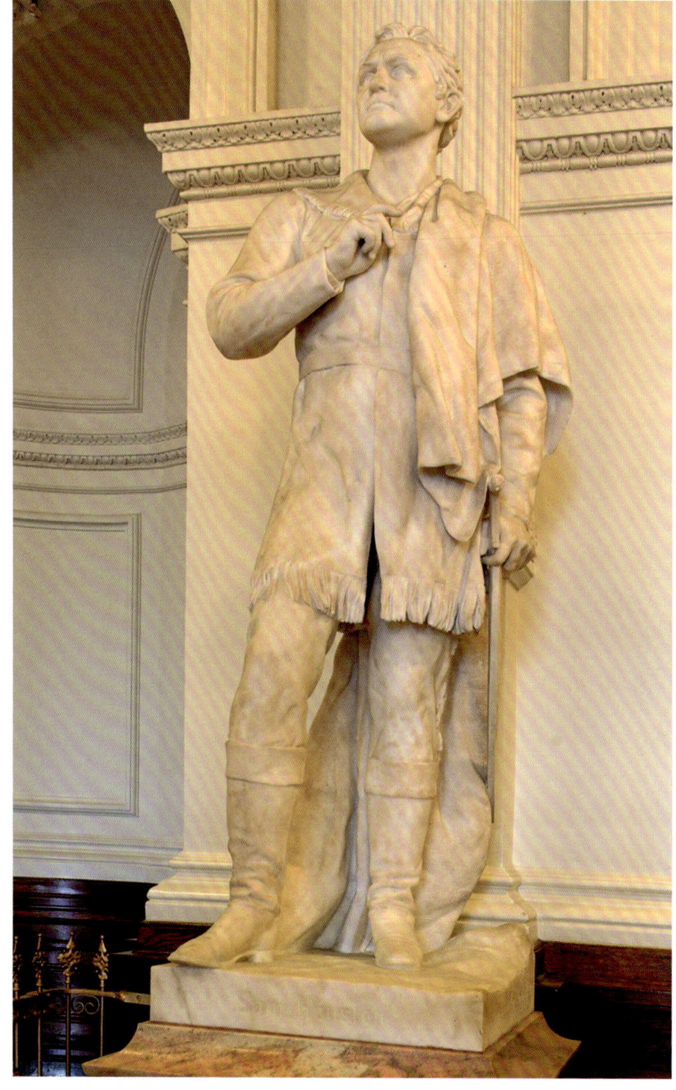

**Figure 3.17.** Elisabet Ney, *Sam Houston*, 1903. Texas Capitol, Austin, Texas. Credit: Photograph by Carol M. Highsmith, 2014. *Marble statue of Sam Houston by Elizabet Ney, unveiled on this spot in the Texas Capitol South Foyer in 1903. Austin, Texas.* The Lyda Hill Texas Collection of Photographs in Carol M. Highsmith's *America Project*, Library of Congress, Prints and Photographs Division.

stripped of the trappings of hereditary aristocracy, rising to his rightful place in democratic society."[27]

Adickes's statue of Houston, in contrast, depicts Houston in his later years, as a dignified statesman:

> The Sam Houston that David chose to depict, was the man in his later years—around age 67. This was not the brash youth who ran off to live with the Cherokees, not even the hero of San Jacinto. This was the Sam Houston recently accused of being a traitor to his Texas and his South.[28]

Linda Wiley goes on to explain that Adickes chose to depict Houston at the end of his political career:

> Here, in the years preceding the Civil War, was perhaps the greatest display of Sam Houston's courage—not the valor of the battlefield, but the courage to stand by one's principles and beliefs. Above all else, Sam Houston believed in the Union and the Constitution. So powerful was this belief, so strong his conviction, that Sam Houston sacrificed his political career and the respect of his fellow Texans in his unsuccessful fight to keep Texas in the Union.
>
> This is the courage for which Sam Houston should most be remembered. . . . By building the statue, David Adickes, himself a champion of these ideals, hoped to revitalize and intensify the message.[29]

Elisabet Ney was not able to complete both the proposed statues in time for the World's Fair. The sculpture of Stephen F. Austin was postponed, but the plaster model of Sam Houston was finished and a huge success at the World's Fair. She later completed statues of both in marble. In Ney's statues, both men are dressed in buckskin and posed in the "contrapposto position of one seeming to mirror the other."[30] One key difference was their height, Houston at six foot two inches was taller than Austin who stood five foot seven inches: "Anyone who disliked the discrepancy, the sculptor was supposed to have said, should take up the issue not with her, but with God."[31]

Like Ney, Adickes would also create a statue of Stephen F. Austin that stands as a kind of bookend to his monumental Sam Houston. *Stephen F. Austin: Father of Texas* is a sixty-foot-tall statue of the man who led the first Anglo settlers to Texas. Adickes designed the statue to be a few feet shorter than Sam Houston in *A Tribute to Courage.* The Austin statue, completed in 2006, is located south of Houston in a county park adjacent to State Highway 288 near Angleton, Texas. The site is on land once granted to Austin and a "focal point for Austin's earliest settlements."[32] Adickes's Austin is dressed in buckskin like Ney's, and, also like hers, he holds his rifle vertically against his body. In Adickes's sculpture, the rifle is fifty-two feet tall. Austin grasps the rifle at the top, holding it at the height of his neck like a tall walking stick in contrast to, and reminiscent of, the cane that steadies Houston in *A Tribute to Courage*. Ney, who was trained as a classical sculptor in a German art academy, renders the early Texans in more relaxed poses than Adickes. Ney's Houston holds his cloak over his shoulder, like Adickes's George H. W. Bush in *Winds of Change*. Ney's *Austin* cradles his rifle in the nook of his arm while he opens a document with his hands. Adickes's figures stand at attention over the landscape. Whereas Adickes depicts Sam Houston with a hint of contrapposto as he seems to be stepping forward with one hand on his hip and one on his cane, Stephen F. Austin is firmly planted, rifle in one hand, and the unopened document rolled in the other (see figures 4.34–4.38).[33]

An art history professor in Kansas has declared that Adickes's "Titan sized likenesses of historical figures may have a big 'gee-whiz' factor, but they're of 'minimal aesthetic interest.'"[34] In fact, the popular, monumental, sculptures, besides being significant to Texans as markers of historical locations, are remarkable technical achievements for an artist trained as a painter, and they are of interest as objects in which popular culture, history, and art intersect. Adickes may not be the Michelangelo of Texas, but it is worth comparing his monumental Sam Houston statue with the statue of David created by Michelangelo Buonarroti in 1504 for the Palazzo della Signoria in Florence, Italy. The most obvious difference between the two statues is the clothing of Houston and the nudity of David. Formally and stylistically, the statues are worlds apart, but functionally, there are similarities. Shortly after the white marble sculpture of David was placed in Florence, a visitor to the city described it as "'phantasm,' as if it were a glowing apparition on the piazza,"[35] and described it as heralding a new moment "in the history of public sculpture" and "in the history of Florentine civic imagery."[36]

John T. Poletti and Rolf Bagemihl, in *Michelangelo's David: Florentine History and Civic Identity,* writes:

> It seems that near-contemporary and late Renaissance viewers differed radically in their reactions to the David from our own modern fascination with the sculpture, which is, it must be recognized, a very recent construction. Indeed, despite the brief attempt to use the David as a positive political symbol when Florence thought it would be the capital of the new Italy, historians of the mid-nineteenth century did not think highly of the statue. William Hazlitt, the British essayist, in fact, was apparently repulsed by the statue when he saw it shortly after Carnavale in 1825: "But what shall we say to a commonplace or barbarous piece of work by Michael Angelo? The David is as if a large mass of solid marble fell upon one's head, to crush one's faith in great names. It looks like an awkward overgrown actor at one of our minor theatres, without his clothes: the head is too big for the body, and it has a helpless expression of distress." Clearly the naked figure "bleached in the open air" and seeming like "a species of huge stone-masonry" before the massive wall of the Palazzo della Signoria was an affront to Hazlitt's notions of classical heroics and accuracy of representation as well as to his aestheticizing sensibilities.[37]

While the average viewer is likely unaware of the cultural significance *David* had at the time of its creation in Florence, its modern cultural significance is relevant to a discussion of Adickes's work. *David* has entered the realm of popular culture as the symbol of Florence, and as an image that stands in for "fine art sculpture" the way that the *Mona Lisa* represents painting. *A Tribute to Courage* quickly became the symbol of Huntsville, Texas, and is associated with the town the way the *David* represents and stands over Florence. Both are iconic images in popular culture, attractions for tourists, and backdrops for photographers.

In 1994, just as he was completing *A Tribute to Courage,* Adickes took a trip to Canada. On his return journey to Texas, he visited Mount Rushmore. Frustrated that he could not get very close to the monument, Adickes conceived the idea of sculpting heads of all the presidents and displaying them in a garden-like setting. He envisioned the heads smaller than those carved into Mount Rushmore, but on a scale that would make them visually as large or even larger when viewers were in close

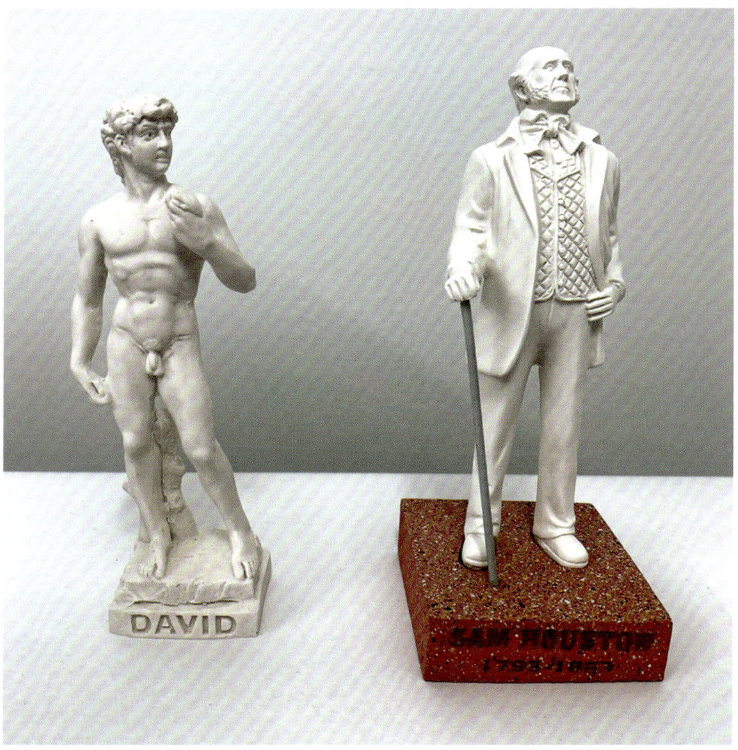


**Figure 3.18.** Souvenirs. Credit: Michael H. Henderson.

proximity. Adickes began carving the giant busts of US presidents in his studio on Summer Street in 1996. He created forty-three plaster molds to cast the portraits of the first forty-three presidents. Most of the busts are sixteen feet tall, but Adickes referred to a poll by historians that ranked the most successful presidents and then made eight of the "best" presidents 10 percent larger. He planned to use the molds to create multiple casts of the heads and place them in "Presidential Parks" around the country and re-create the experience of Mount Rushmore in a more intimate setting. As Adickes completed each bust, they were placed in the parking lot outside his studio. The heads, with the Houston skyline behind them, became a tourist attraction before they were ever transported to the parks.[38]

Adickes financed the first park himself, on property located near Mount Rushmore in Lead, South Dakota. The park was open from 2003 to 2010 and featured the busts placed on winding trails with information about each president. Adickes planned on recovering his costs through admission fees, but the park proved to be financially unsustainable due to poor attendance. The sculptures have remained on the site, and Adickes hopes to eventually relocate them to a new spot that will be more accessible to tourism. A second set of heads was purchased by a developer who opened another park in Virginia not far from colonial Williamsburg. The Virginia Presidents Park

> opened to the public in 2004 with the intention of teaching visitors, especially children, about America's journey and the part each president played. An open-air museum covering 10 acres of land, the park included manicured walking paths and informational signs about history.
>
> If the park were closer to the bigger tourist destination of Colonial Williamsburg, it might have drawn larger crowds. Instead, the attraction resided behind a motel and a wooded area. After a $10 million investment and six years of operation, poor attendance forced the park to shut down in 2010.[39]

When the Virginia park closed, the property was sold and the heads were moved and stored in a nearby field. Adickes had designed the heads so they could be moved and transported safely, but the proper procedures were unknown to the movers who seriously damaged the sculptures in the process of moving them. The movers punctured and cracked the hollow sculptures, which left them susceptible to weather damage and decay. Even though they are not accessible to the public, they have become a source of fascination in their unmaintained state. The cracked, stained, and decaying heads have been featured in articles and photo essays in the *Smithsonian Magazine* and the *New York Times Magazine*.[40] The property is not open to the public, but a local photographer is providing private and small group tours. In their state of decay, they have become fascinatingly photogenic and have been used as backdrops by fashion photographers and filmmakers.[41]

A third set of presidents is located in the yard of Adickes's studio along with *Charlie Chaplin* and the recently finished, thirty-six-foot-tall *Conductor* (a companion piece to *Virtuoso*), waiting for a home. The presidents' heads are demonstrative of the challenges Adickes has faced in placing his monumental public work. He often designs and creates what he envisions

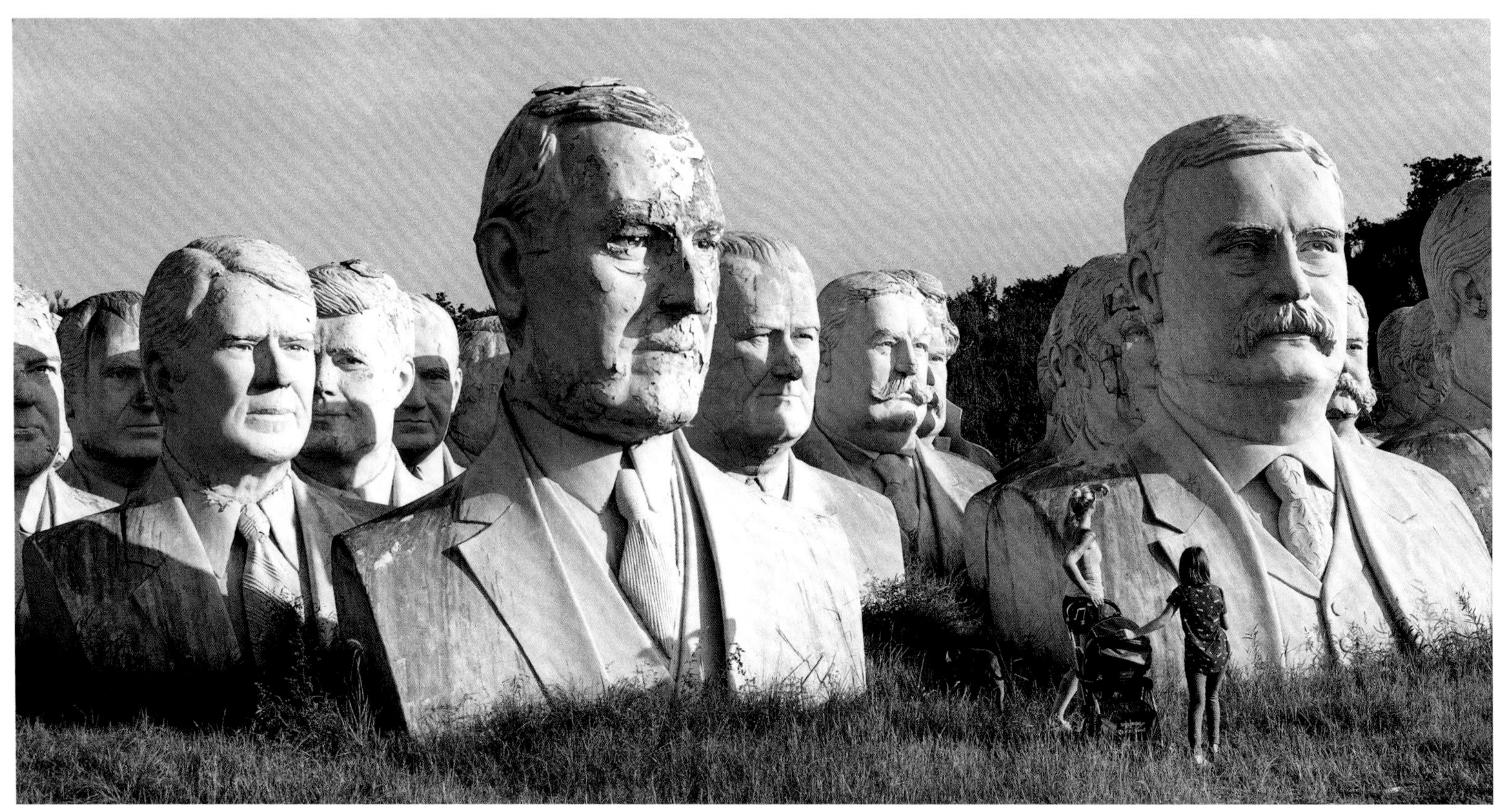

**Figure 3.19.** David Adickes. *From left to right: Herbert Hoover, Richard Nixon, Jimmy Carter, John F. Kennedy, Calvin Coolidge, Woodrow Wilson, Lyndon B. Johnson, William Howard Taft, Theodore Roosevelt and Chester A. Arthur, Industrial Park, Virginia, 2019*. Credit: Photograph © Hannah Price, 2019.

as an artist and then seeks an owner, or a public site, later. *Big Alex*, *Stone Trumpet*, and *A Tribute to Courage* are examples of works that have challenged Adickes in his attempts to place them on public sites (see figures 4.74–4.81).

Unused property adjacent to freeways has proven to be some of the most successful locations for Adickes's work. Just north of downtown Houston, at the tangled intersection of Interstates 10 and 45, Adickes has placed eighteen-foot-tall busts of George Washington, Abraham Lincoln, Stephen F. Austin, and Sam Houston. The busts are mounted on pedestals with the title *A Tribute to American Statesmanship*, but the sculptures (located at an infamous traffic bottleneck) are nicknamed *Mount Rush Hour* in popular lexicon. The one-third-acre lot was donated to Harris County, designated "American Statesmanship Park," and is maintained by the county. About three million cars pass by the sculptures each week.[42]

In 2011, Adickes created a giant concrete sculpture of the words "We Love Houston." The piece was inspired by the Hollywood sign on the hillside in Los Angeles, and the iconic "I Love New York" slogan. (The word "love" in Adickes's piece, like the Milton Glaser "I Love New York" design, is replaced by the image of a heart) (see figures 4.50–4.56). Each letter is eight feet tall and five feet wide, the fronts of the letters are white, and the edges are painted in bright colors. The sculpture was originally placed where it was visible from Interstate 10 just north of downtown Houston, but when condominium construction began nearby, it had to be relocated to accommodate "new housing developments and the safety of folks taking photos."[43] The piece was moved to the "EaDo International Promenade" in "8th Wonder Brewery's backyard in March 2018, where the sign found a safe, accessible home that also provides a great view of the city."[44] The sculpture is not far from and is a companion piece to Adickes's *The Beatles*, which is also located at this site.

Adickes has used text as an element in his work since he incorporated words from Michener's novel in his portrait of Michener in the early 1960s (see figure 2.11). In another three-dimensional text-based work, Adickes renders the word "ART" as a giant thirty-five-foot-tall sculpture on a base covered in letters listing the names of famous artists and concluding with "your name here." *ART* was installed in 2015 at the entrance to "Art Alley" at the Silos at Sawyer Yards, a large art complex that includes exhibition spaces and artists' studios as well as shops and restaurants. The converted Silos and warehouses are a few blocks from his former studio, where Adickes's sculptures first attracted art crowds to the area[45] (see figure 4.20). The text sculptures deepen the connection between Adickes's work and pop art, such as Robert Indiana's *LOVE* sculpture and the graphic designs of Milton Glaser. They also provide further opportunities for viewers to engage with the work by posing for photographs and sharing images on social media.[46]

In 2018, after the condominium development that necessitated the move of the *We Love Houston* sculpture was completed, Adickes placed a new sculpture in the same location beside Interstate 10. The new piece, *Art Is Everywhere in Houston*, was made of letters that spelled almost just that (Art Everywhere Houston), and was roughly the same size as the previous sculpture. In 2020, in response the COVID-19 pandemic, Adickes revised the sculpture to read *We Are All in This Together Houston.* Around the same time, the heads of the American Statesmen on nearby "Mount Rush Hour" were fitted with giant face masks to promote public health and safety. The popularity of Adickes's works, demonstrated through their prevalent appearances on Instagram, Facebook, and YouTube, supports their use as positive and self-affirming images of civic responsibility and pride (see figures 4.57 and 4.60–4.64).

Other recent sculptures by Adickes have stylistic qualities associated with pop art. *Three Colorful Friendly Trees* is a ten-foot-tall cast concrete sculpture of three abstracted trees. The trees are painted red, yellow, and blue and are rendered in a flat cartoon-like style that refer back to some of Adickes's earlier landscapes but are also reminiscent of the style of Keith Haring. The sculpture was included in *True North*, an annual yearlong exhibition of sculptures on the esplanade along Heights Boulevard in Houston. The large, but more humanly scaled, sculpture invited social engagement in its placement on a heavily traveled walking and running path (see figures 4.11–4.13).

*Onward* is a fifteen-foot-tall, sixteen-foot-long concrete statue of Sam Houston on horseback. The piece was commissioned by the city of Baytown, Texas, and placed in the center of an intersection in a traffic roundabout. Sam Houston is "depicted on horseback, much like Enrico Filiberto Cerrachi's Sam Houston Monument that has been on display near Hermann Park since 1925. In Adickes' piece titled 'Onward,' he is riding Saracen, his horse that was killed at San Jacinto in 1836 and the decisive battle in the war for Texas Independence"[47] (see figures 4.58–4.59).

In the sculpture, Sam Houston looks in the direction of the battle of San Jacinto, which took place across Galveston Bay from where the statue is placed. The statue is more stylized than the heads of the presidents and the other sculptures of Houston and Austin. The concrete is smooth, and the forms are simplified, giving the sculpture a cartoon-like quality, more similar to Adickes's sculptures of musicians. Unlike the angular geometry in *The Beatles*, the horse and the figure in *Onward* are more fluid and curvilinear. The style is reminiscent of the work of Iwao Takamoto, an animator who worked on Walt Disney films in the 1950s and Hanna-Barbera cartoons in the 1960s and later.[48] Takamoto designed many of the characters for the Saturday morning *Scooby-Doo* series. Adickes's sculpture of Houston on horseback would not seem out of place in one of Hanna-Barbera's cartoons.

When his work was ignored by art critics and curators in the 1980s, Adickes made his work relevant and visible by placing it in public spaces and increasing its scale and dimension. His work is popular and perfectly suited for viewers to engage with and become part of through social media. His whimsical giant sculptures express his love of music, and they embrace and are embraced by popular culture.

Adickes's monumental sculptures of Texas heroes and US presidents mythologize political figures uncritically. The characters come with complicated political histories, and their reputations are evolving in the public consciousness. However they are thought of, they will be thought of often, as long as the giants that David Adickes has placed along our paths remain standing. His positive, sometimes kitschy, always popular sculptures will continue to entertain.

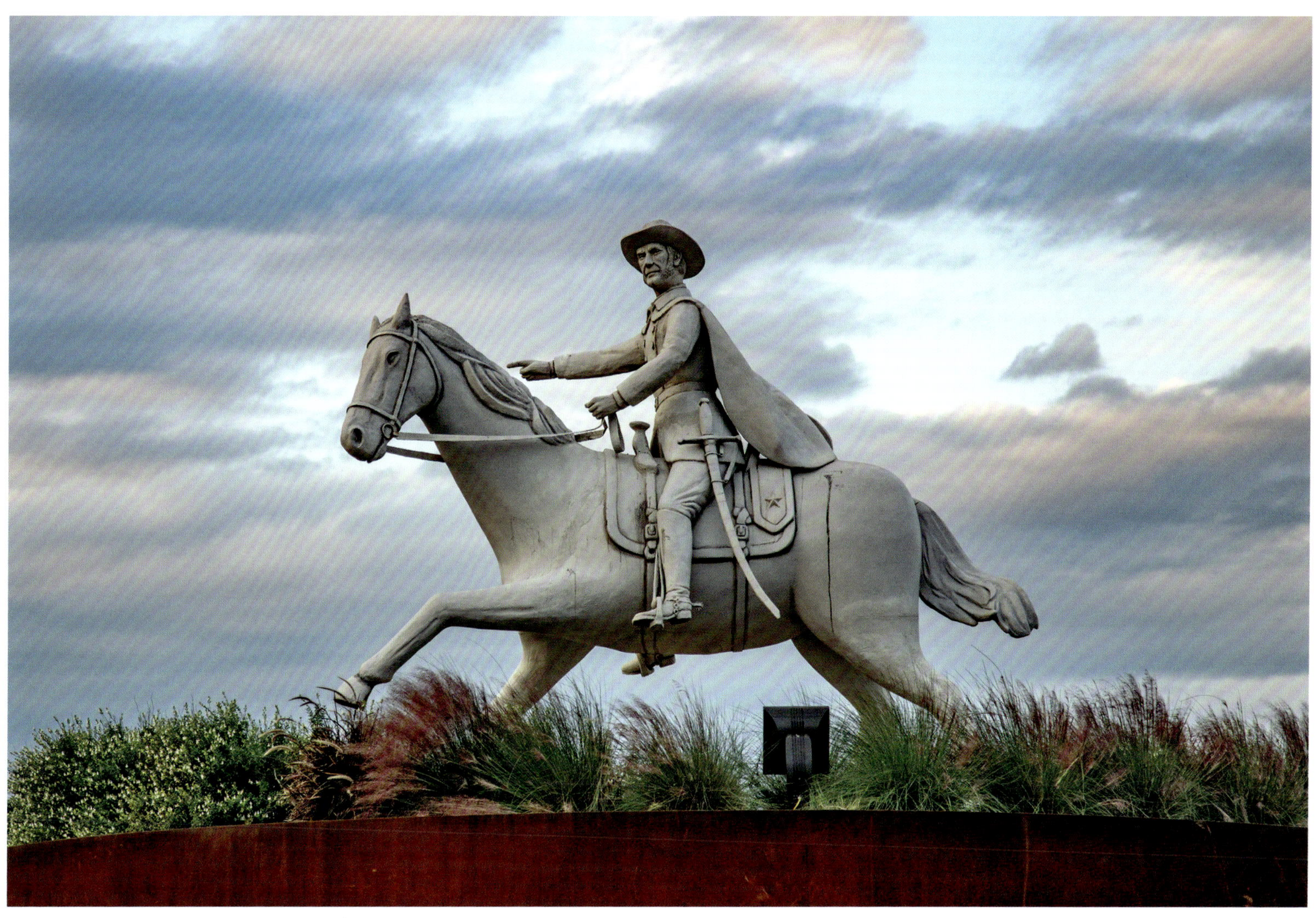

**Figure 3.20.** David Adickes, *Onward,* 2018. Credit: Rebecca Finley.

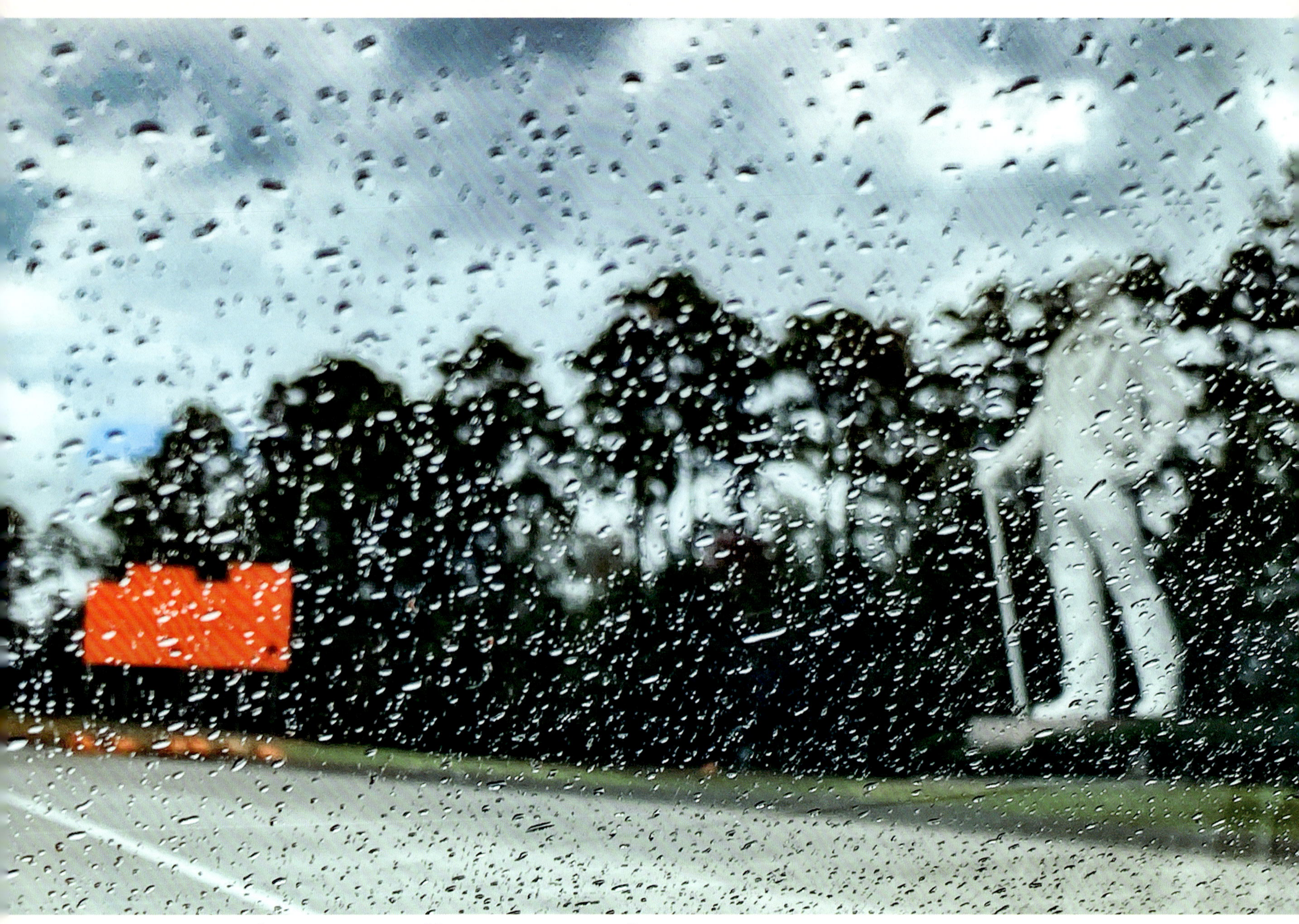

**Figure 4.1.** *A Tribute to Courage*, viewed from my car, I-45 Huntsville, Texas.

# Chapter 4

## Living among Giants

### *The Public Art of David Adickes*

Rebecca Finley

The first time I encountered a sculpture by David Adickes was in Houston at the George Bush Intercontinental Airport during a layover. I had no idea who Adickes was but was intrigued by the piece. It struck me as humorous seeing our forty-first president's bronze jacket flapping in the nonexistent airport wind. Upon further inspection I noted that George Bush was holding a book that displayed the title of the piece, *Winds of Change*. It suddenly made sense. I later learned that the work made its debut at the 1992 Republican Convention in Houston and moved in 1997 to the airport when it was renamed after the former president. This was years before I took my position teaching photography in Huntsville, Texas, at Sam Houston State University and learned more about the artist who made this piece along with *A Tribute to Courage*, the monumental statue of Sam Houston I passed on I-45 everyday going to work.

Not long after accepting my position at SHSU, I found myself on a committee charged with the placement of a smaller version of *A Tribute to Courage* on our campus. The committee chose a spot in the center of campus with the thought that students would want to make photographs with it. We were not wrong. It is a rite of passage to have graduation photographs taken with Sam. We recommended that the university maintain a green space around it to give a similar feeling as its larger counterpart who appears to be coming out of a wooded area. It felt important to create an environment for Sam Houston.

As an alumnus of SHSU himself, David Adickes is a celebrity in Huntsville as well as in Houston and East Texas. His works can be found in many public spaces in the region where some serve as meeting locations and major tourist attractions, such as the *We Love Houston* sculpture or *The Beatles* statues, both located at 8th Wonder Brewery. Others are quiet landmarks that catch the viewer by surprise, such as *Big Alex* who sits on top of a building in the Montrose District in Houston. *Virtuoso* offers a calm breath in downtown Houston, and *We're All in This Together Houston* offers a sign of hope to those driving through Houston on I-10 during the COVID-19 pandemic.

My photographic series, *Living among Giants*, examines the interaction between David Adickes's work and the environments in which these pieces are placed. While most of the images focus on Adickes's large public artworks, I also photographed in his studio and home where I found some of the work to be placed in curious juxtapositions with other items. I investigated ways in which his giant sculptures interact with nature, architecture, people, animals, and objects. With the smaller works and paintings, I found their meanings to change depending on objects placed around them. Adickes's work doesn't ever blend into these spaces. The landscape and/or architecture is always secondary to these giants.

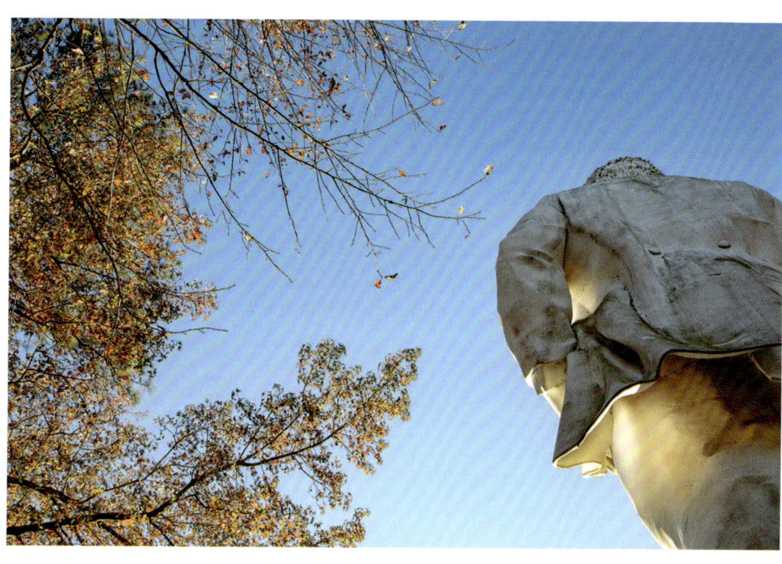

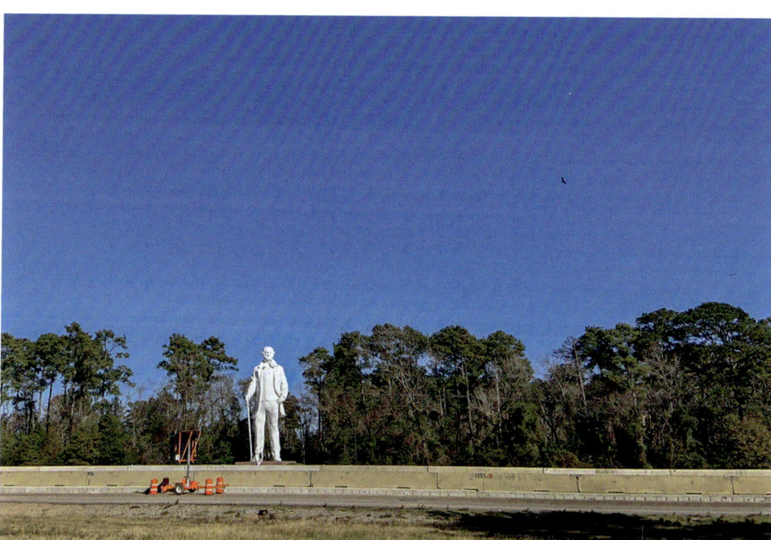

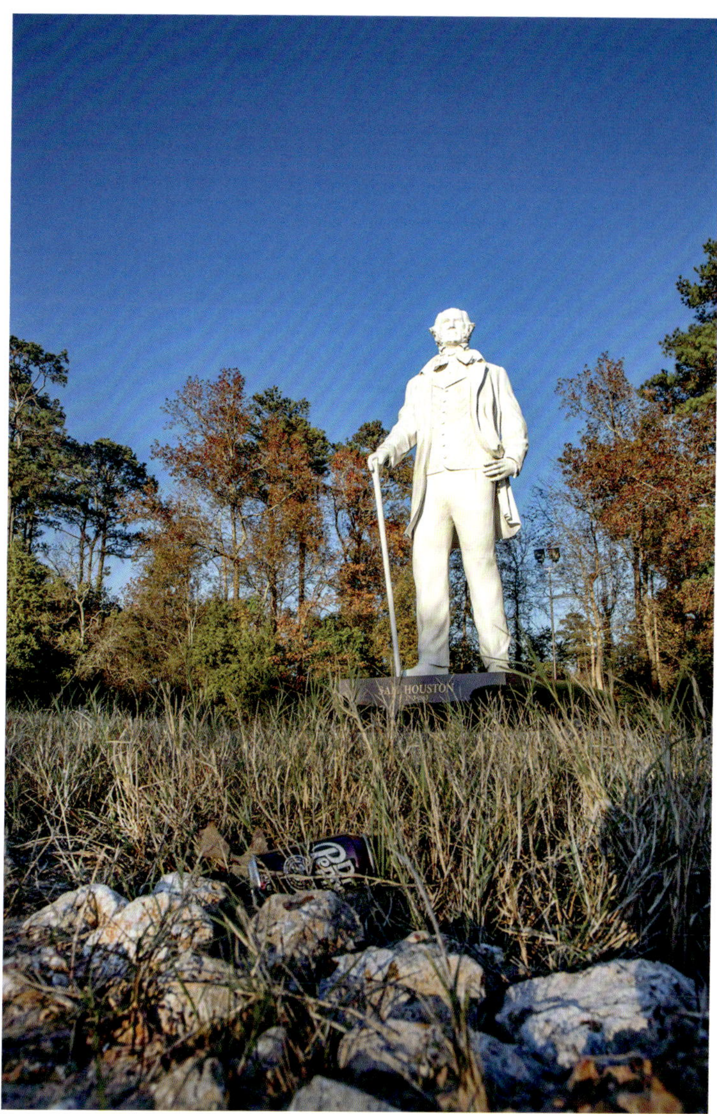

**Figures 4.2, 4.3, and 4.4.** *A Tribute to Courage*, Sam Houston Statue and Visitor Center, Huntsville, Texas.

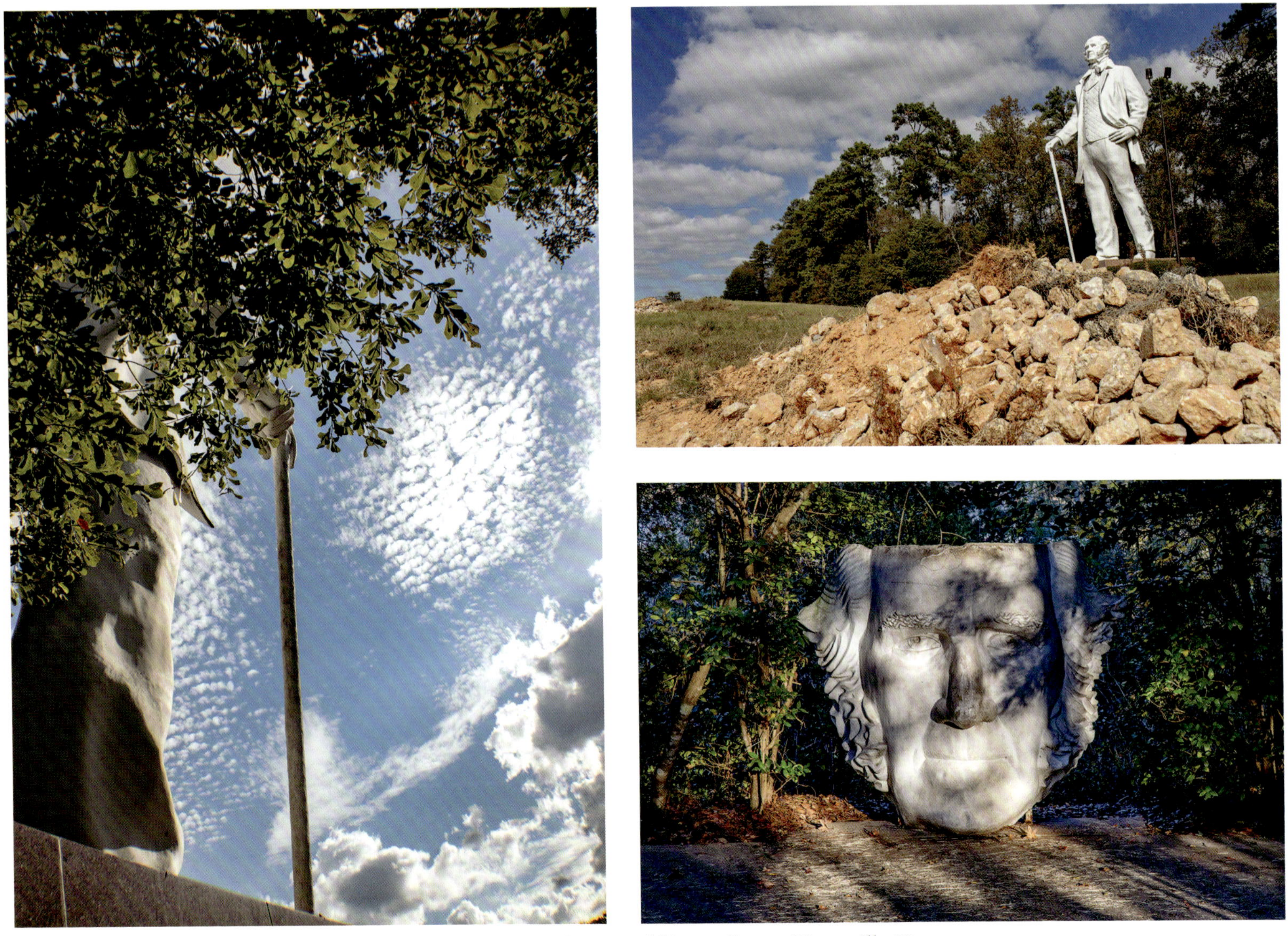

**Figures 4.5, 4.6, and 4.7.** *A Tribute to Courage,* Sam Houston Statue and Visitor Center, Huntsville, Texas.

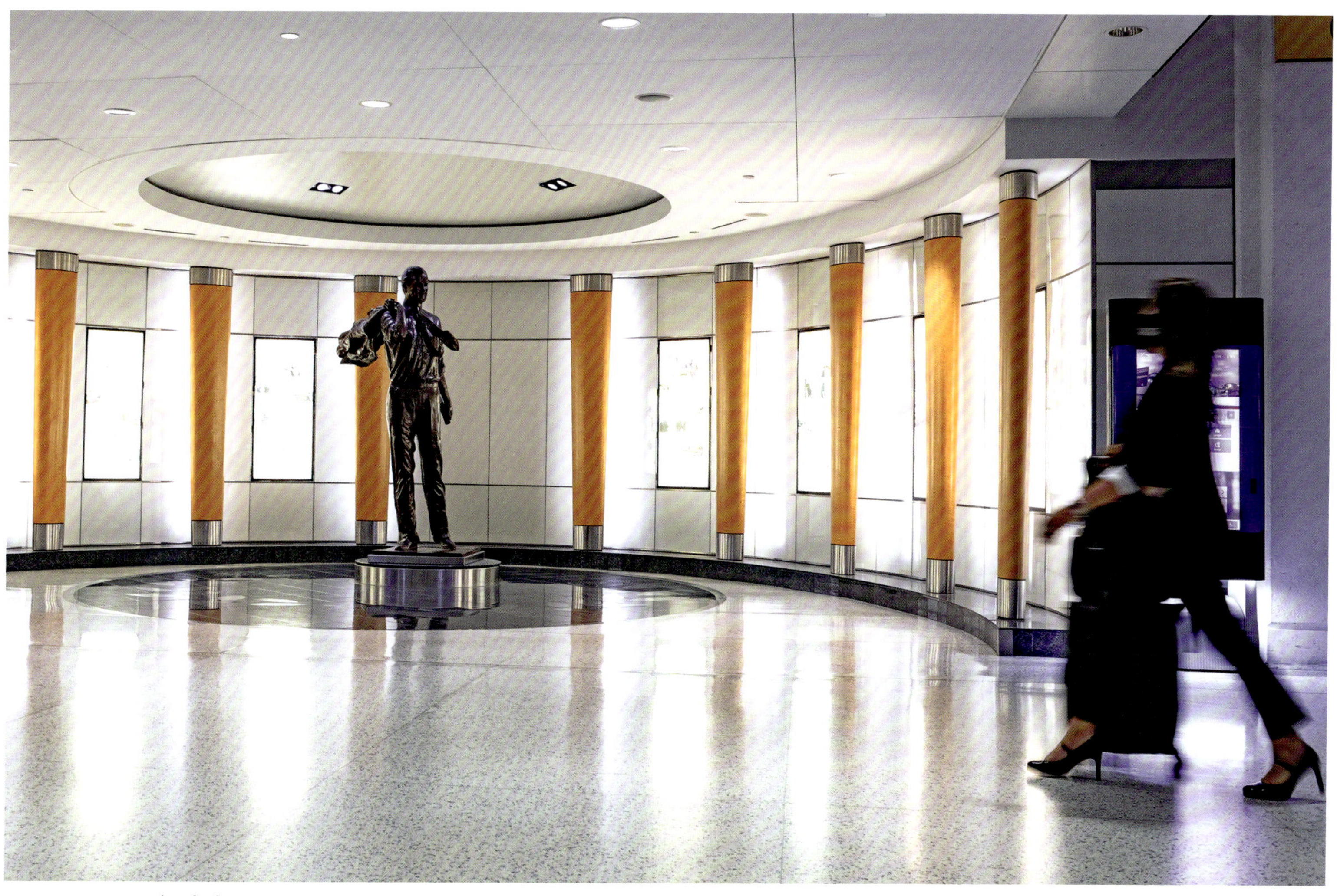

**Figure 4.8.** *Winds of Change,* George Bush Intercontinental Airport, Terminal C, Houston, Texas.

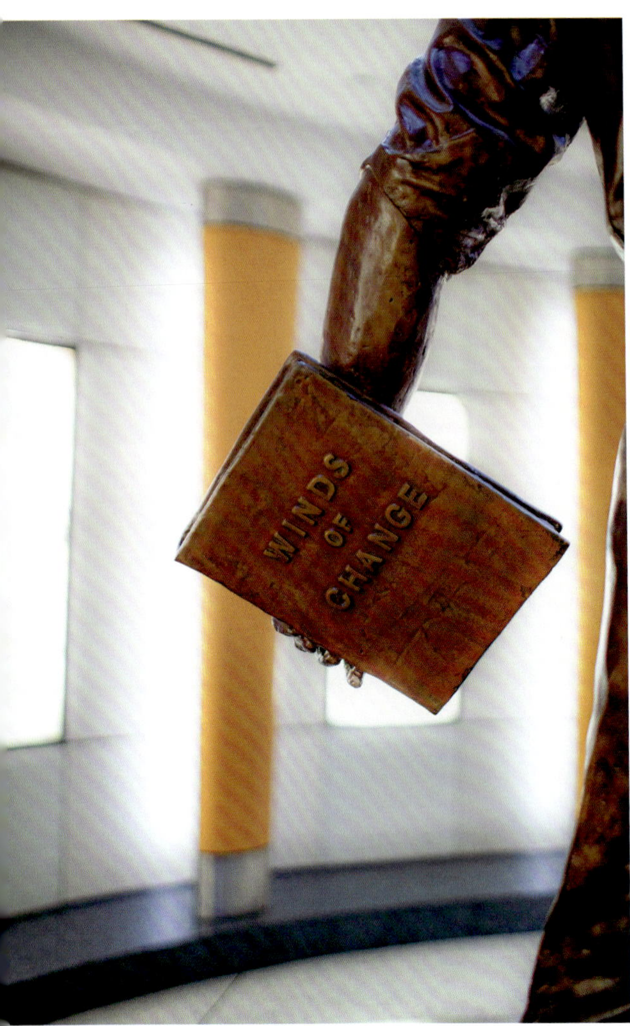


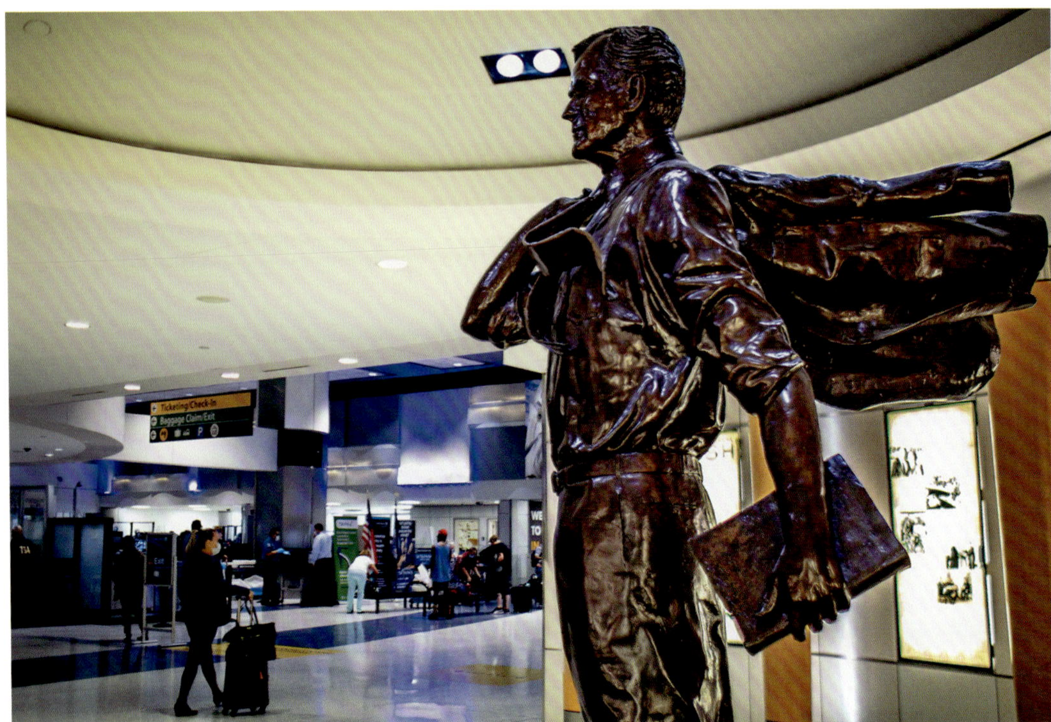


**Figures 4.9 and 4.10.** *Winds of Change,* George Bush Intercontinental Airport, Terminal C, Houston, Texas.

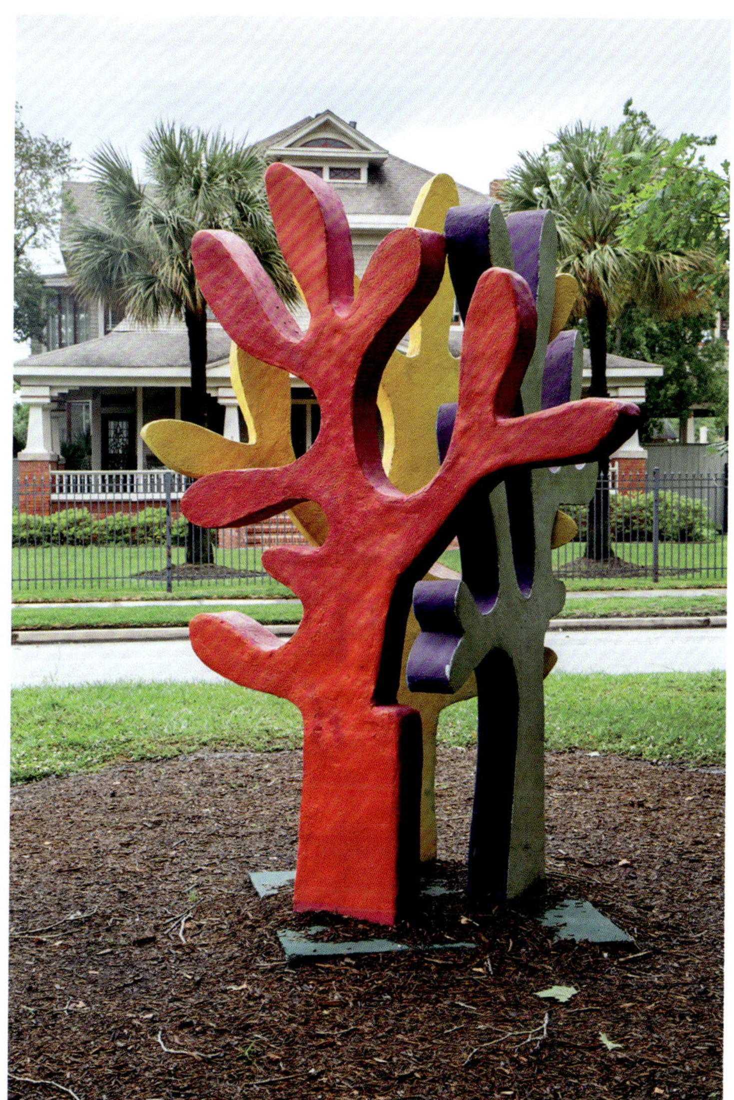

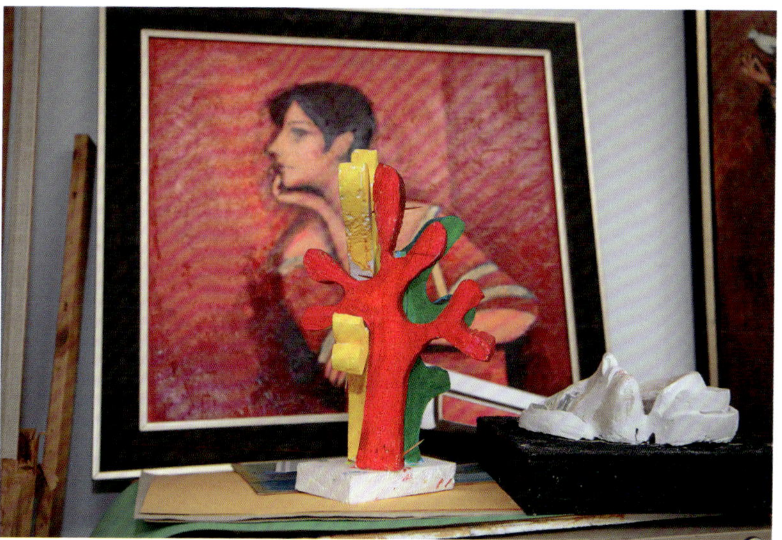

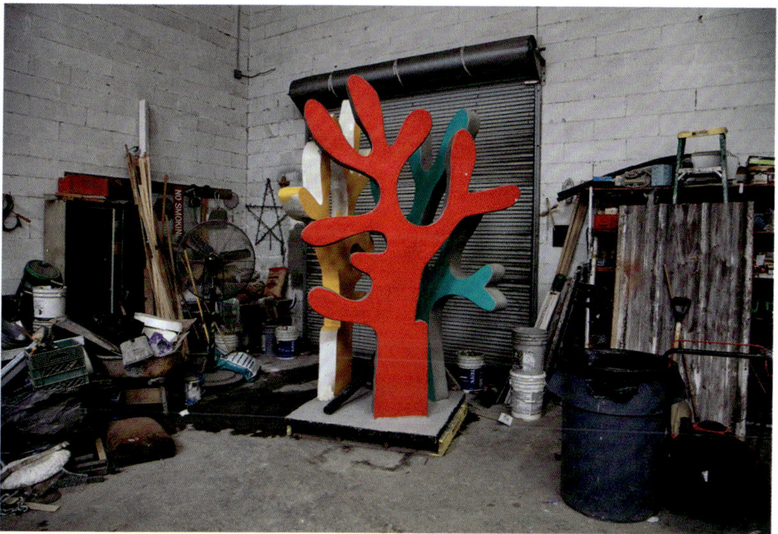

**Figures 4.11, 4.12, and 4.13.** Three views of *Three Colorful Friendly Trees.* Public sculpture at Paul Carr Jogging Trail Park, David Adickes's home, and in his studio, Houston, Texas.

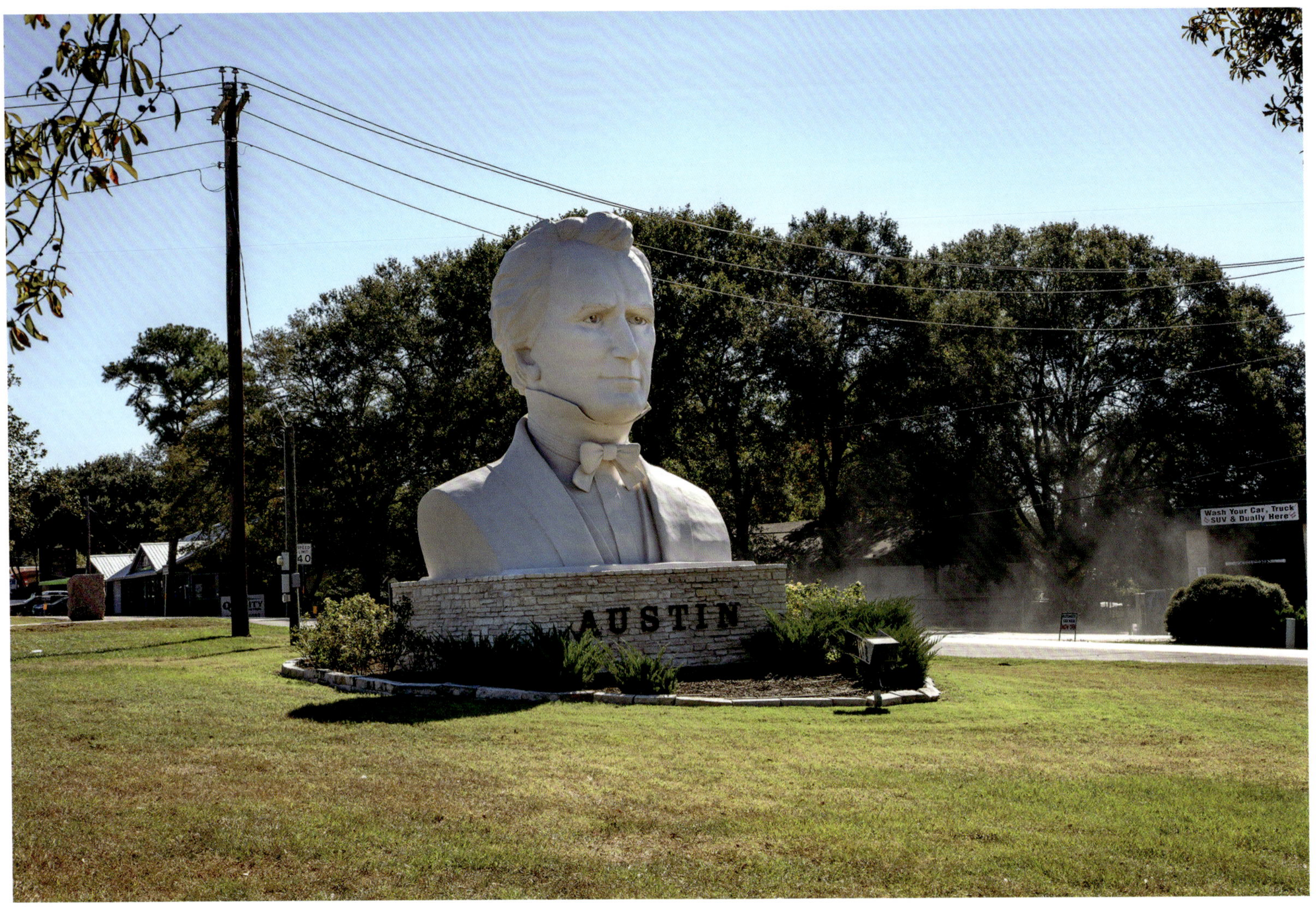


**Figure 4.14.** *Bust of Stephen F. Austin* and carwash in Bellville, Texas.

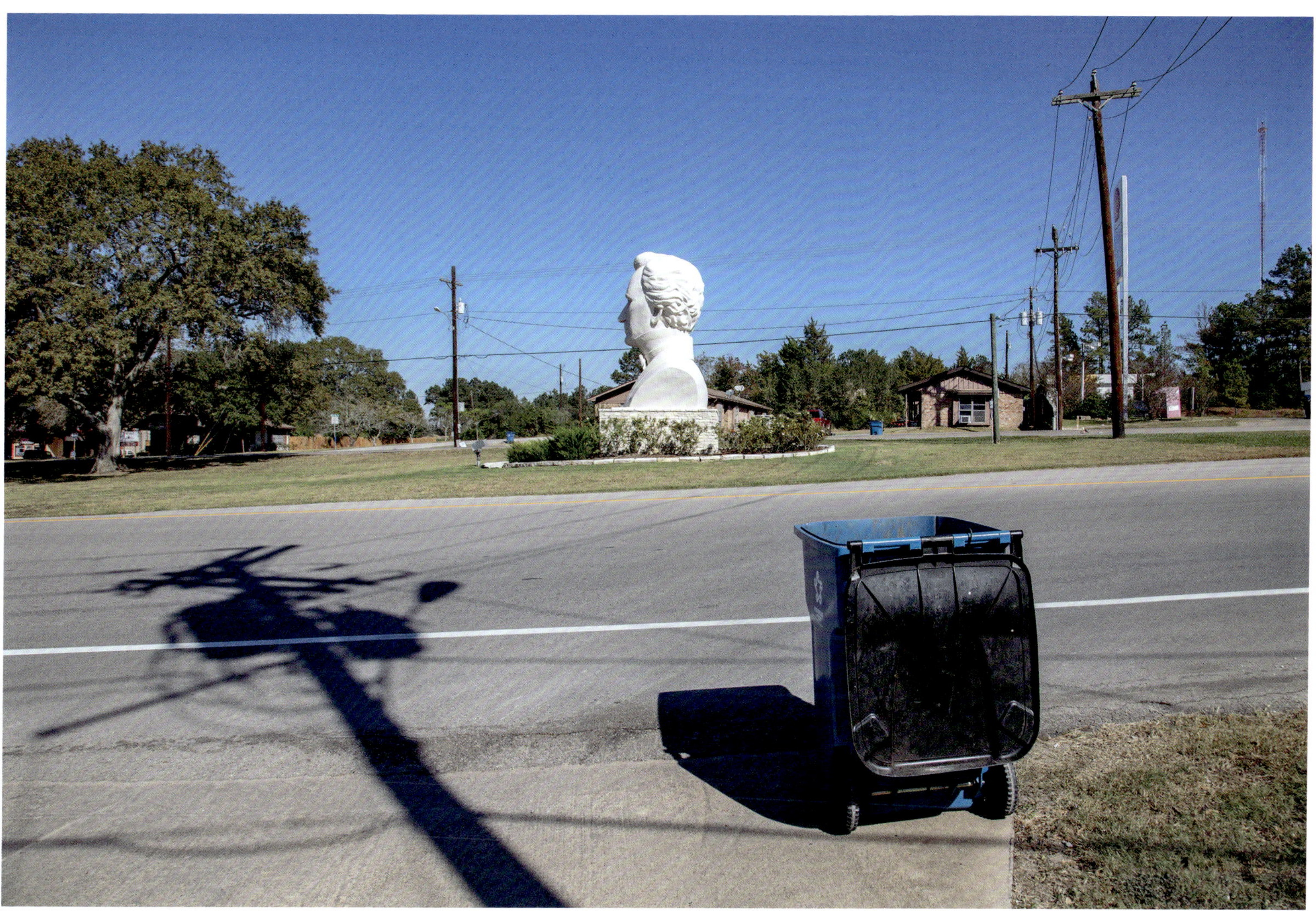

**Figure 4.15.** *Bust of Stephen F. Austin* in Bellville, Texas, viewed from a neighborhood driveway.

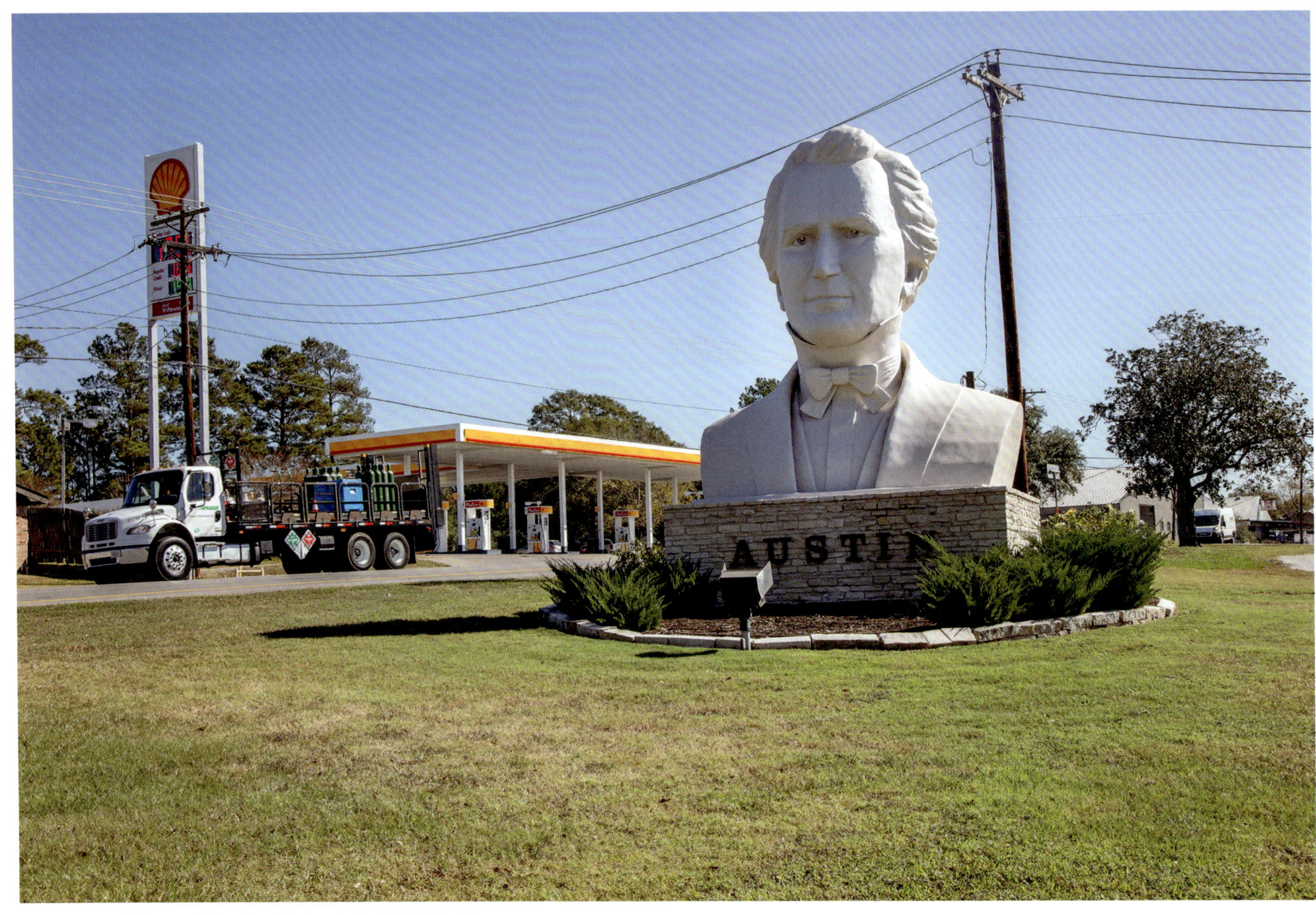

**Figure 4.16.** *Bust of Stephen F. Austin* in Bellville, Texas.

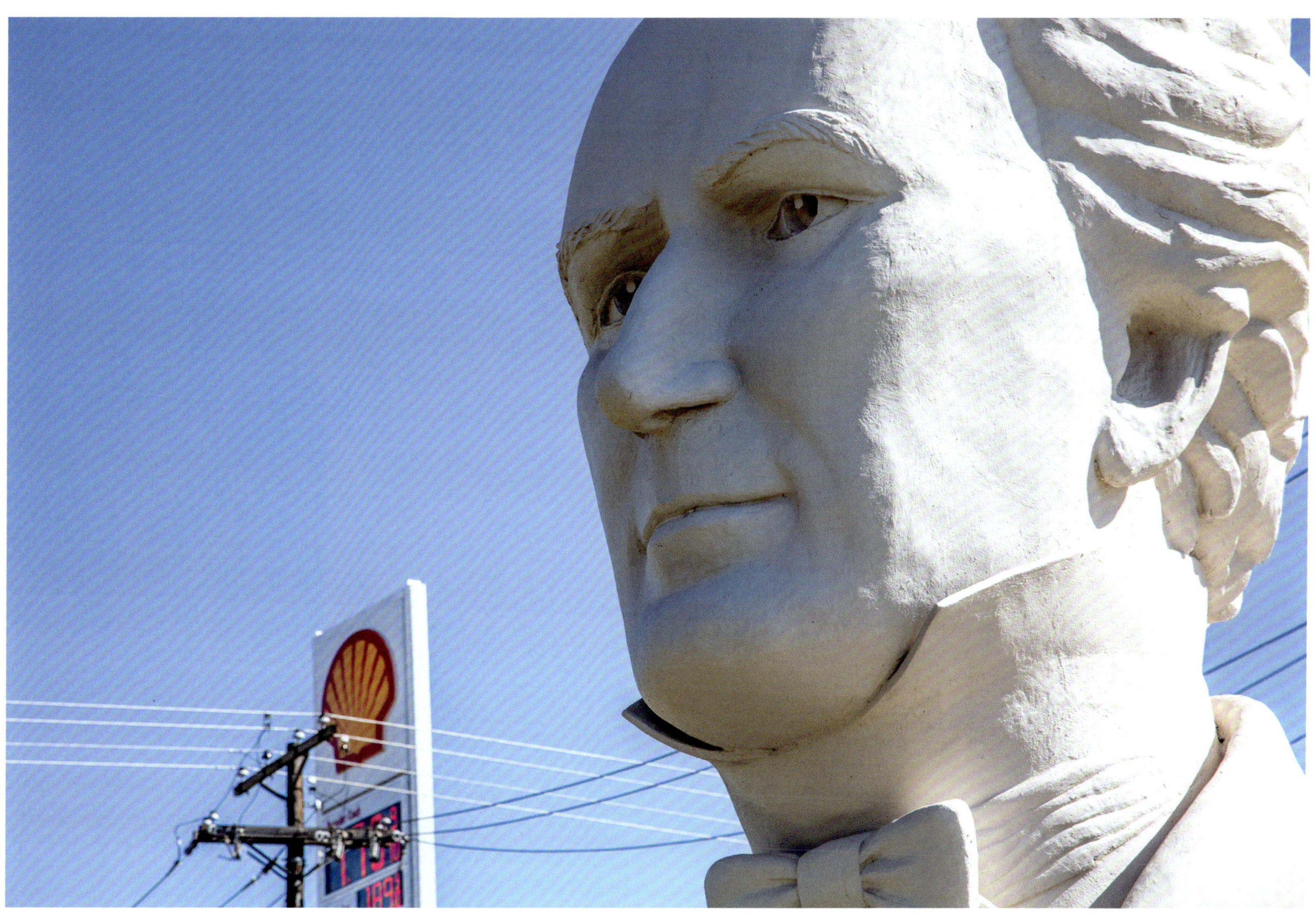

**Figure 4.17.** *Bust of Stephen F. Austin* in Bellville, Texas.

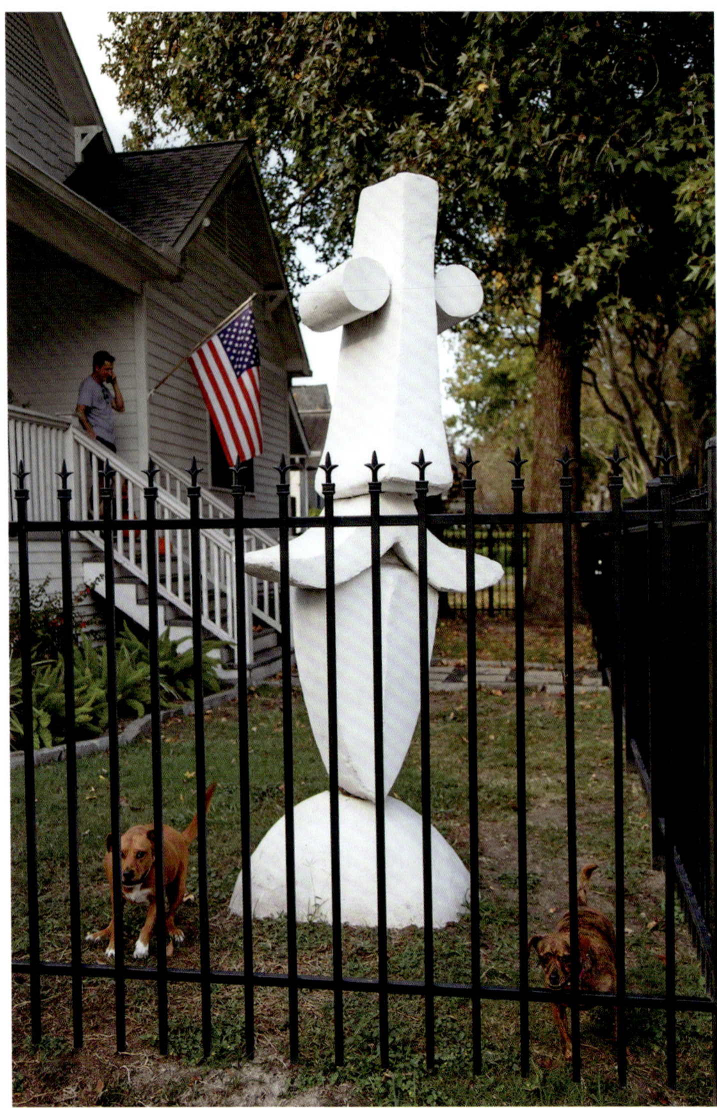

**Figure 4.18.** A privately owned sculpture in a Houston, Texas yard.

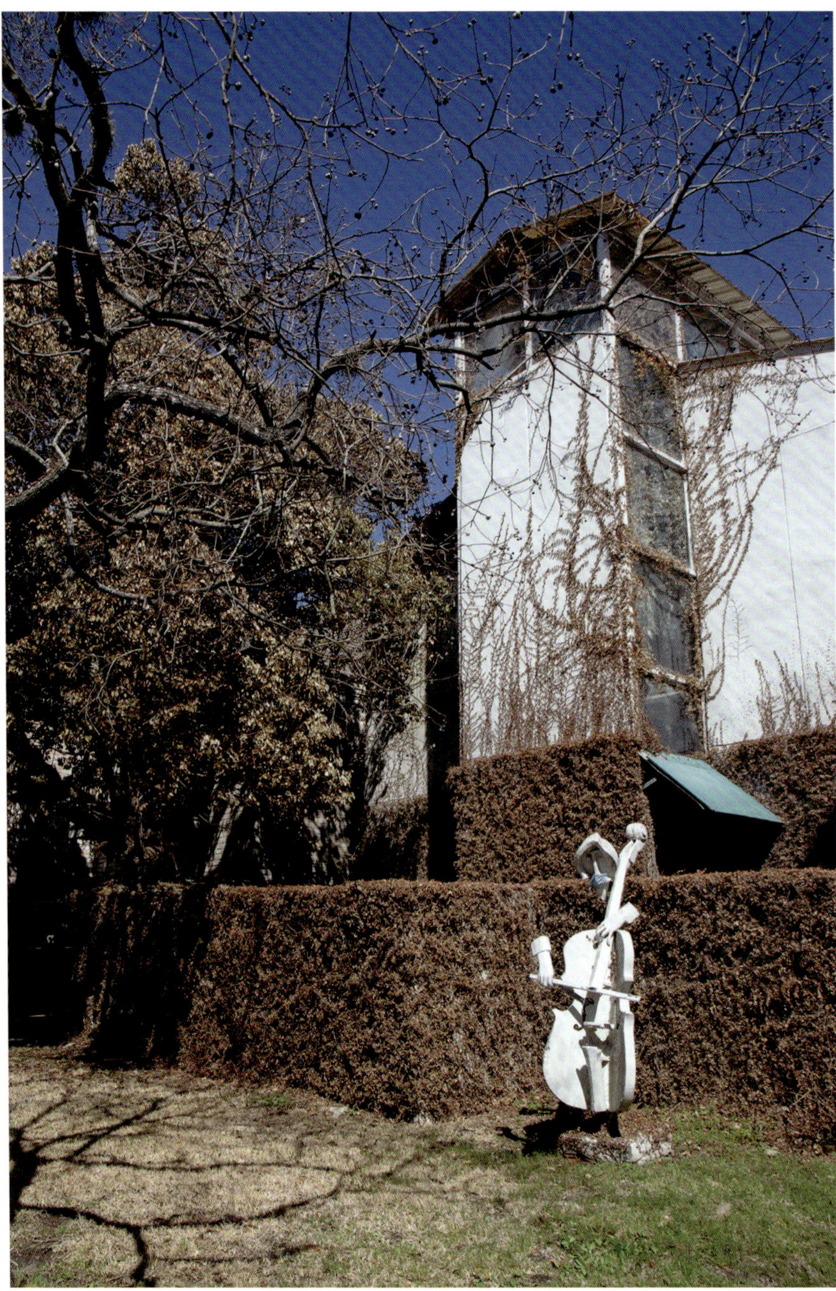

**Figure 4.19.** *Virtuoso* wearing a mask in David Adickes's yard, Houston, Texas.

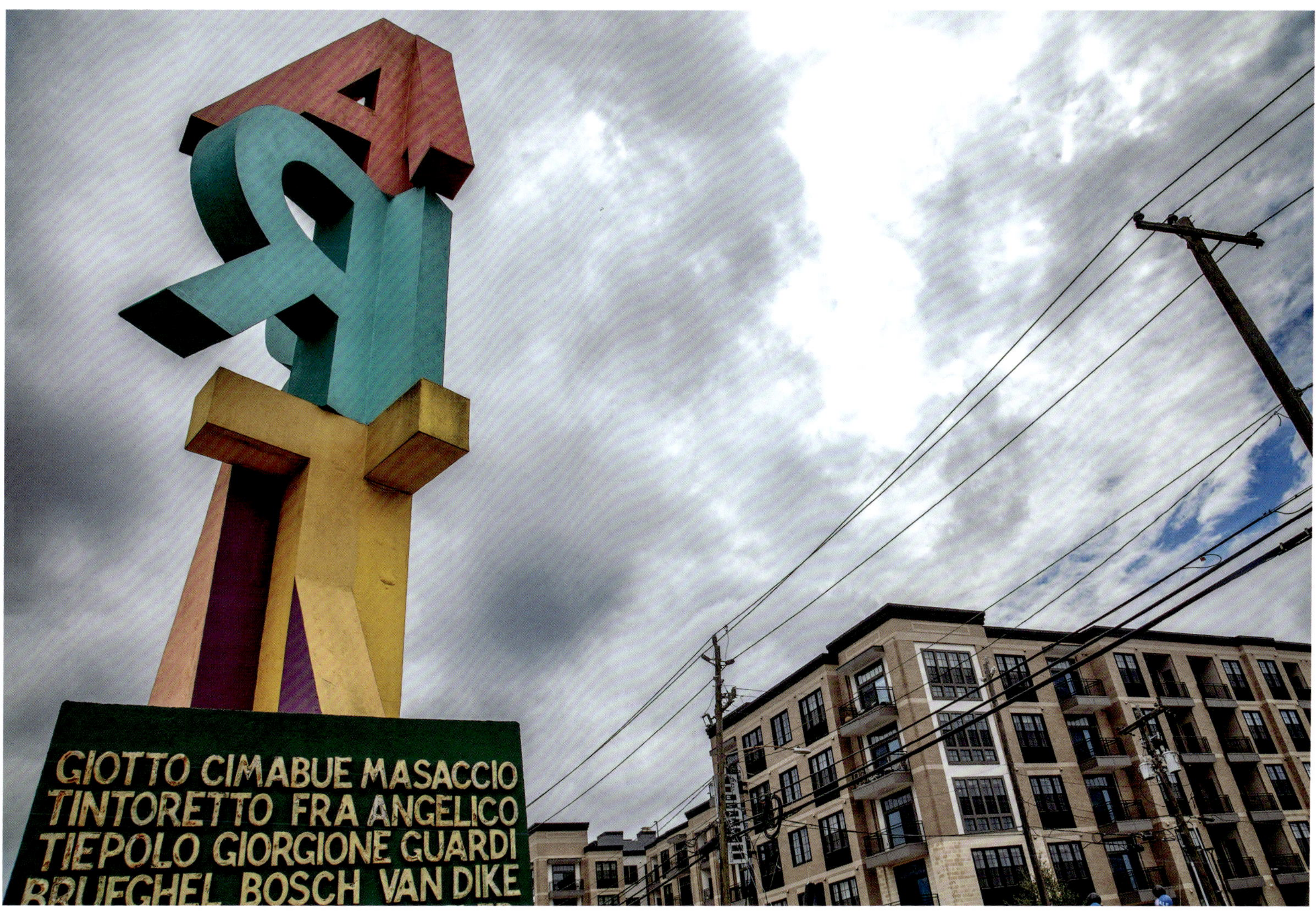

**Figure 4.20.** *ART* in front of Sawyer Yards in Houston, Texas.

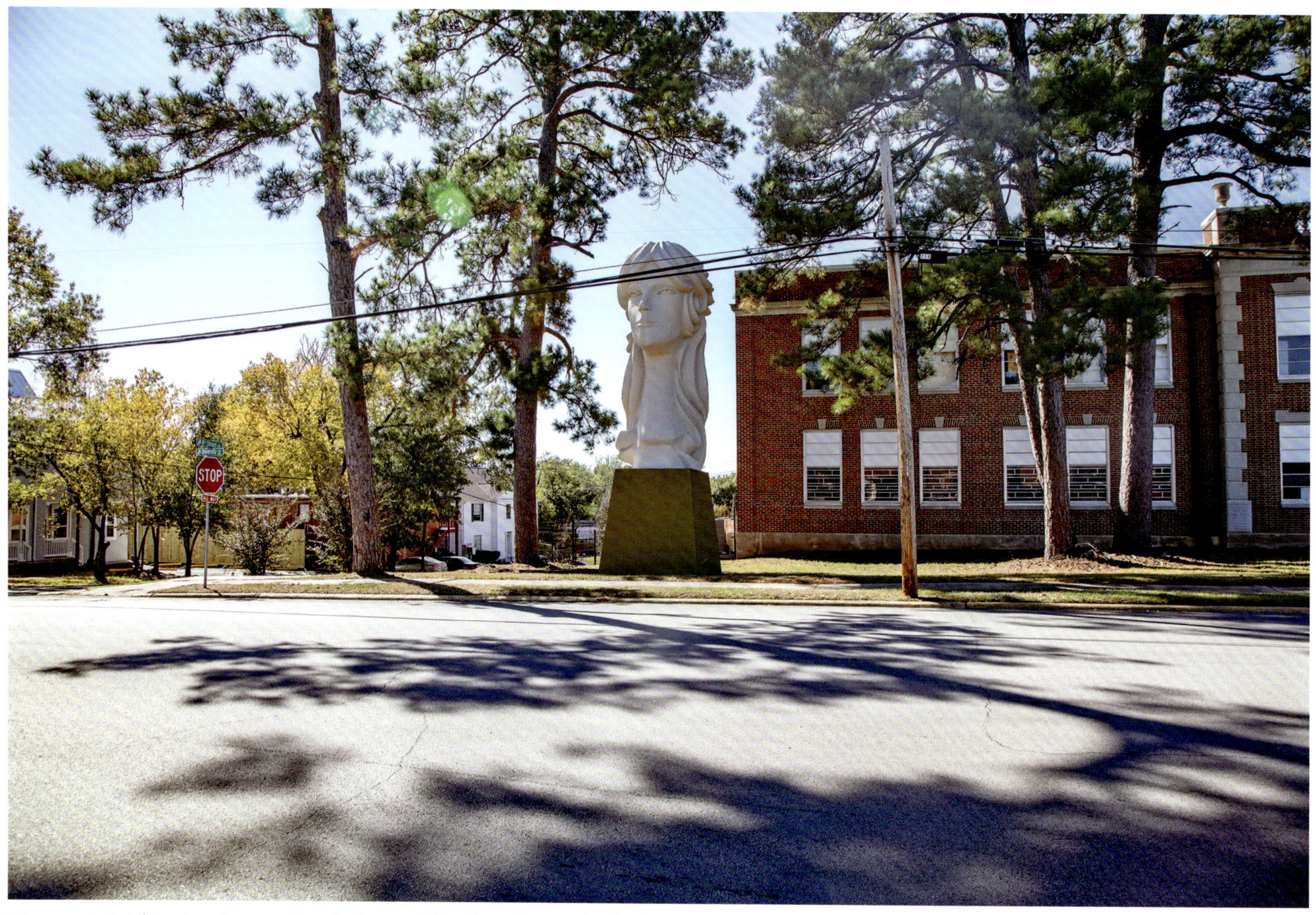


**Figure 4.21.** This giant bust resides in front of Adickes's former high school in Huntsville, Texas.

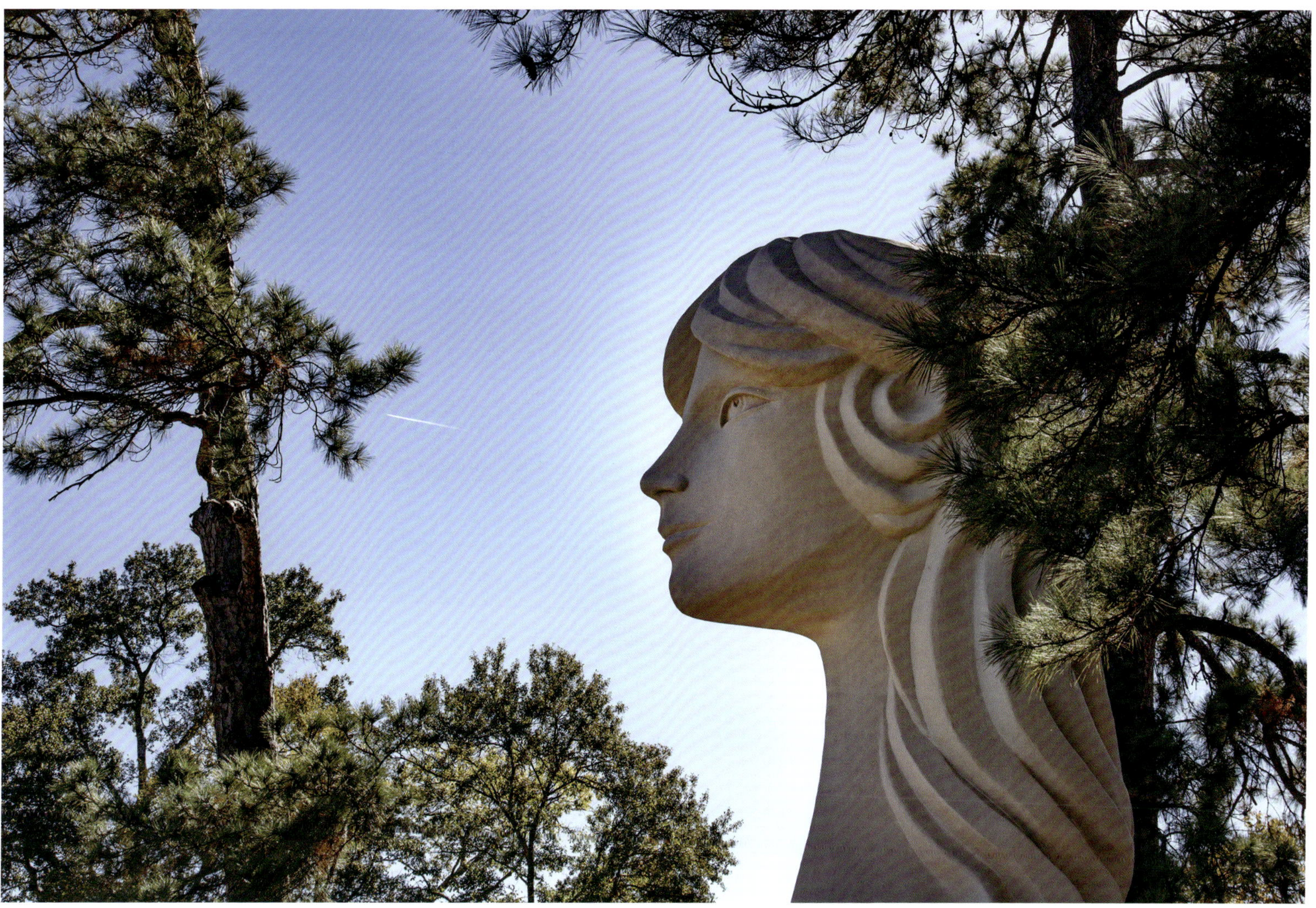

**Figure 4.22.** A plane flies over Huntsville, Texas.

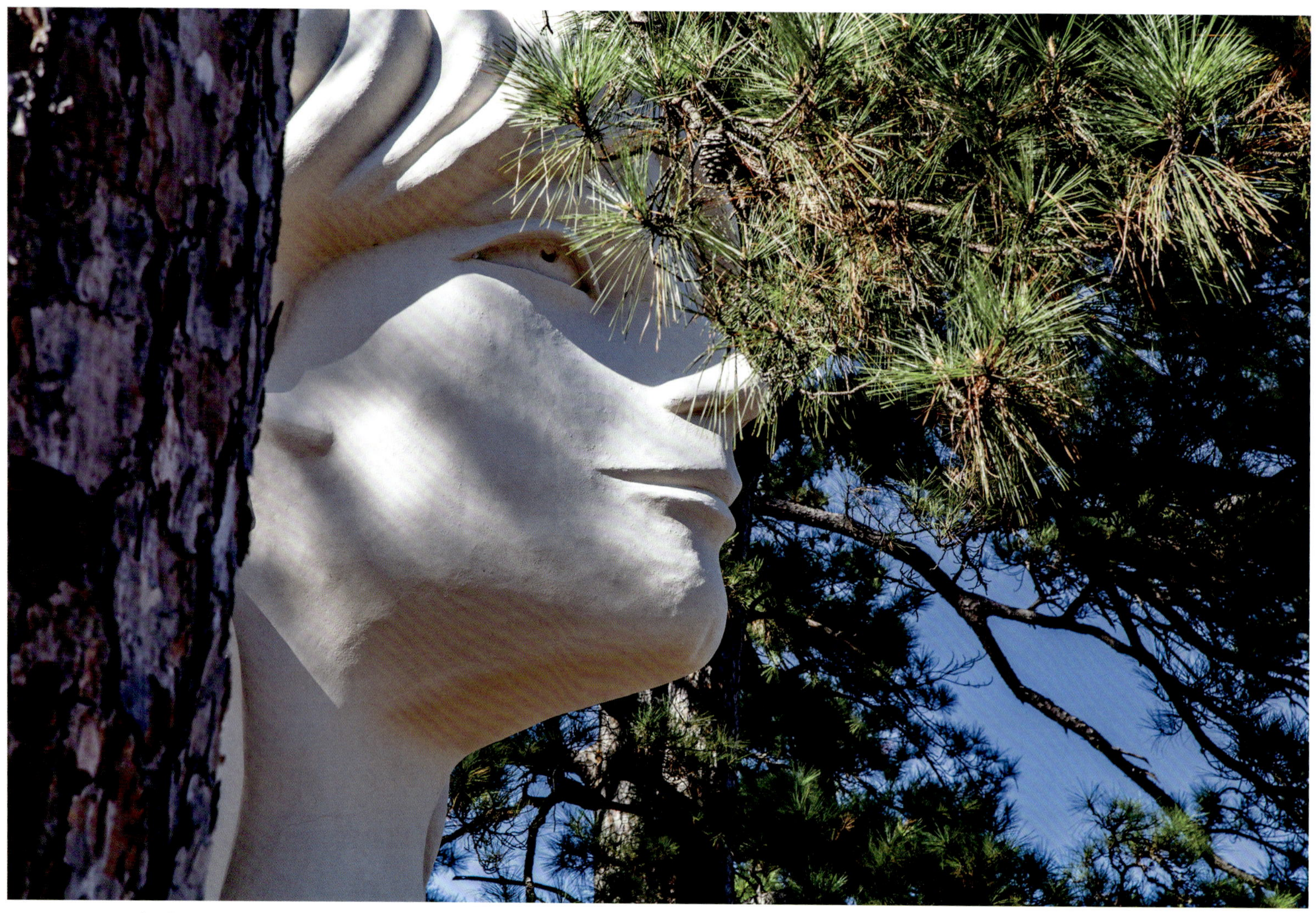

**Figure 4.23.** The bust surrounded by trees in the summer, Huntsville, Texas.

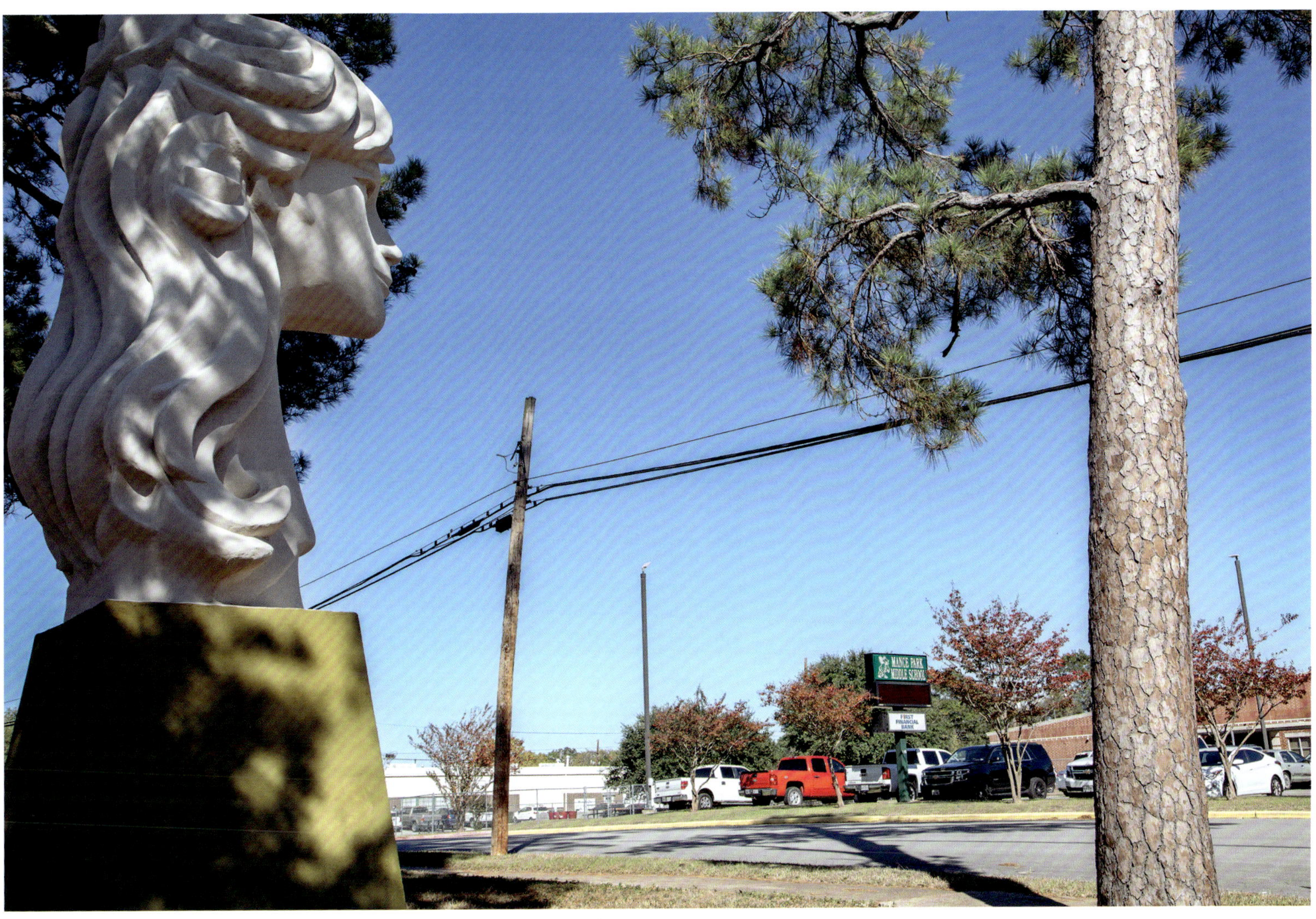


**Figure 4.24.** She overlooks Mance Park Middle School, Huntsville, Texas.

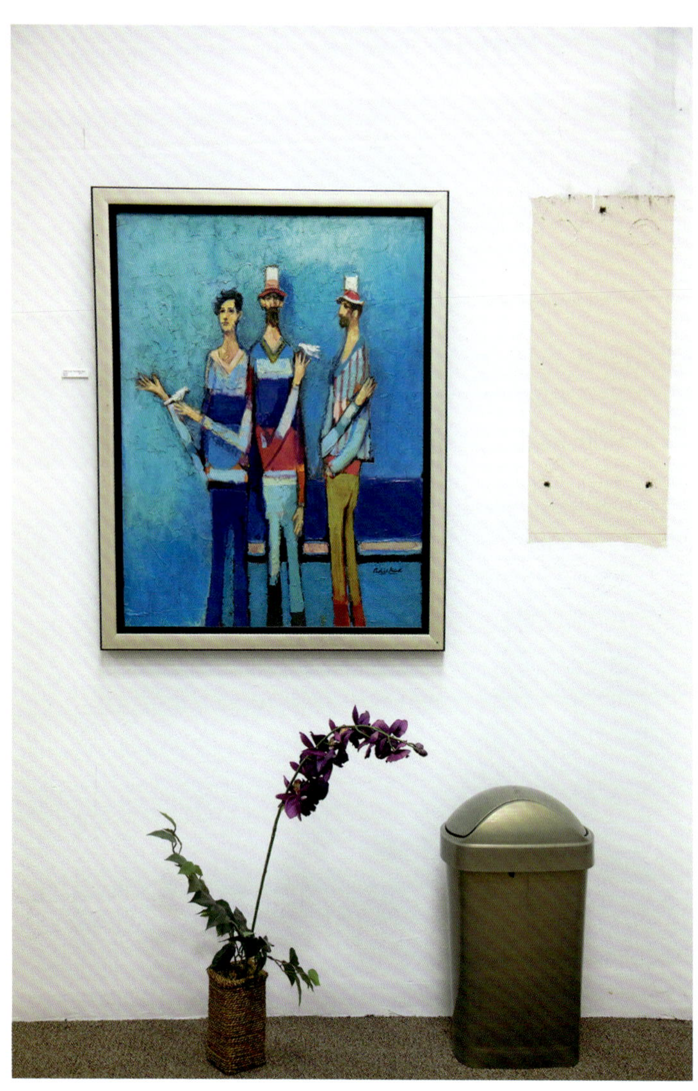

**Figure 4.25.** Inside the Adickes Foundation galleries, Huntsville, Texas.

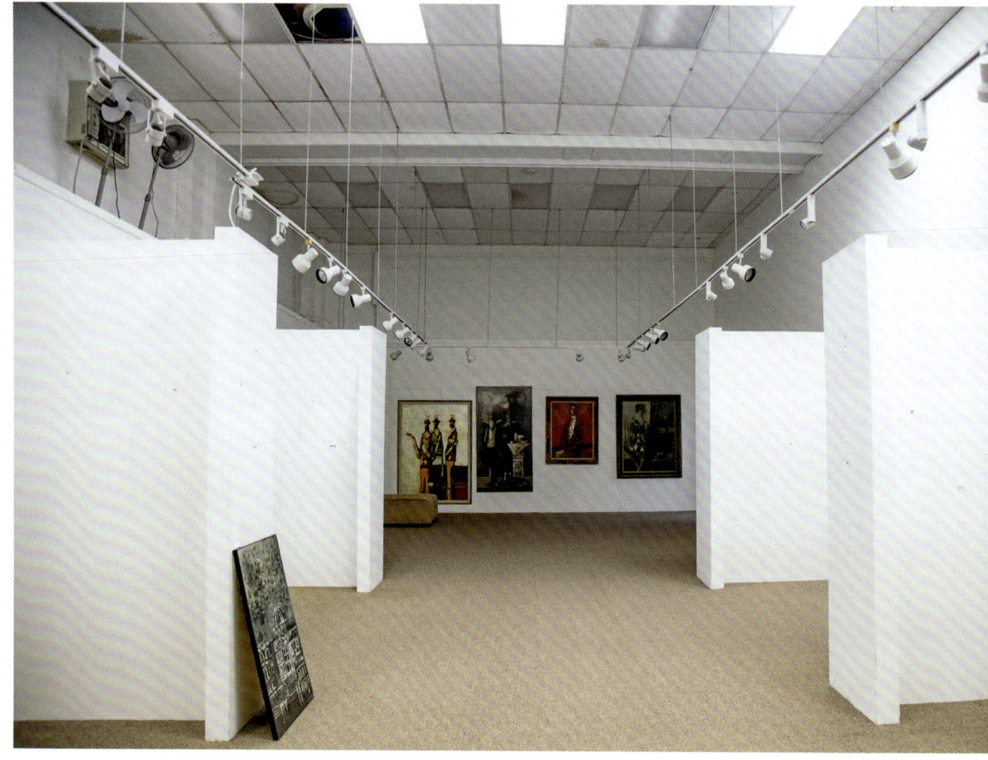

**Figure 4.26.** These images were taken as Adickes was moving out of his galleries in the Huntsville High School.

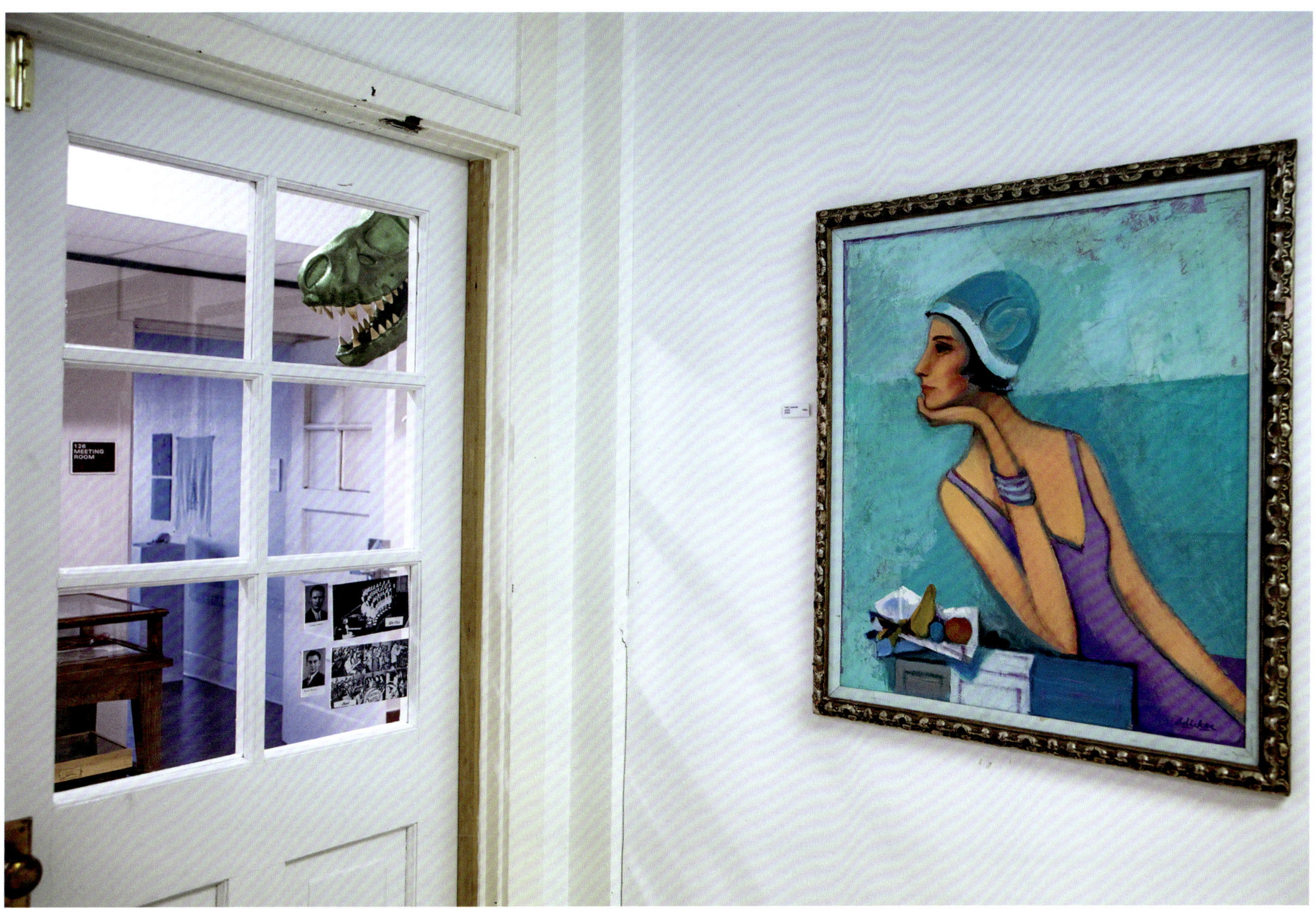


**Figure 4.27.** Art and Science meet in the final days of the Adickes Foundation's location in Sam Houston State University's Natural Science and Art Research Center, Huntsville, Texas.

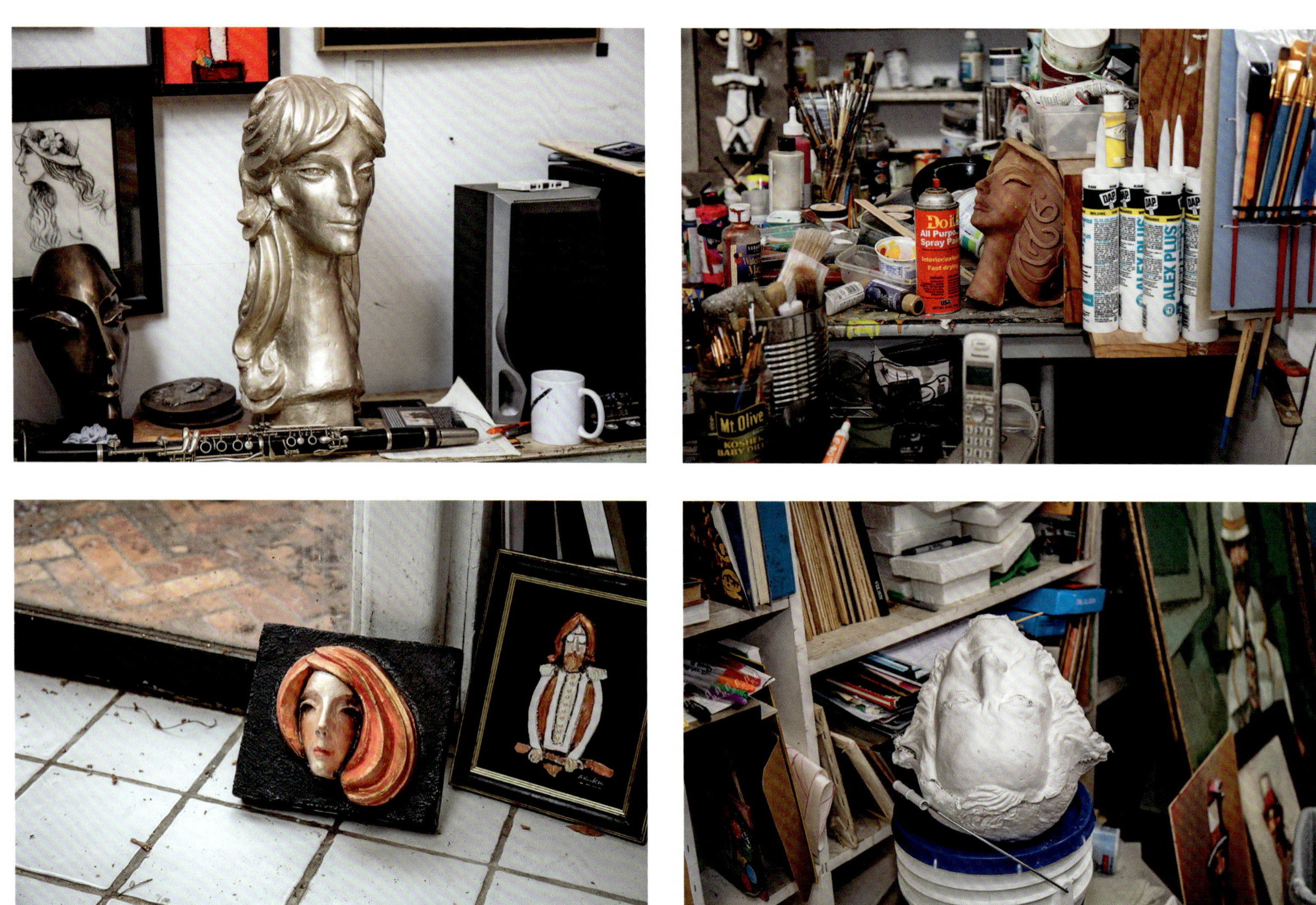


**Figures 4.28, 4.29, 4.30, and 4.31.** David Adickes's work in his home/studio in Houston, Texas.

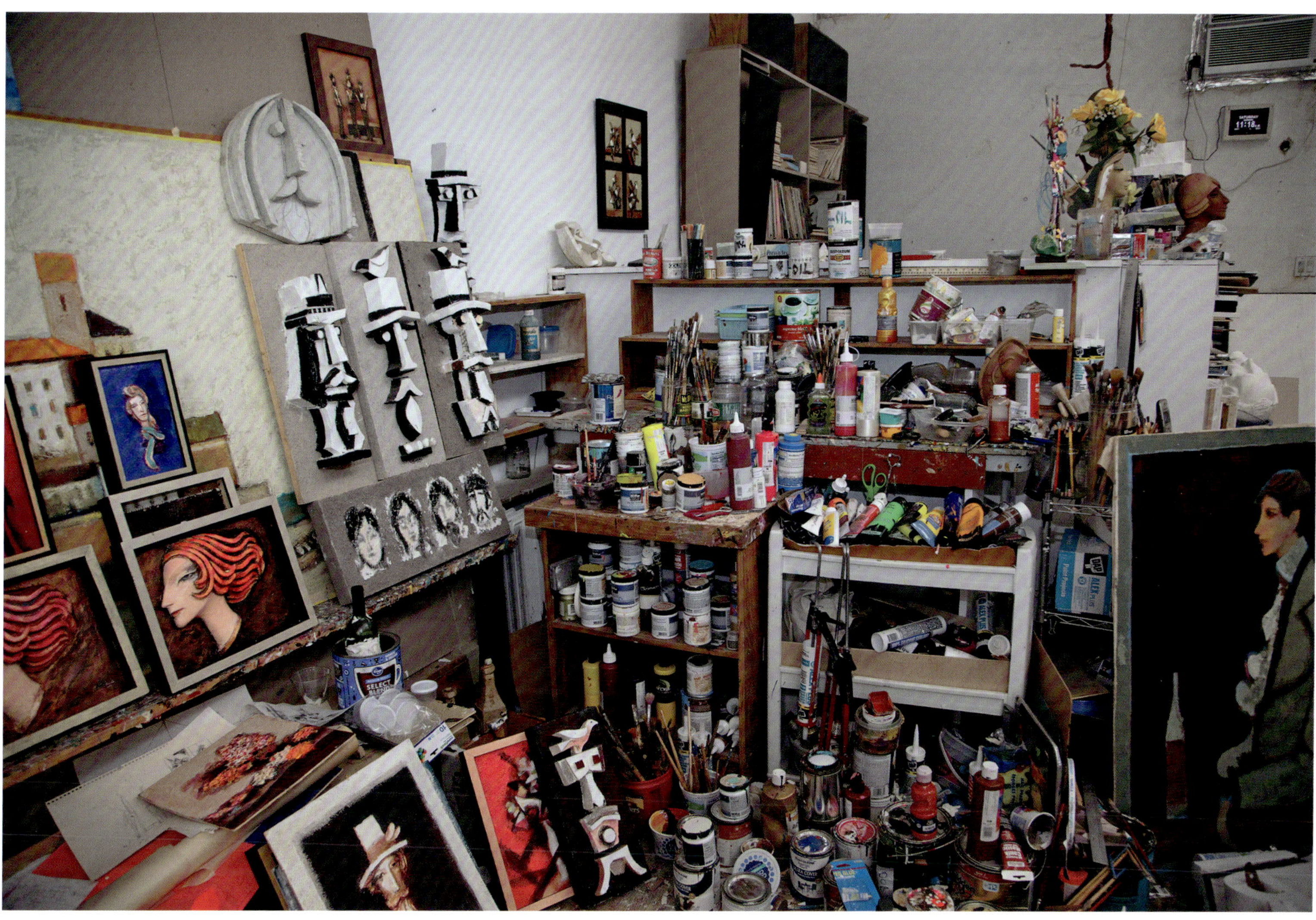

**Figure 4.32.** Upstairs in David Adickes's home/studio in Houston, Texas.

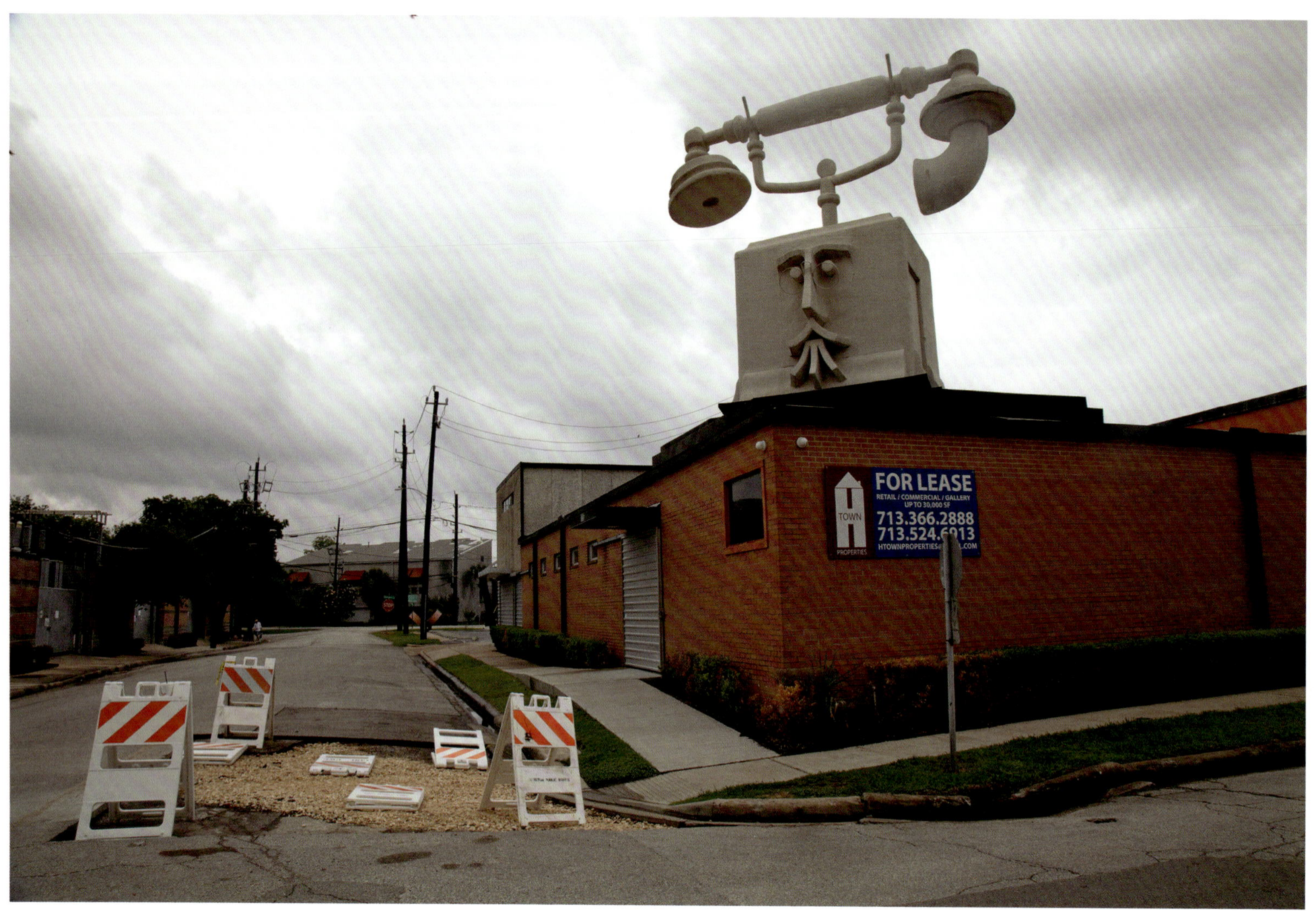


**Figure 4.33.** *Big Alex* in Houston, Texas.

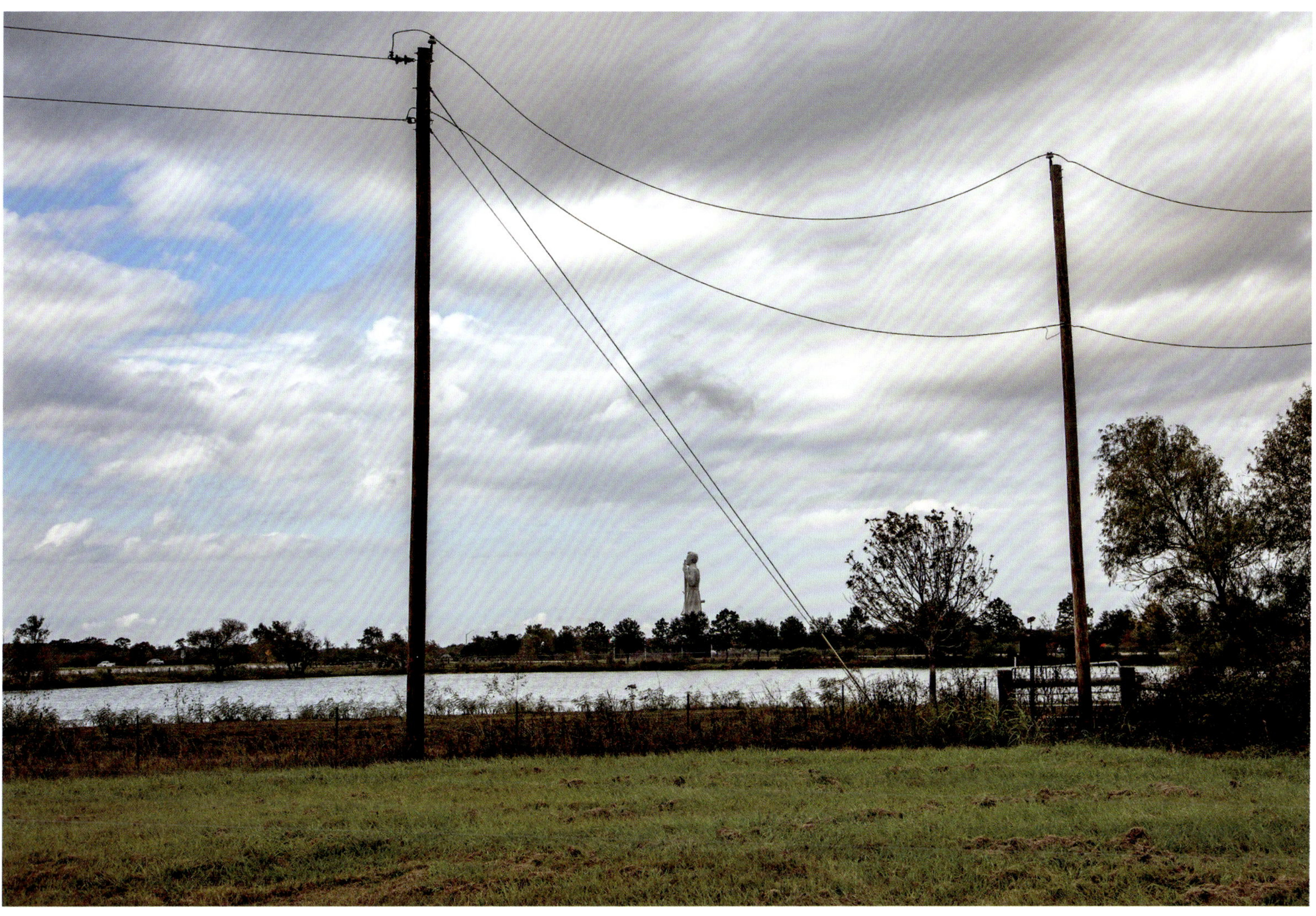

**Figure 4.34.** A view from a distance of *Stephen F. Austin* at Munson Historical County Park, Angleton, Texas.

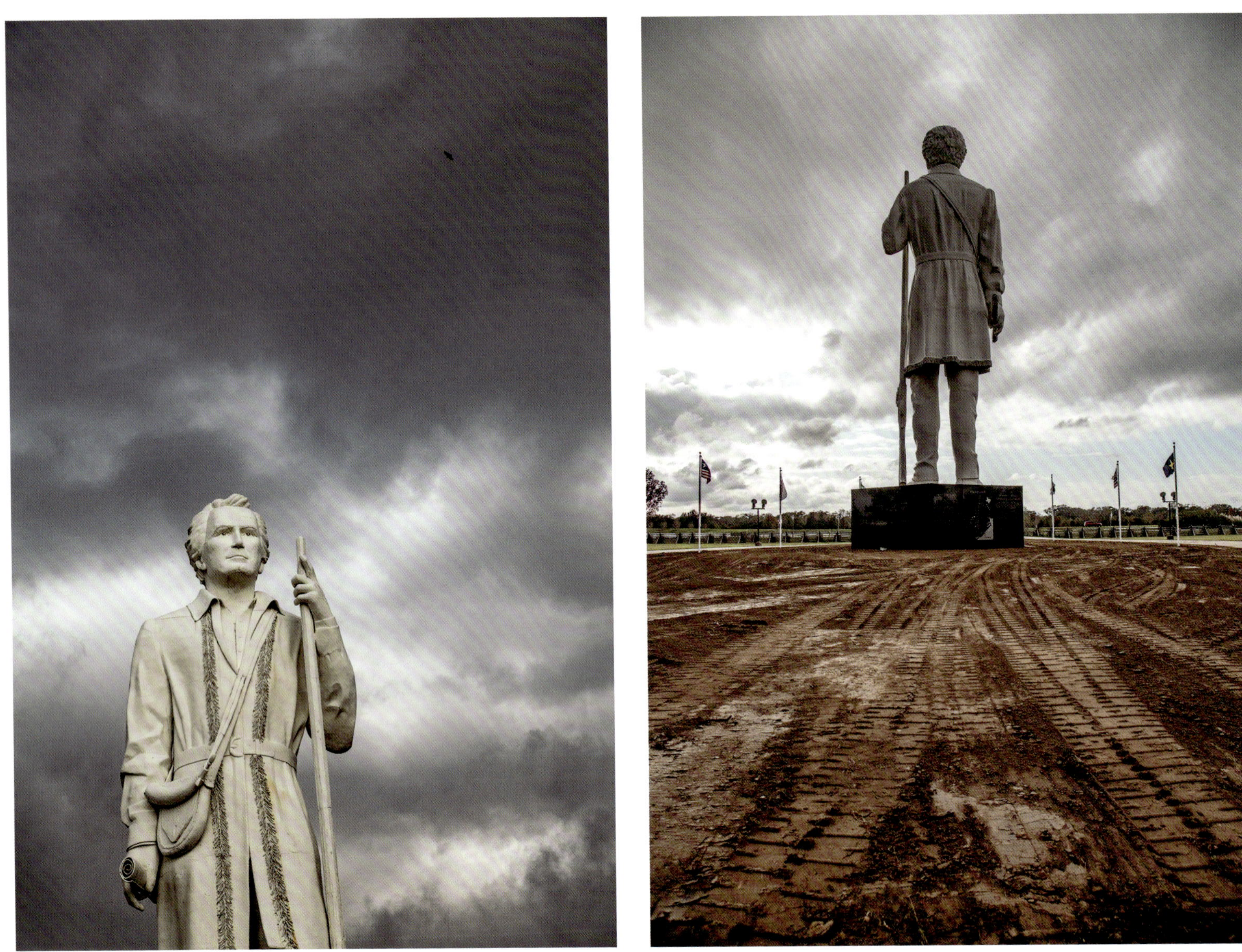

**Figures 4.35 and 4.36.** *Stephen F. Austin* at Munson Historical County Park, Angleton, Texas.

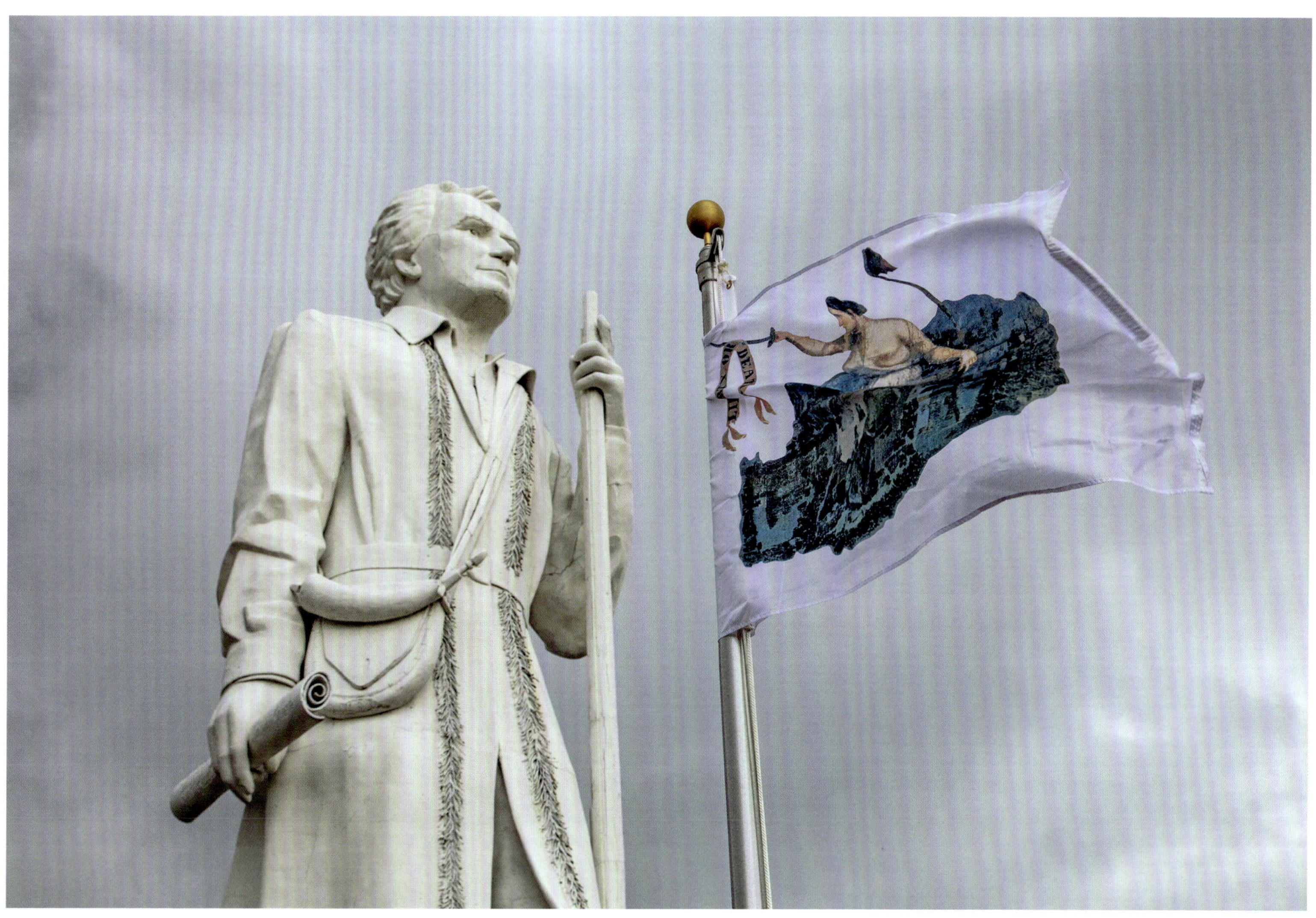

**Figure 4.37.** *Stephen F. Austin* and a flag commemorating the Battle of San Jacinto, Angleton, Texas.

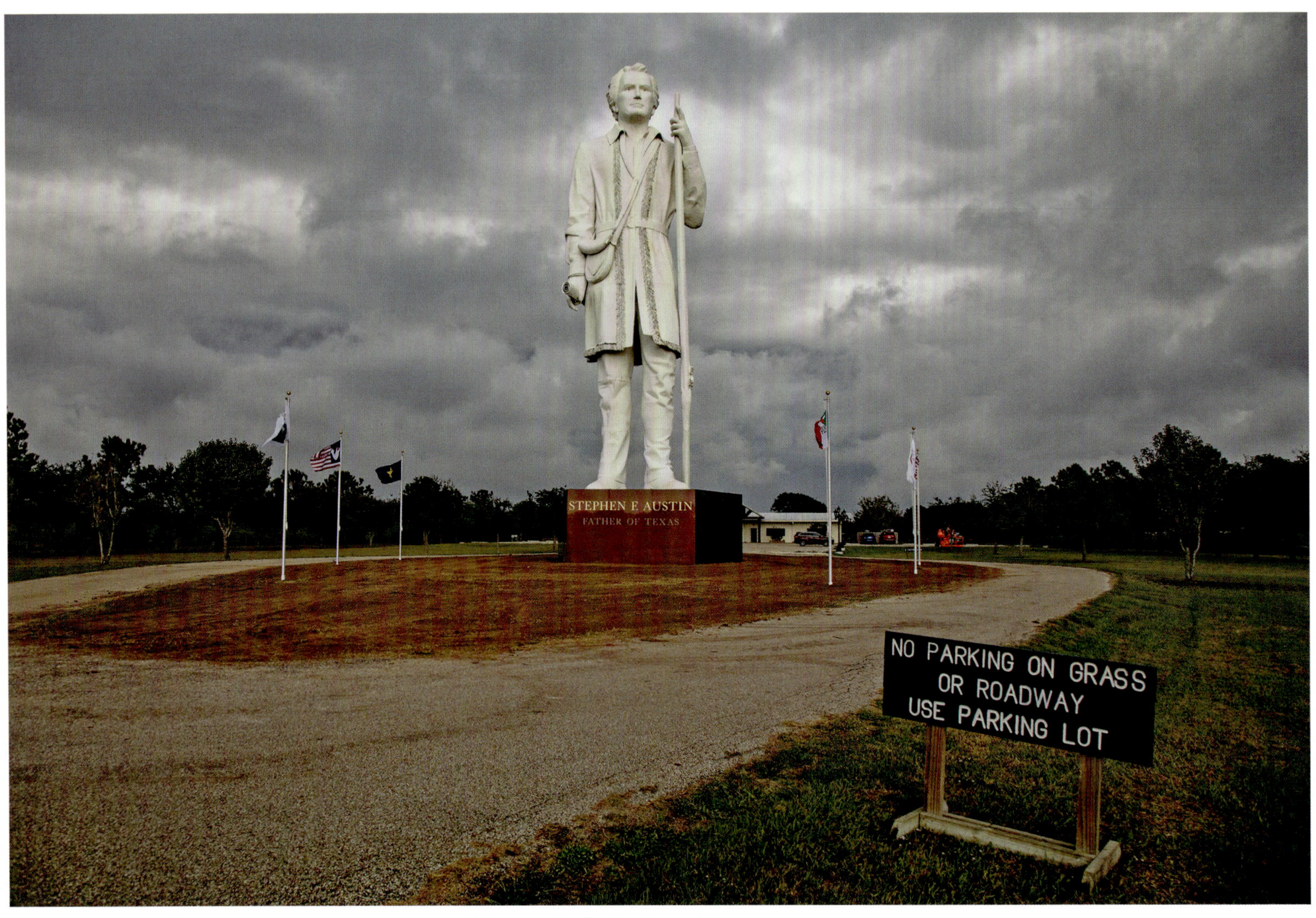


**Figure 4.38.** *Stephen F. Austin* at Munson Historical County Park, Angleton, Texas.

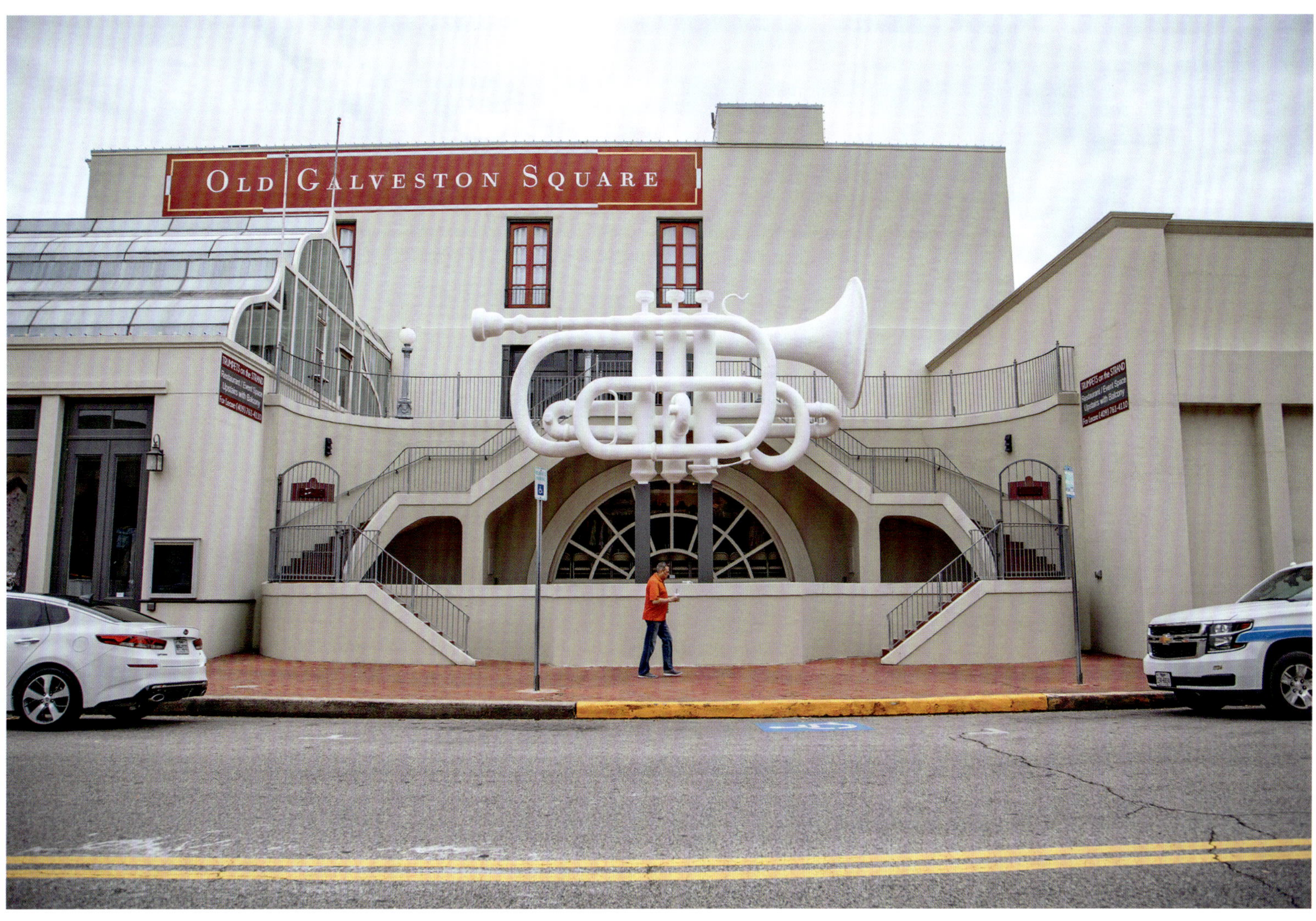


**Figure 4.39.** *Cornet*, Galveston, Texas.

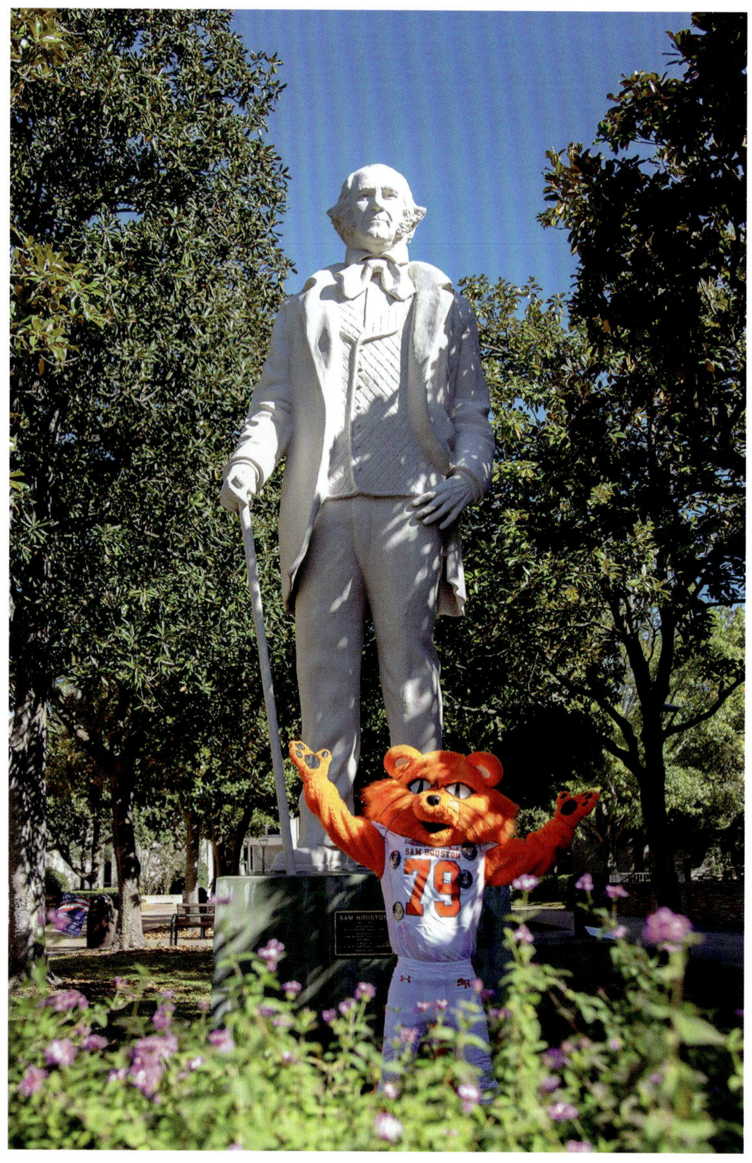


**Figure 4.40.** *Sam Houston* is prominently featured on the campus of Sam Houston State University. Mascot, Sammy Bearkat.

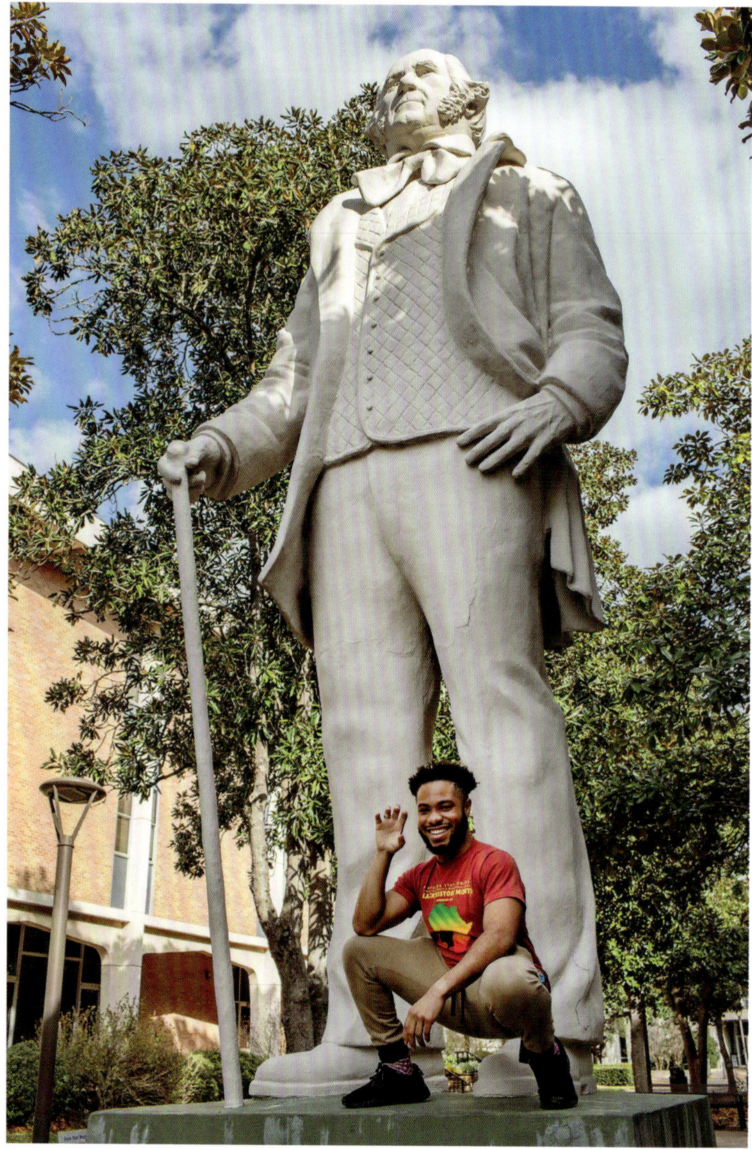

**Figure 4.41.** A student poses with Adickes's sculpture in Huntsville, Texas.

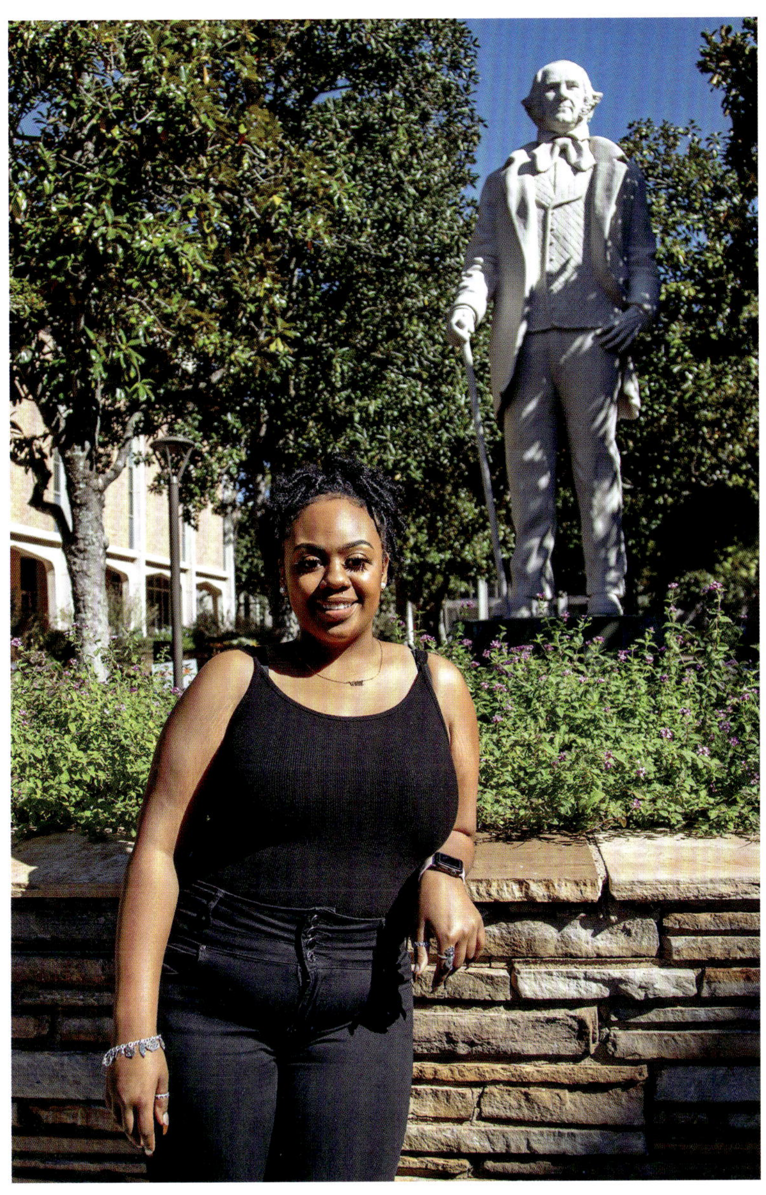

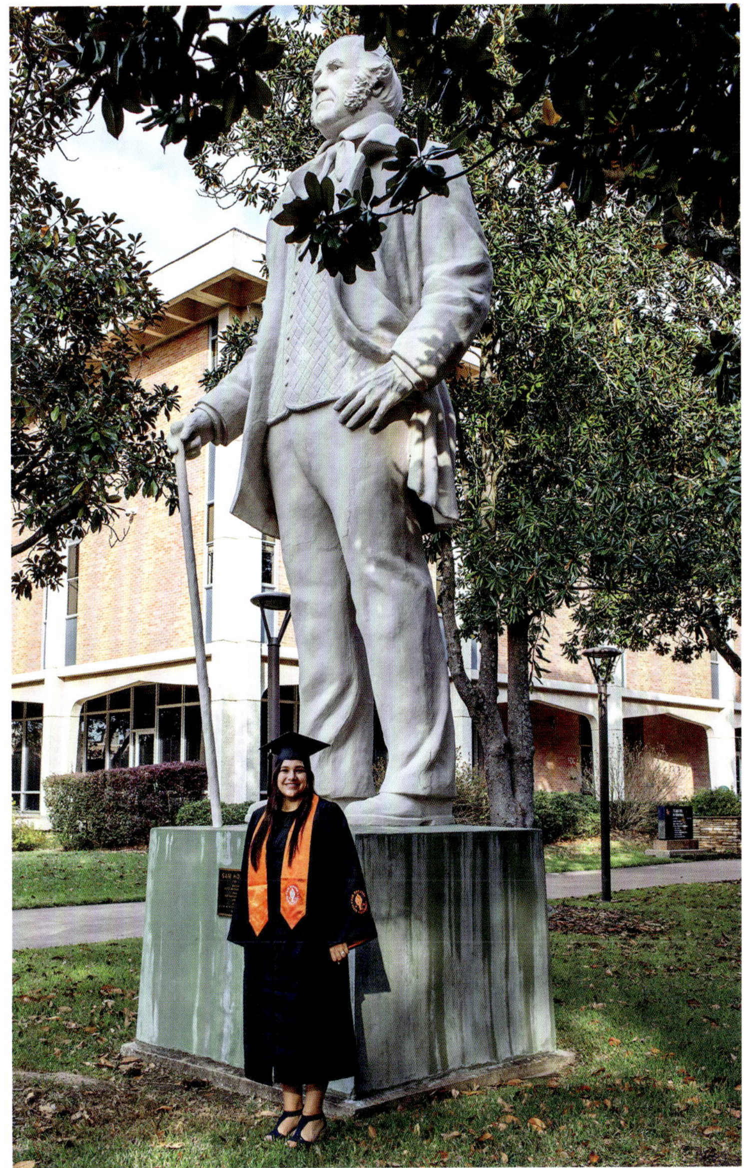

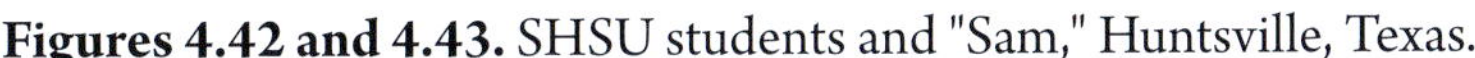

**Figures 4.42 and 4.43.** SHSU students and "Sam," Huntsville, Texas.

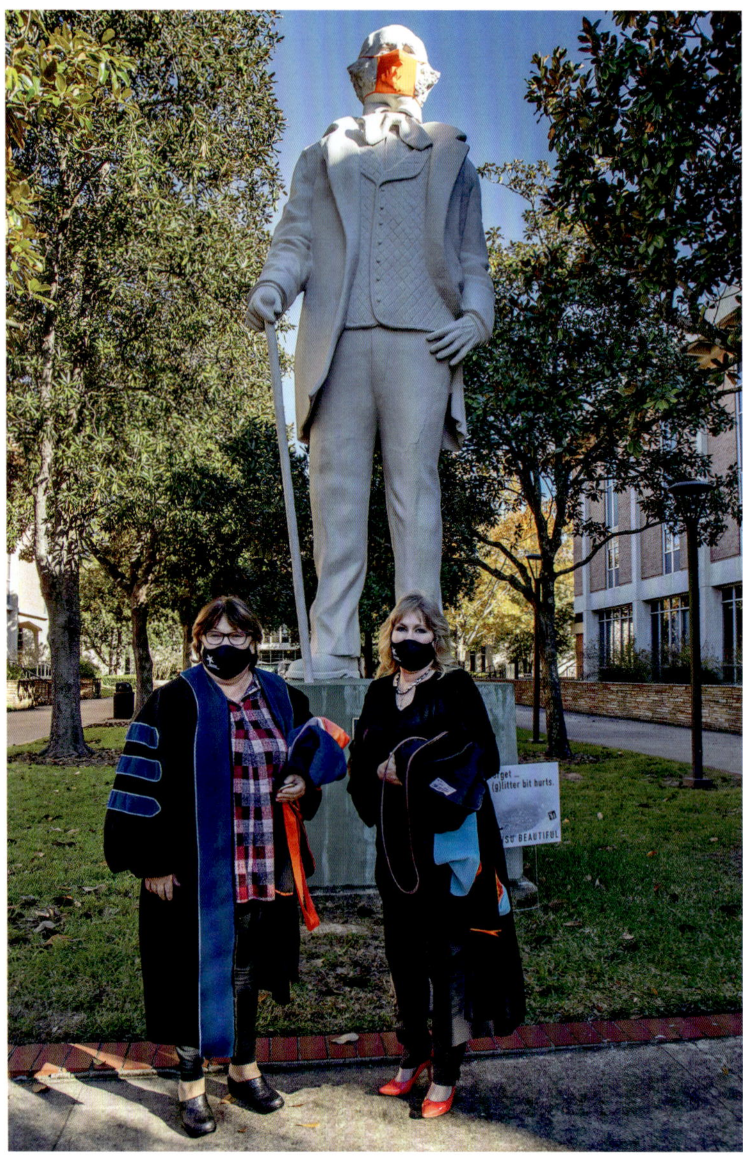


**Figure 4.44.** Barry Doss, costume designer for the Department of Dance at SHSU, created a mask for *Sam Houston* to encourage students and faculty to wear masks on campus.

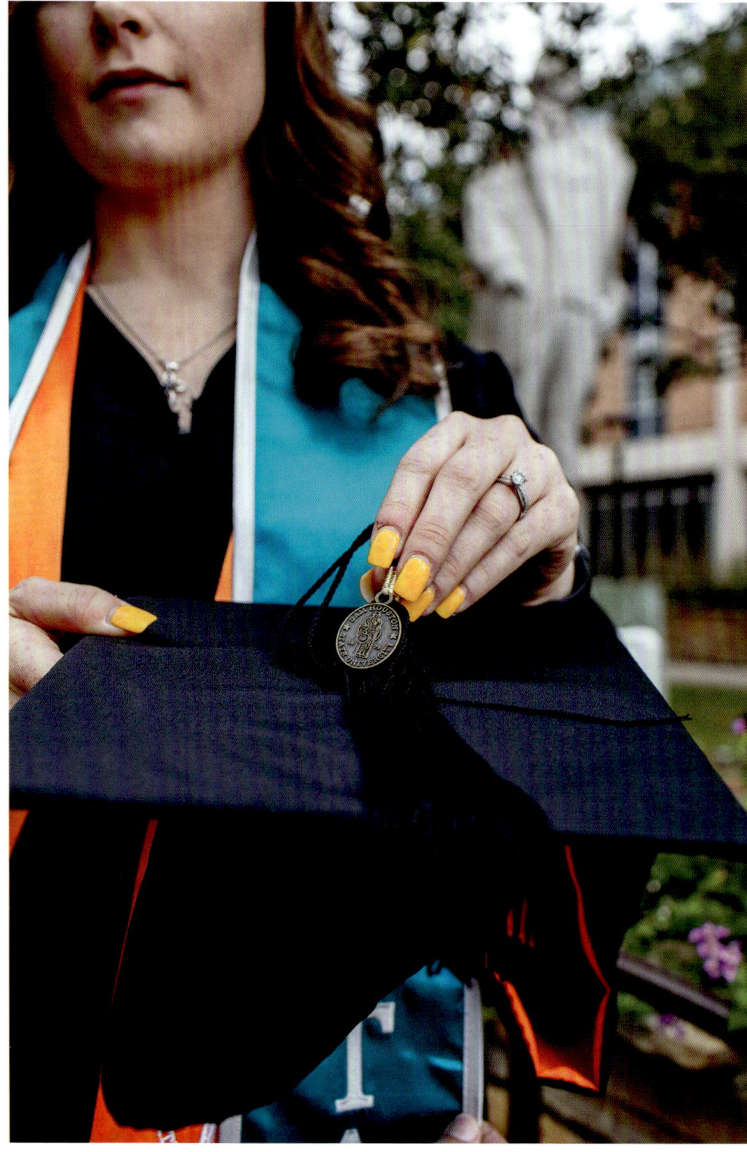

**Figure 4.45.** After graduation ceremonies, the *Sam Houston* statue is a popular photography spot at Sam Houston State University.

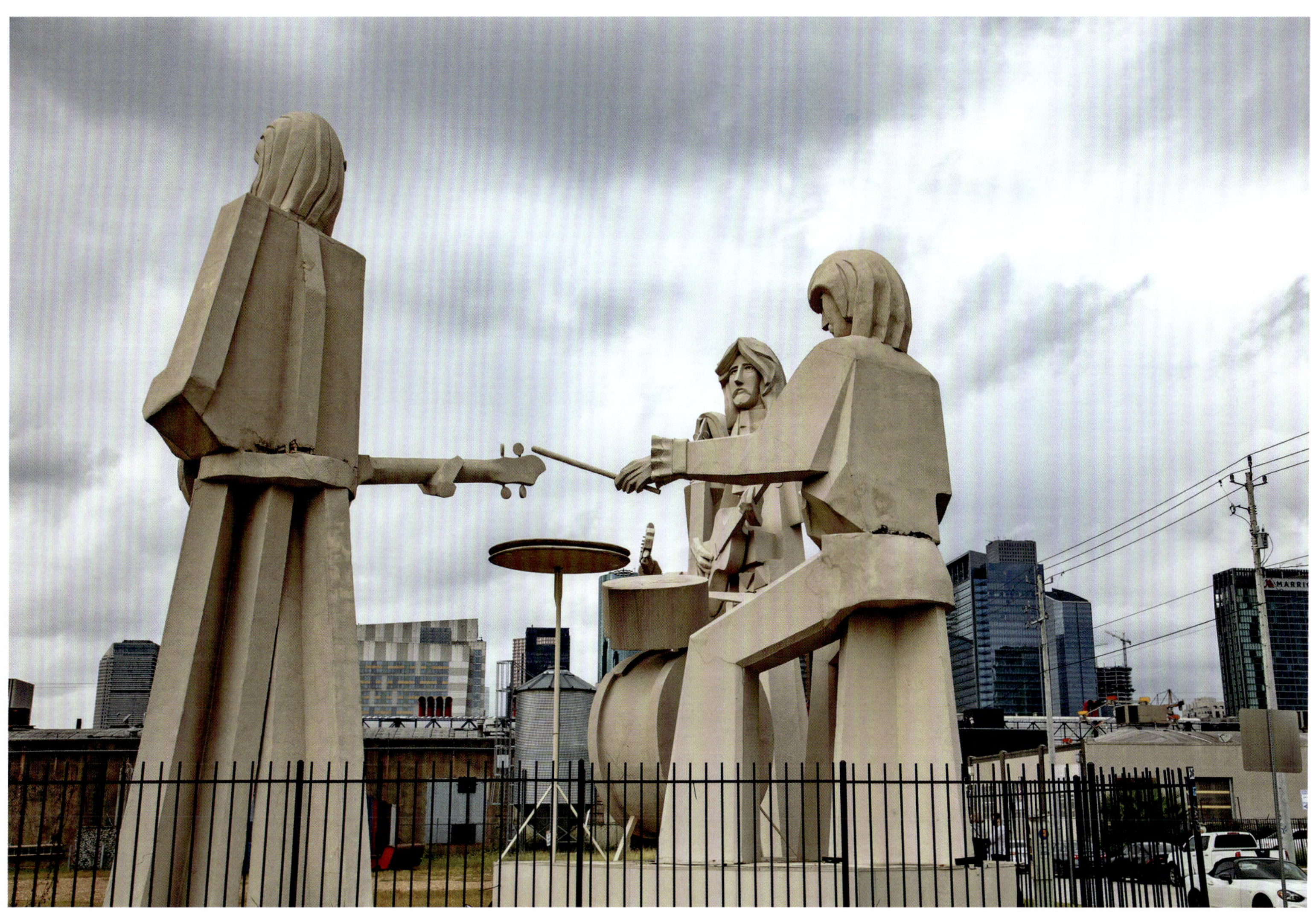

**Figure 4.46.** *The Beatles*, 8th Wonder Brewery, Houston, Texas.

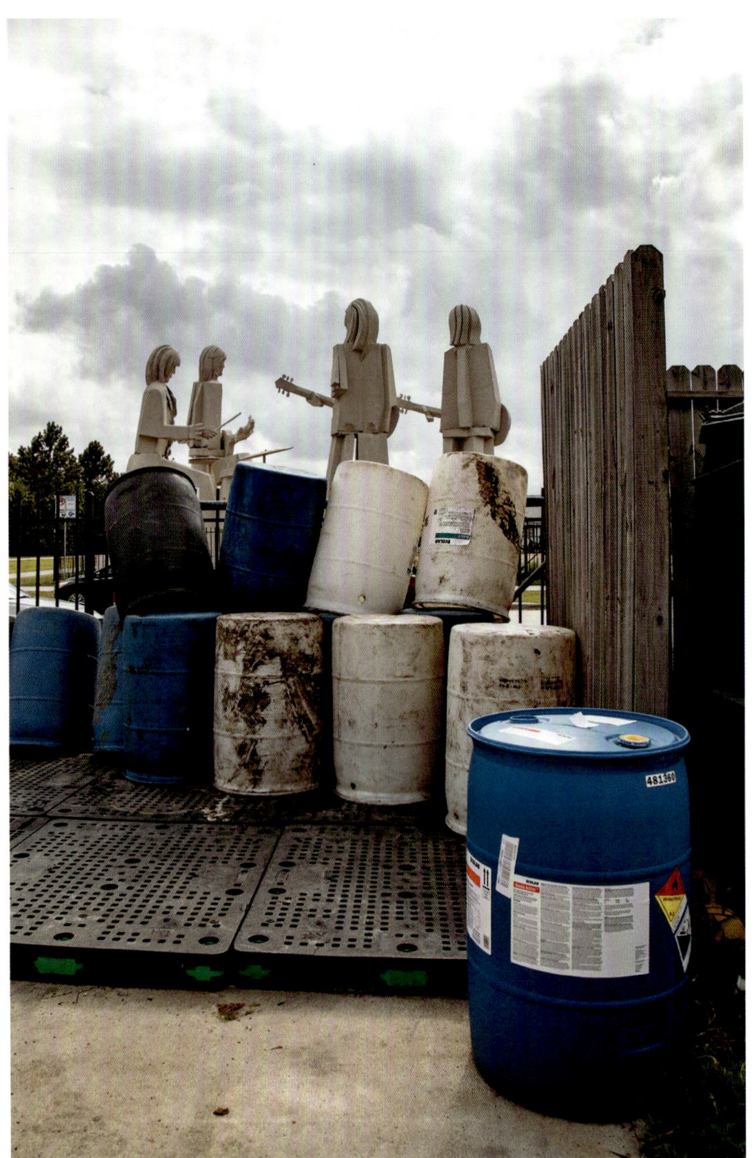

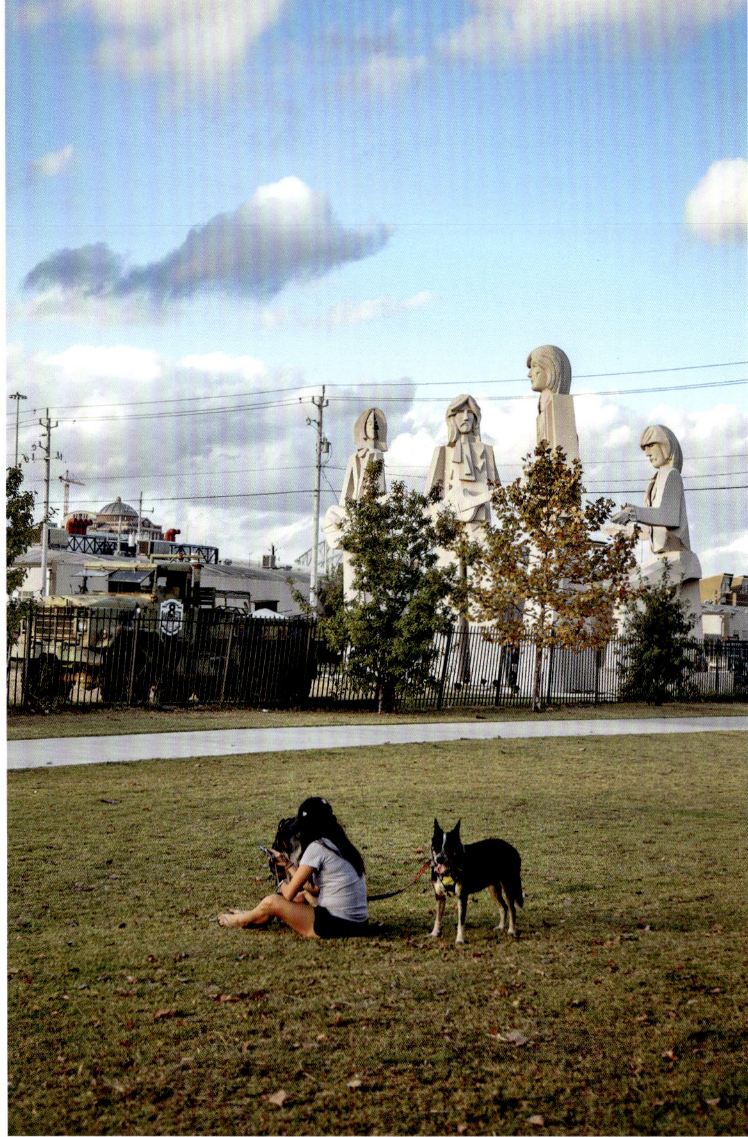

**Figures 4.47 and 4.48.** Views of *The Beatles* from across the street, east downtown Houston, Texas.

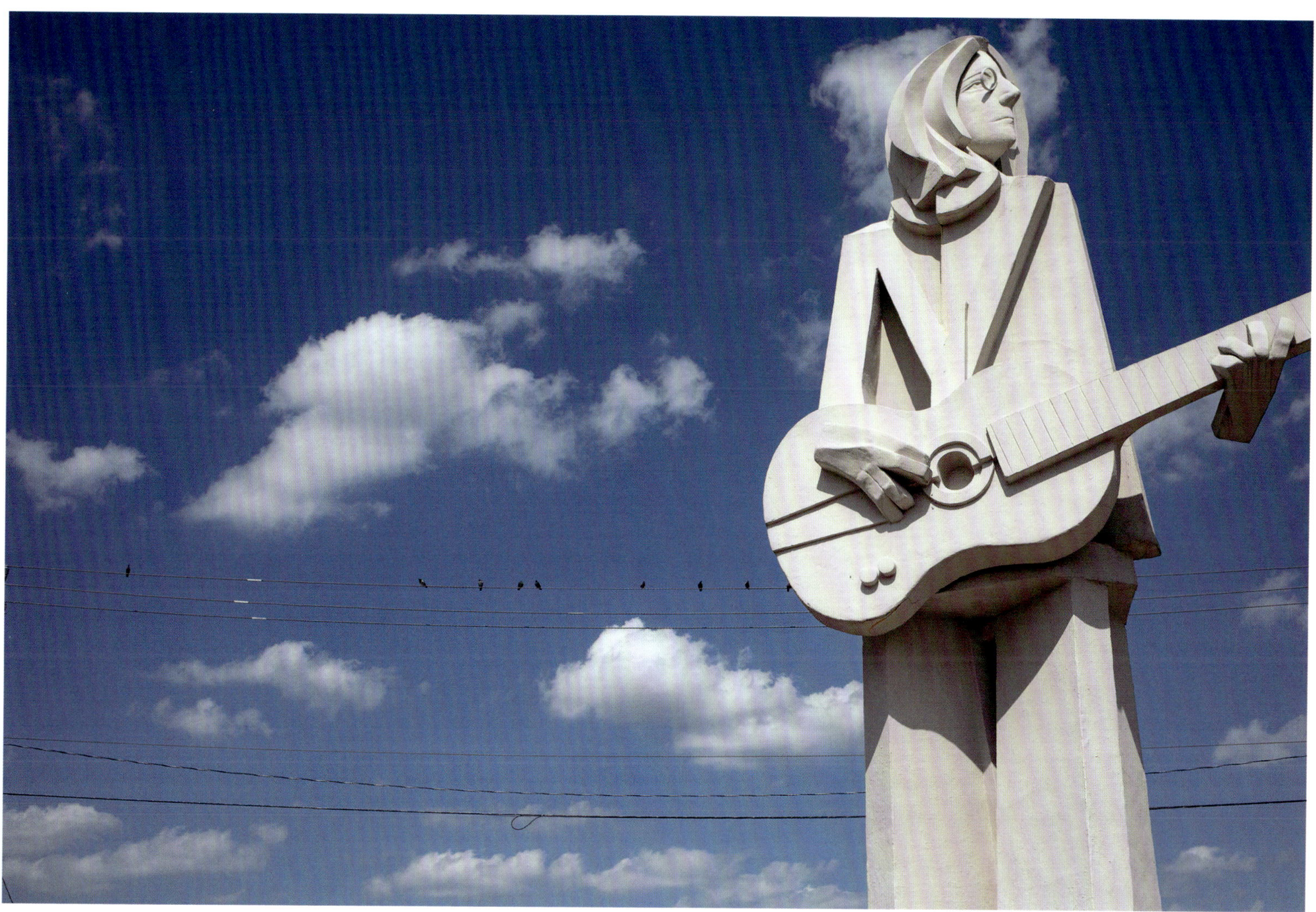

**Figure 4.49.** John Lennon and birds, 8th Wonder Brewery, Houston, Texas.

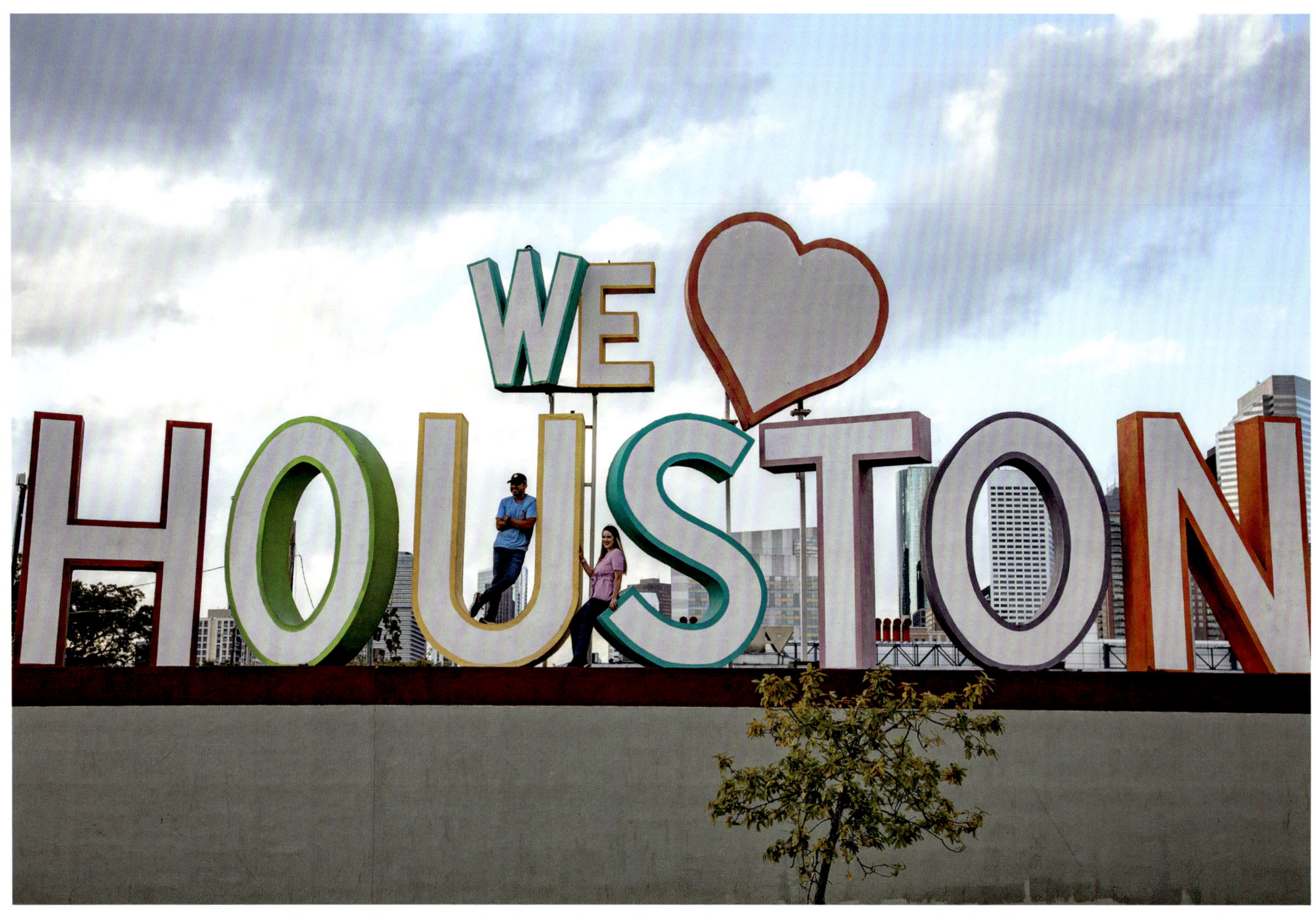


**Figure 4.50.** *We Love Houston* shares its location with *The Beatles* at 8th Wonder Brewery in Houston. This has become an iconic spot for photographs in the city.

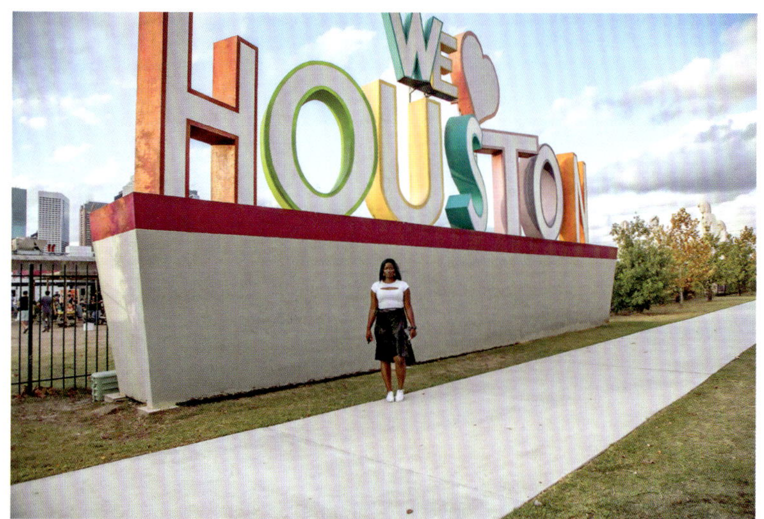

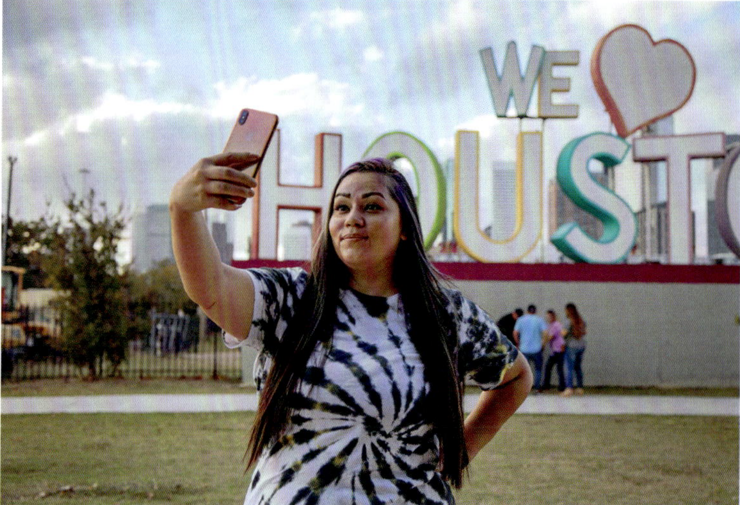

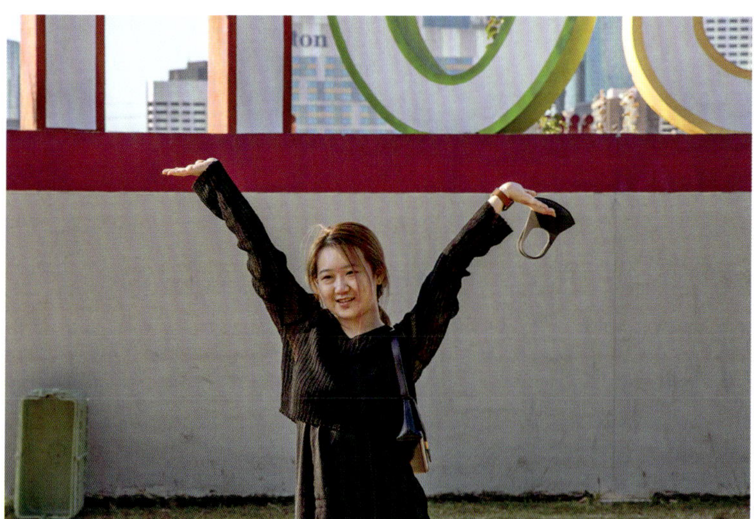
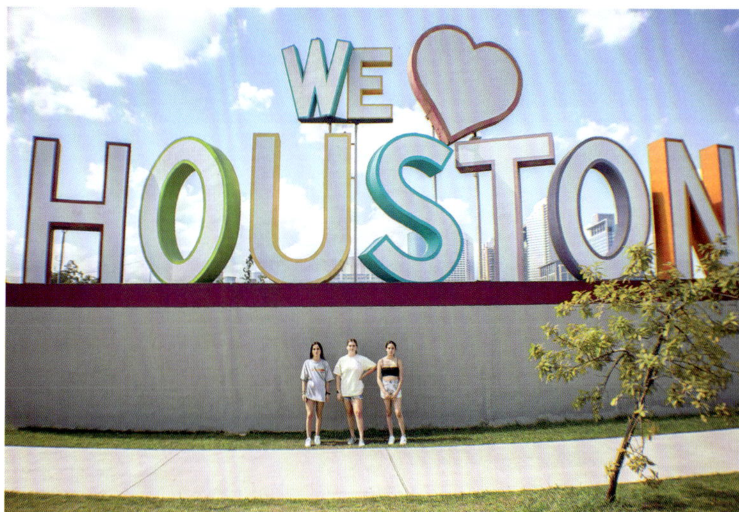


**Figures 4.51, 4.52, 4.53, and 4.54**. People posing with *We Love Houston* in Houston, Texas.

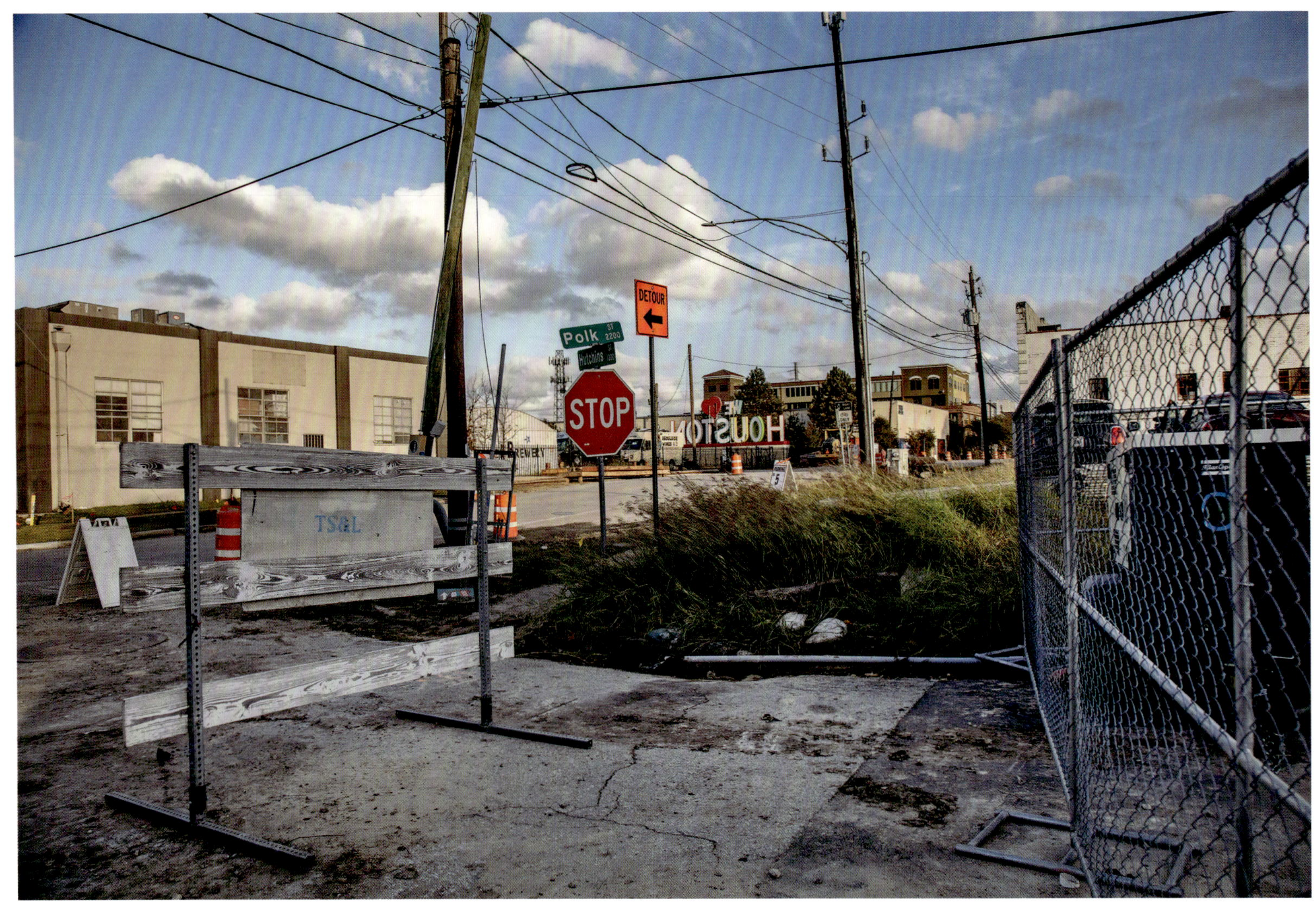


**Figure 4.55.** East downtown Houston, Texas views of *We Love Houston*.

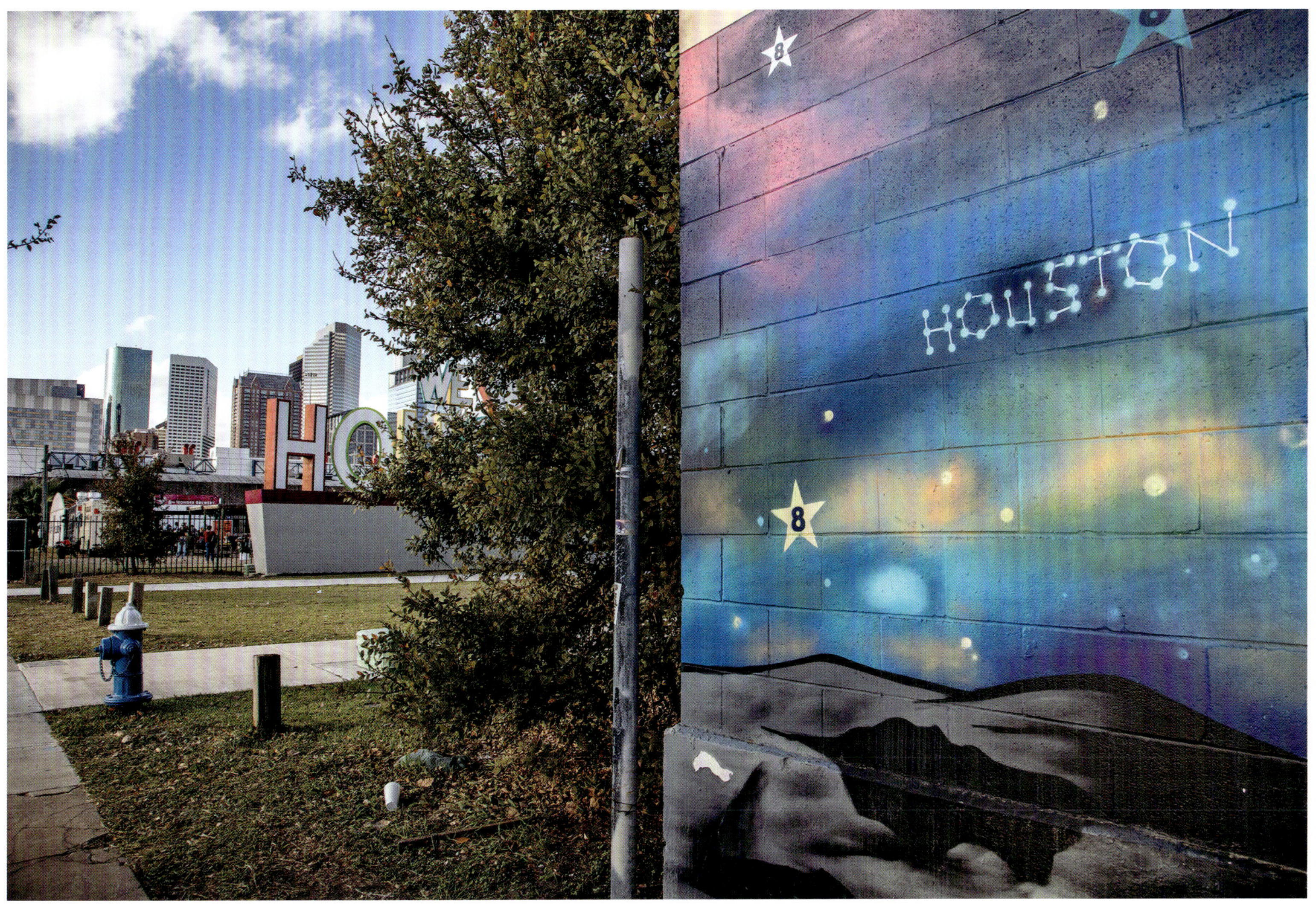


**Figure 4.56.** East downtown Houston, Texas views of *We Love Houston*.

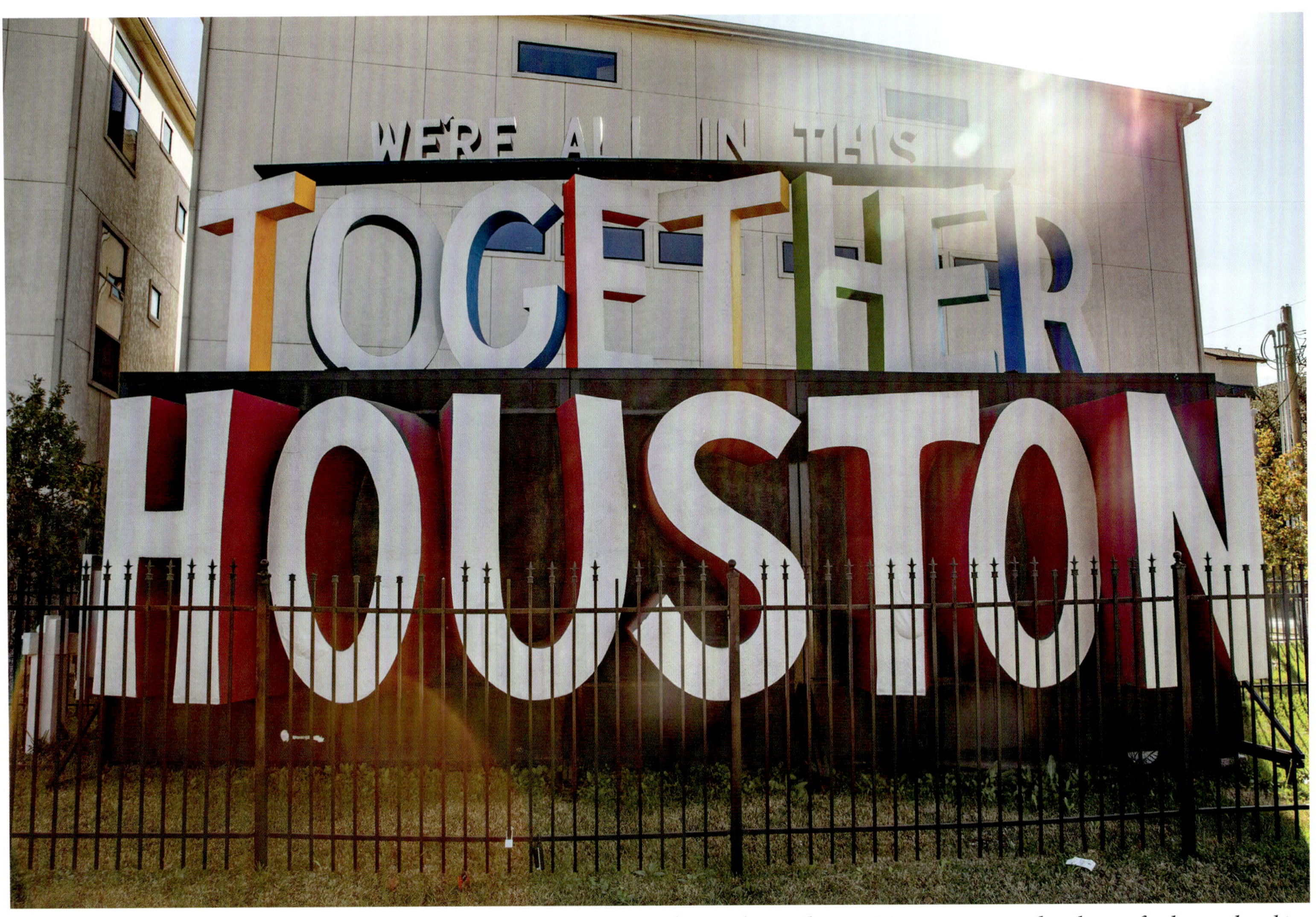


**Figure 4.57.** *We're All in This Together, Houston*, replaced the *Art Is Everywhere* sculpture during COVID-19. It resides along a feeder road and is visible from the Katy Freeway through Houston.

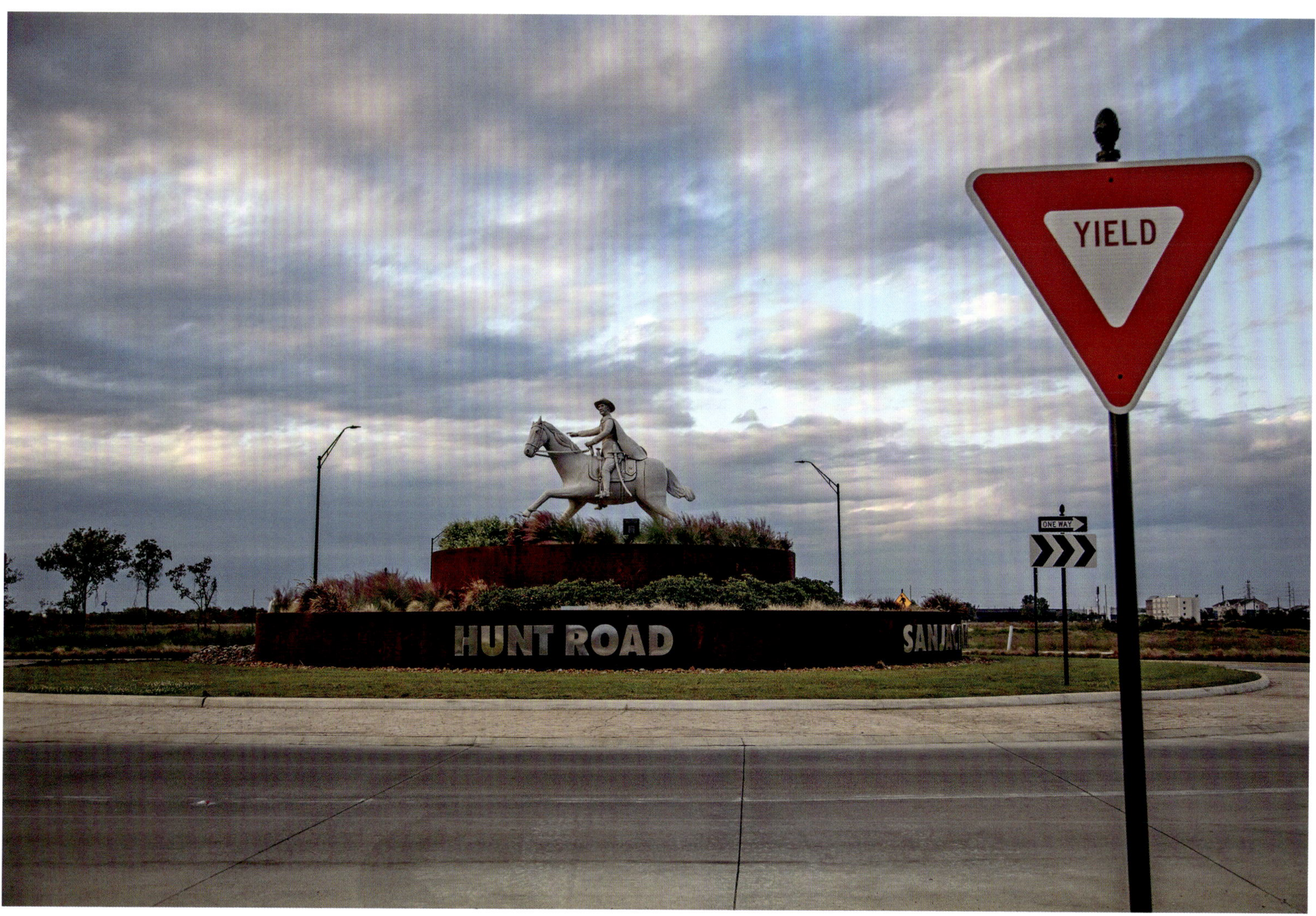


**Figure 4.58.** *Onward,* sculpture of General Sam Houston in Baytown, Texas.

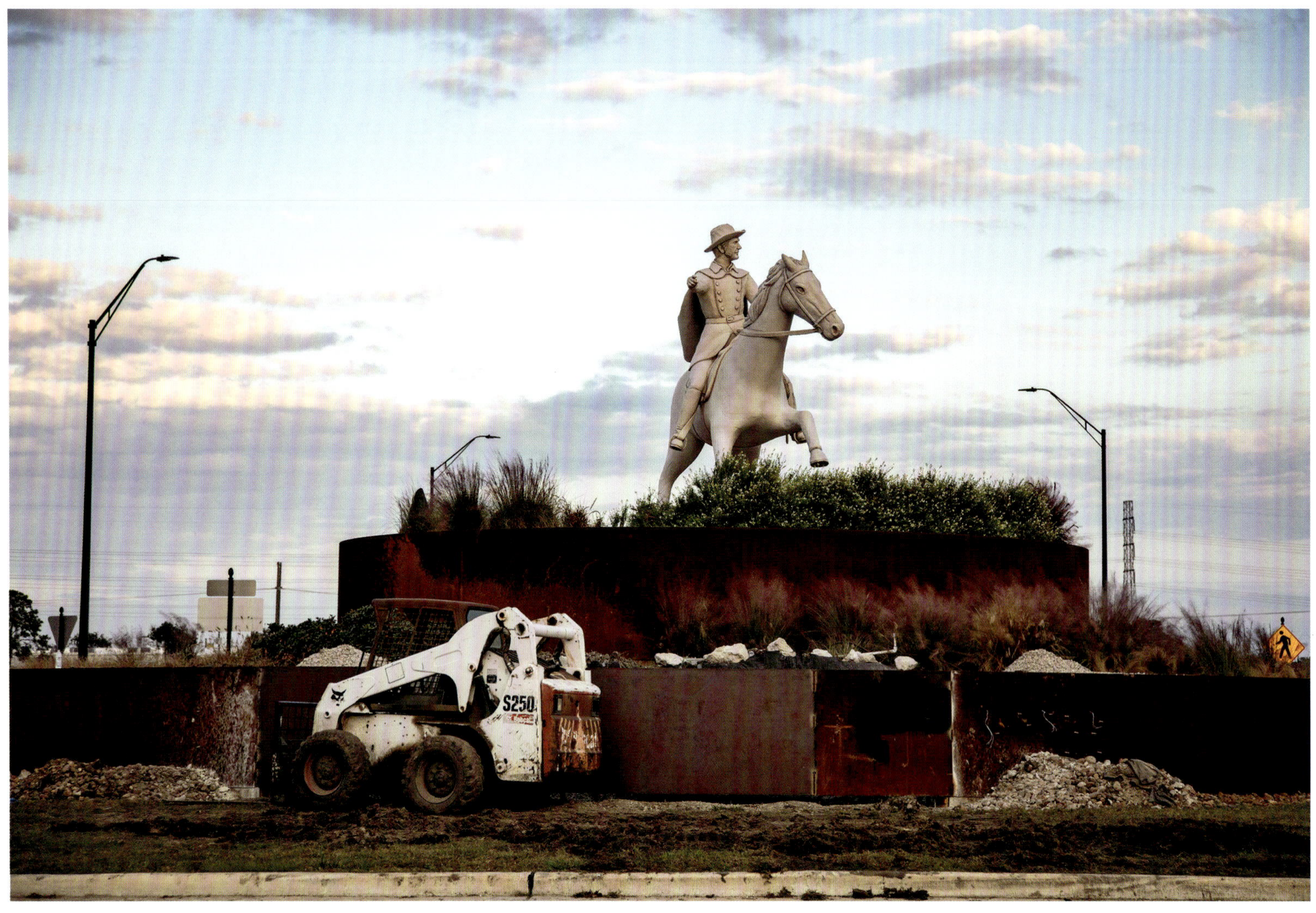


**Figure 4.59.** *Onward*, sculpture of General Sam Houston in Baytown, Texas.

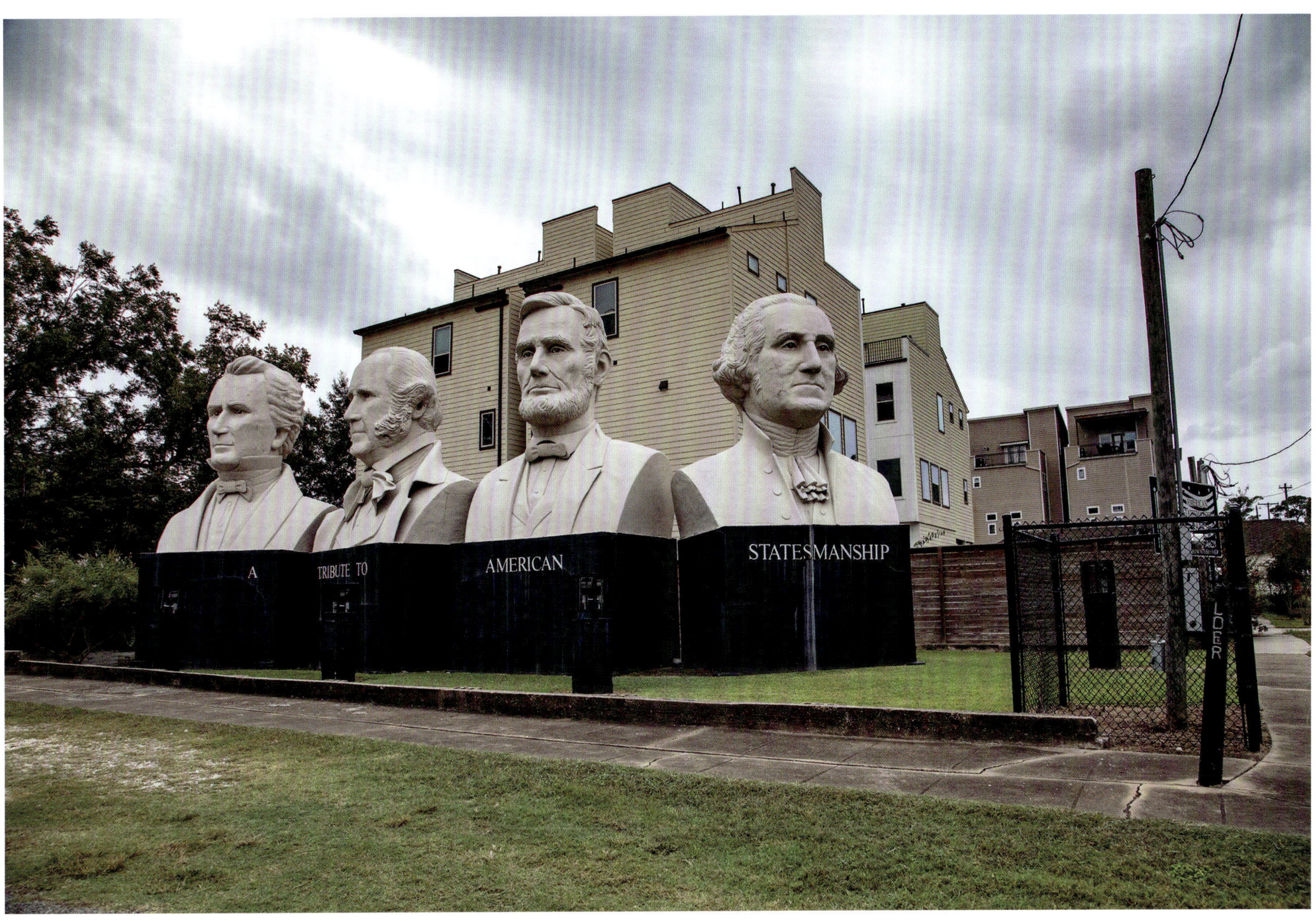


**Figure 4.60.** American Statesmanship Park, Houston, Texas.

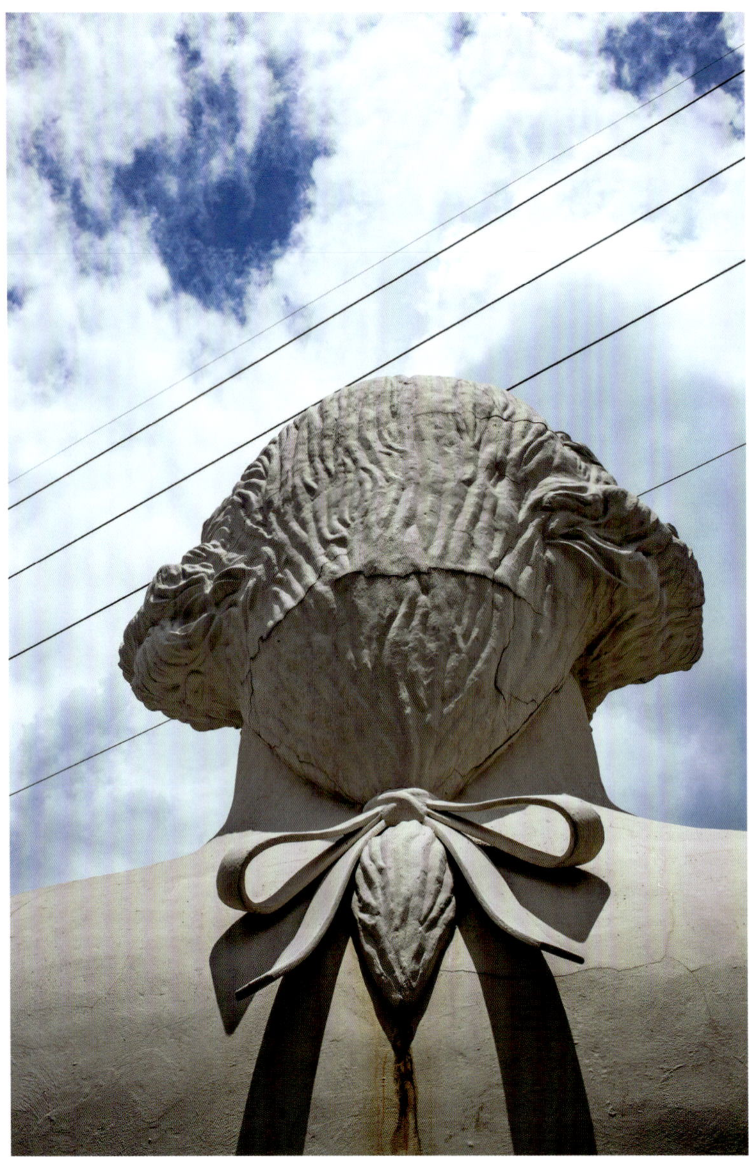

**Figure 4.61.** The back of *George Washington*'s head, American Statesmanship Park, Houston, Texas.

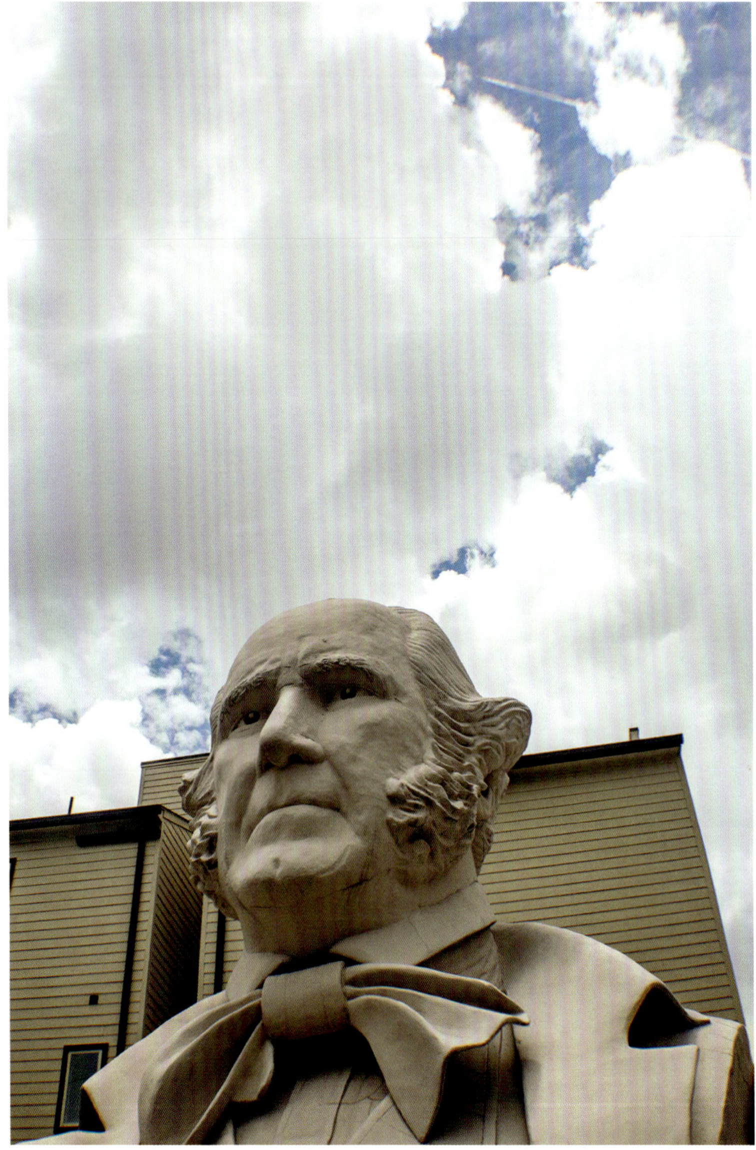

**Figure 4.62.** *Sam Houston*, American Statesmanship Park, Houston, Texas.

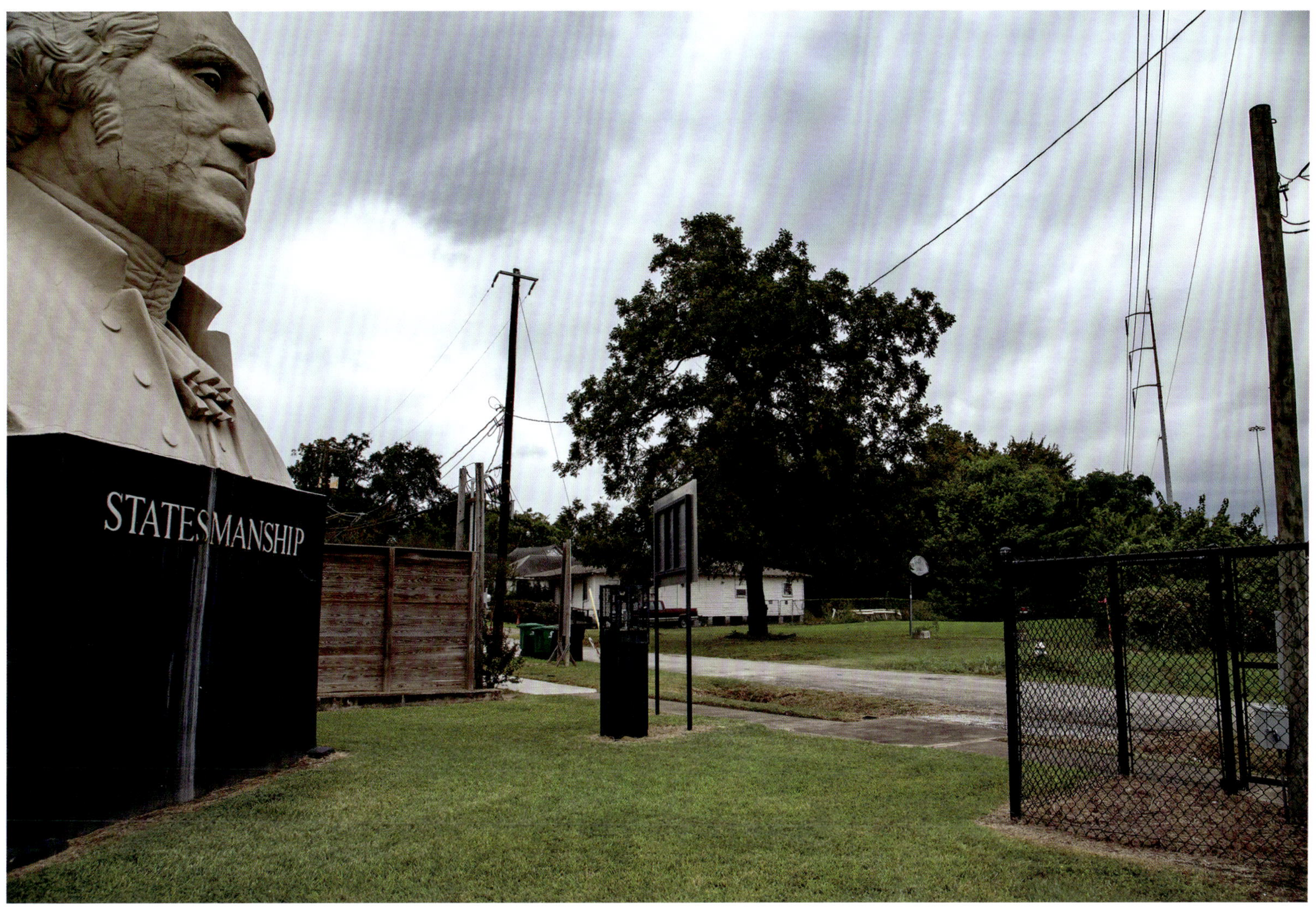


**Figure 4.63.** Neighborhood view of American Statesmanship Park, Houston, Texas.

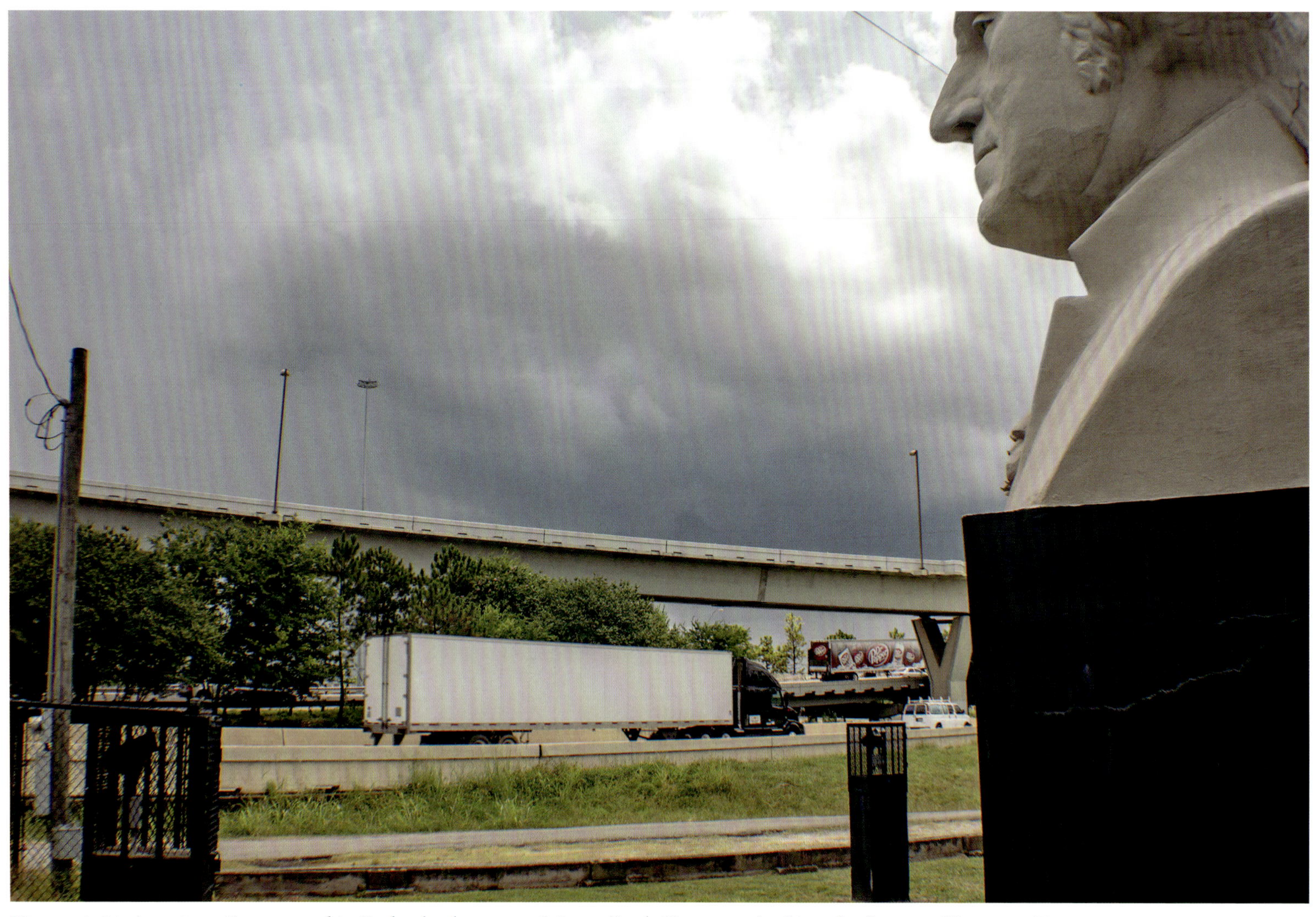

**Figure 4.64.** American Statesmanship Park, also known as Mount Rush Hour, overlooking the freeway, Houston, Texas.

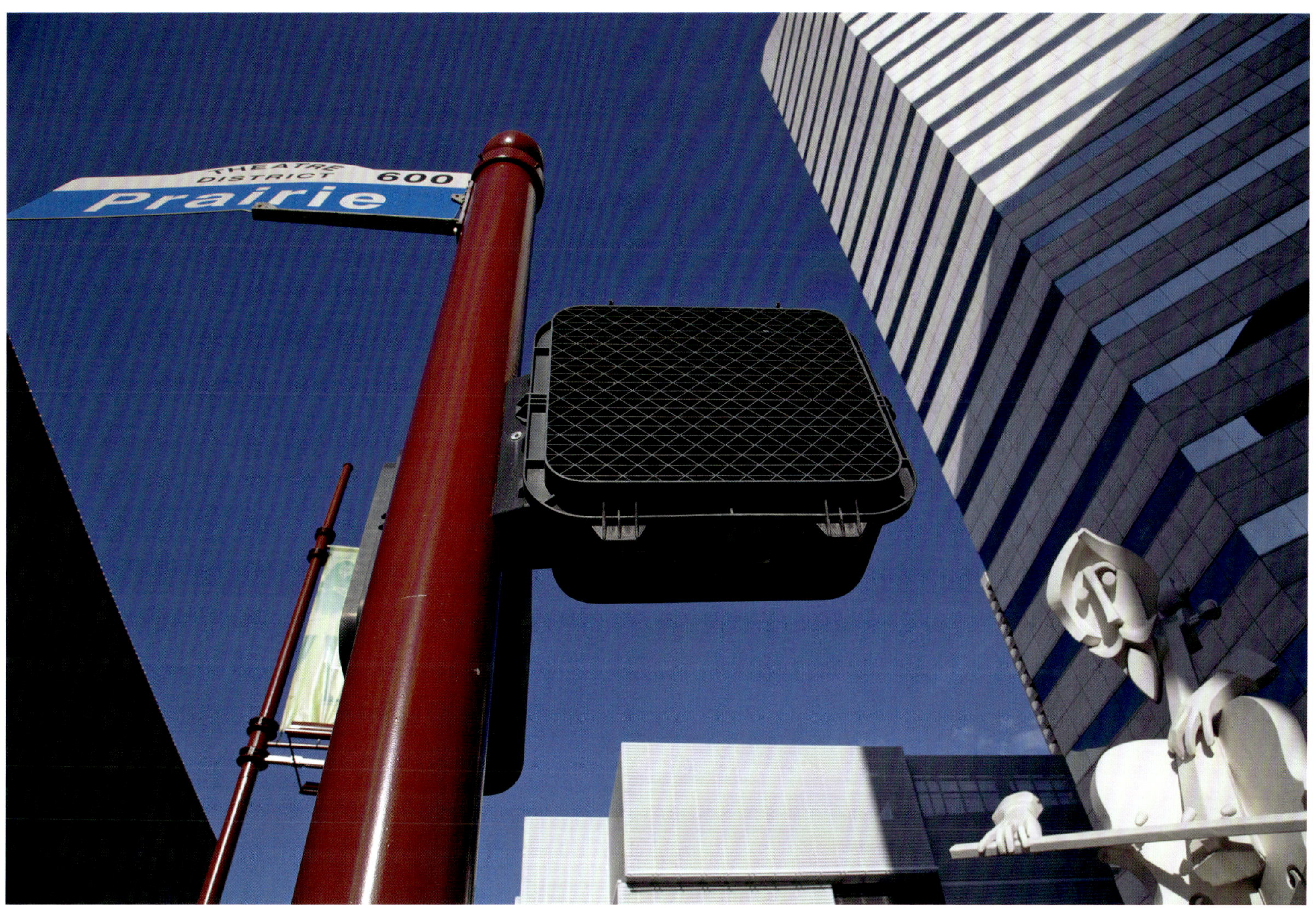


**Figure 4.65.** *Virtuoso*, downtown Houston, Texas.

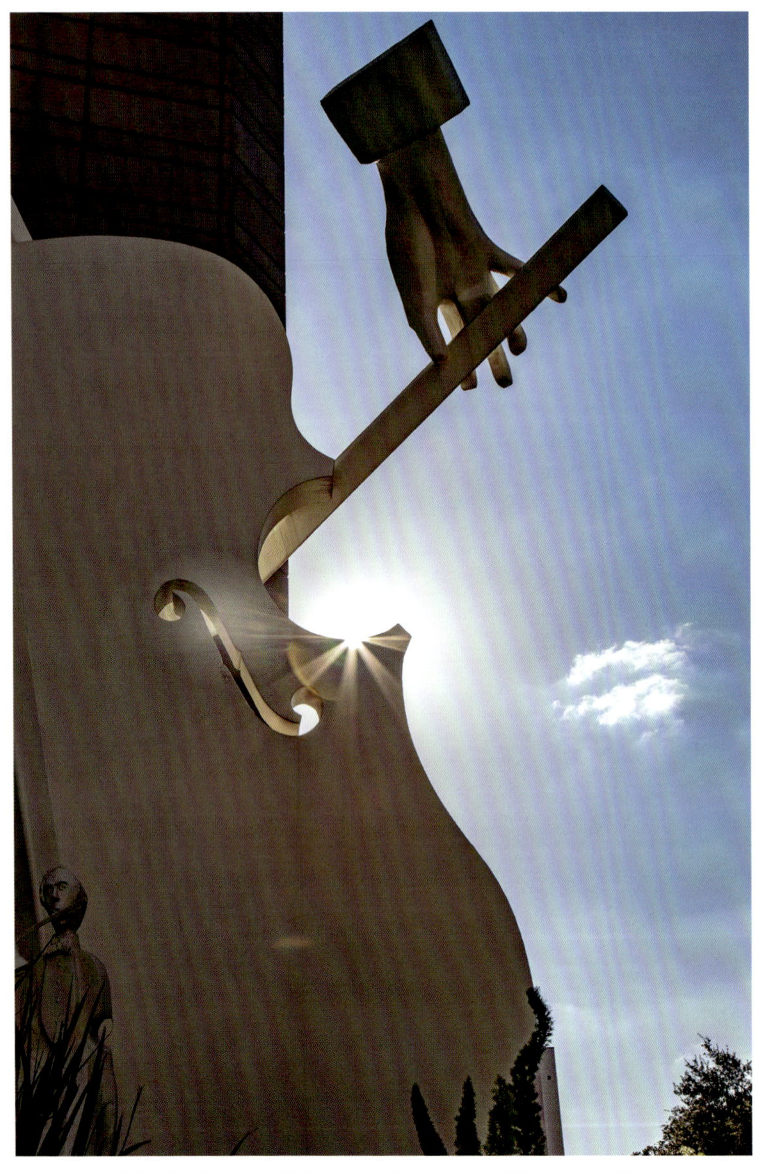

**Figure 4.66.** The hand of *Virtuoso*, downtown Houston, Texas.

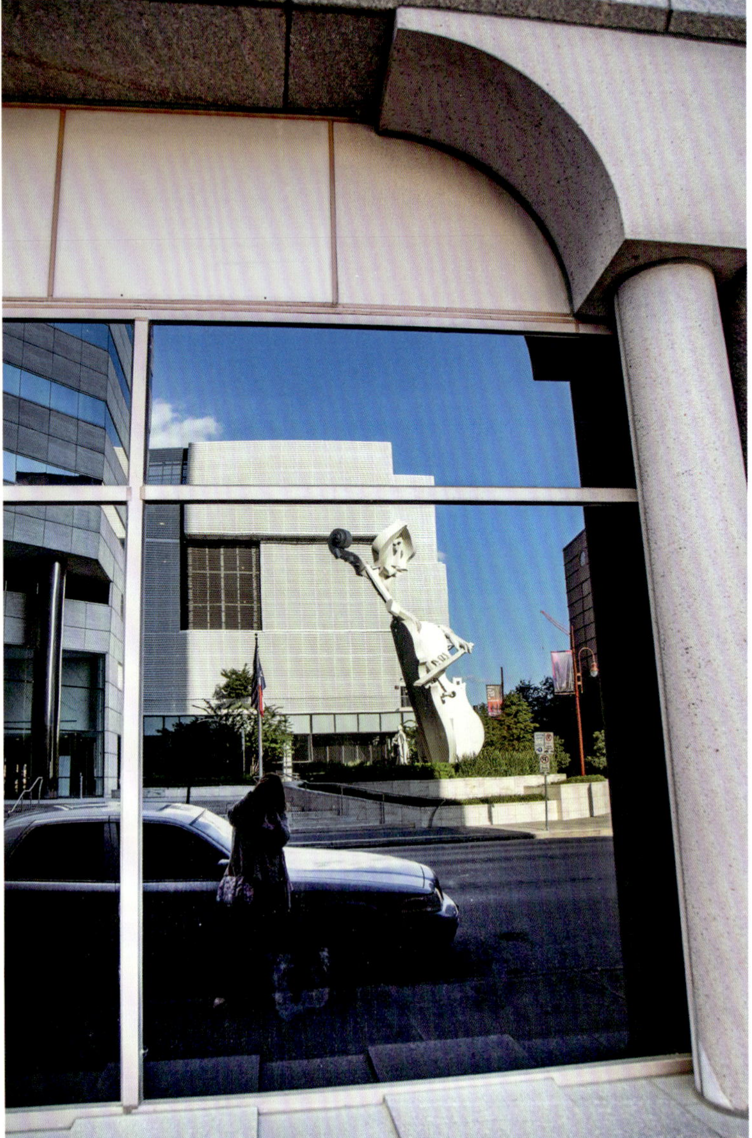

**Figure 4.67.** Self-portrait with *Virtuoso*, downtown Houston, Texas.

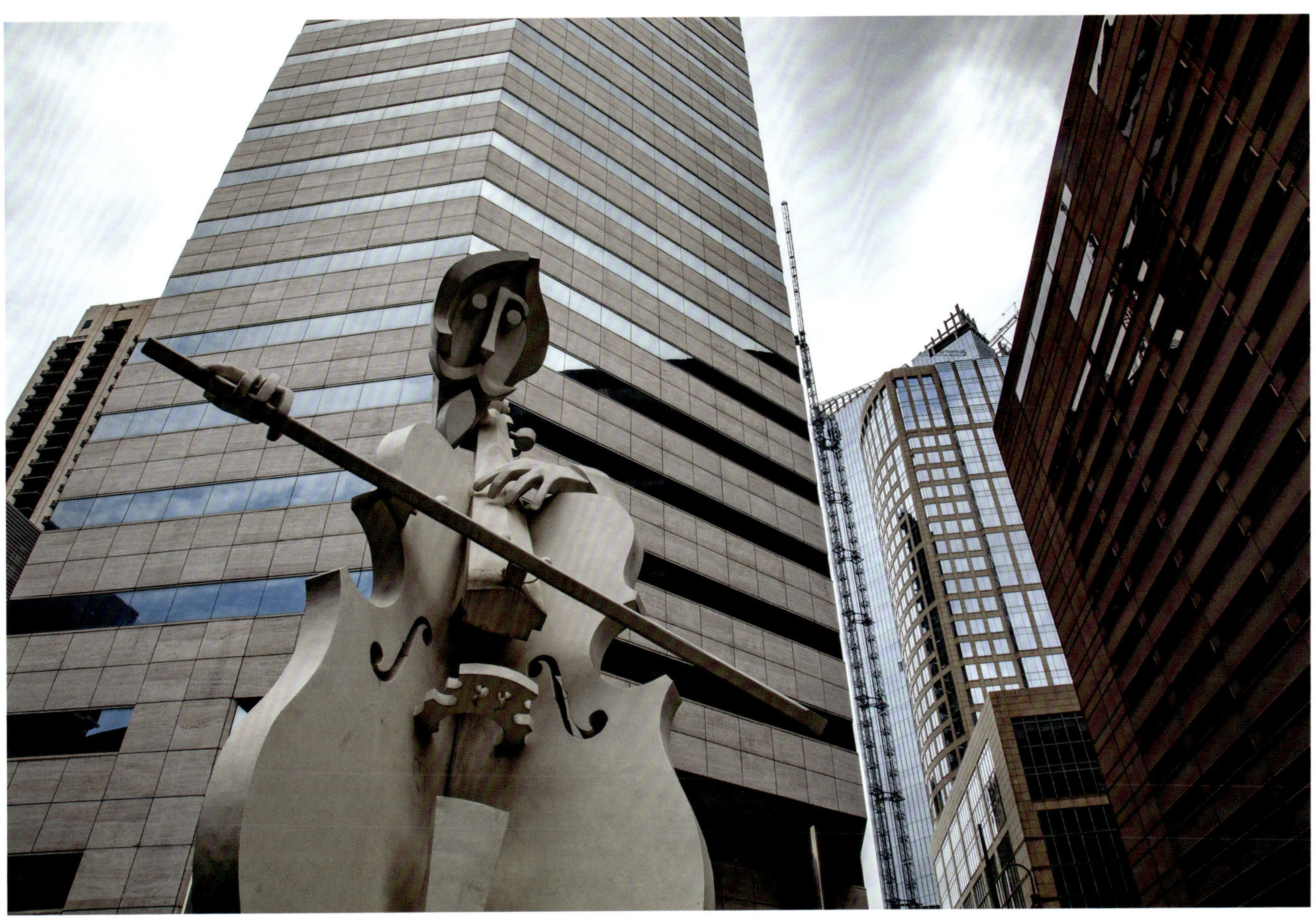

**Figure 4.68.** Classic view of *Virtuoso*, downtown Houston, Texas.

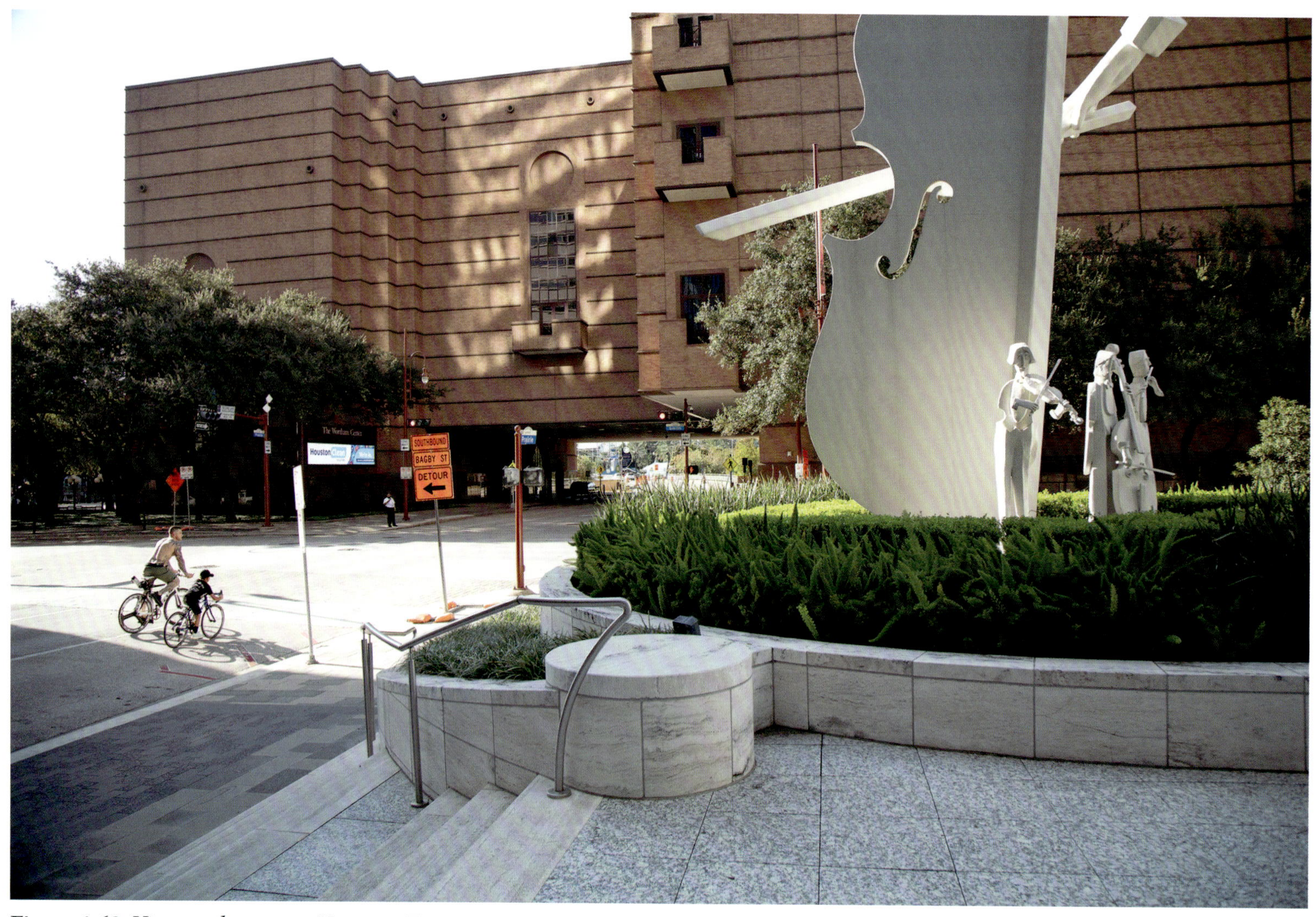


**Figure 4.69.** *Virtuoso,* downtown Houston, Texas.

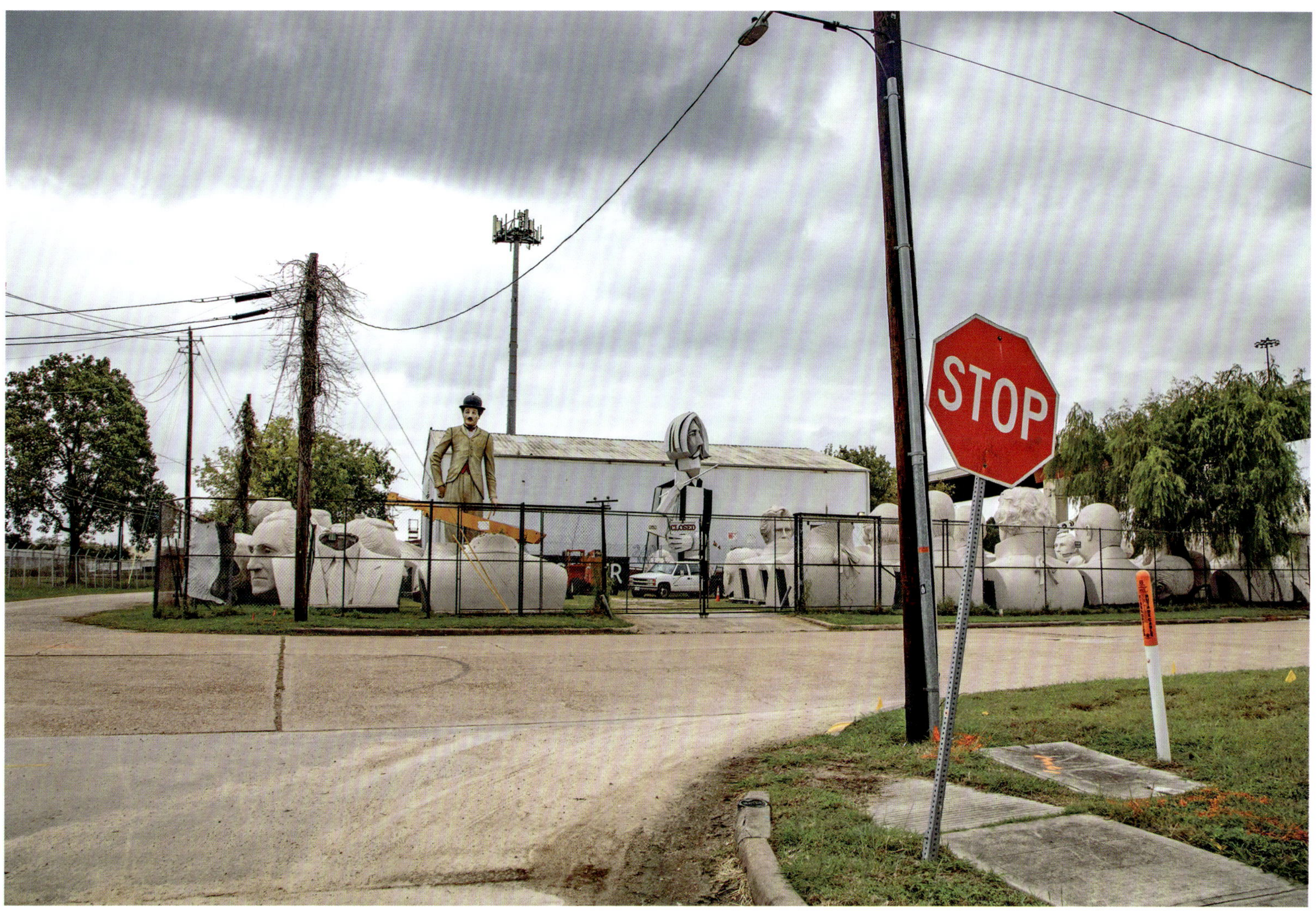


**Figure 4.70.** Adickes Sculpture Works Studio in Houston.

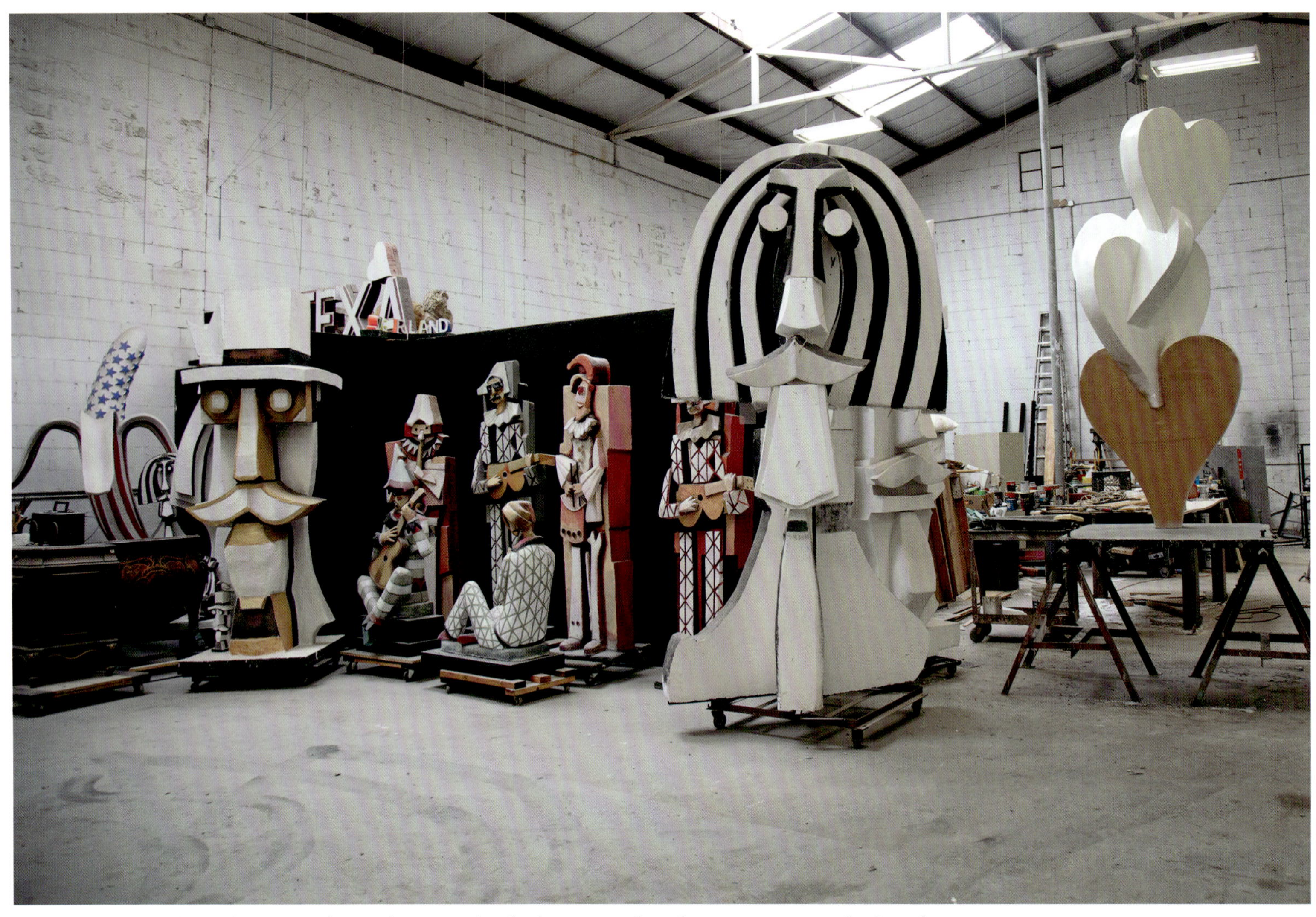

**Figure 4.71.** Inside Sculpture Works Studio many finished pieces and works in progress can be found.

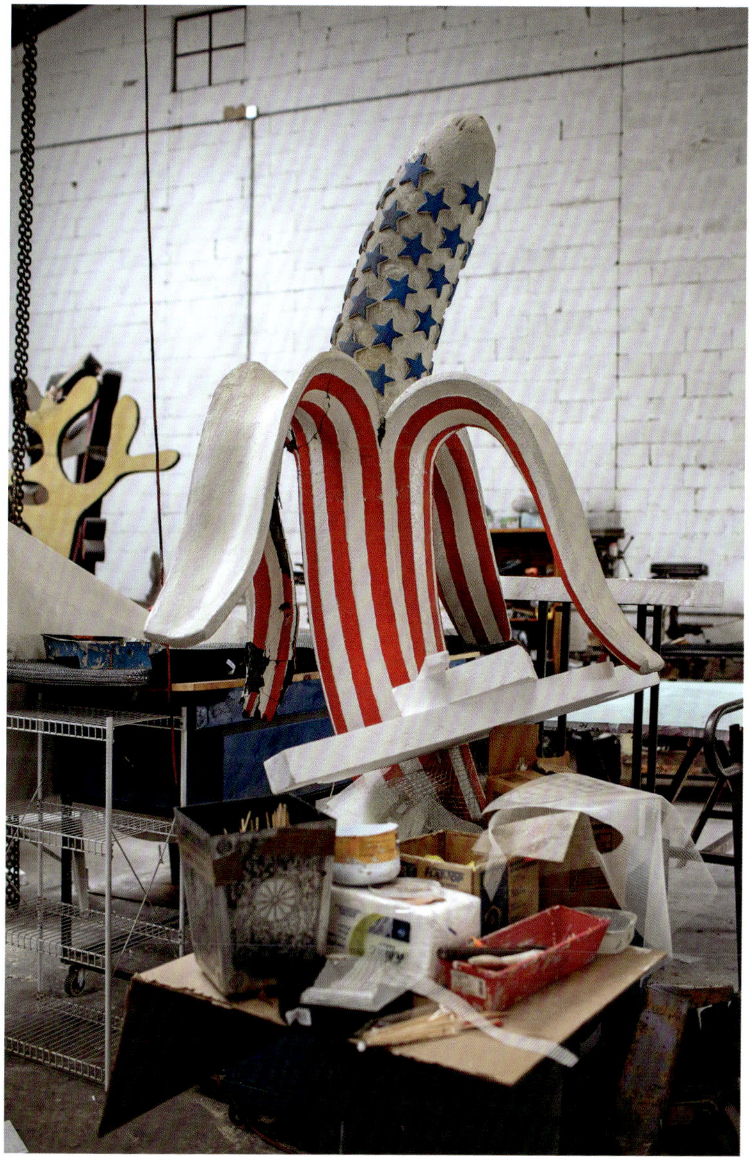

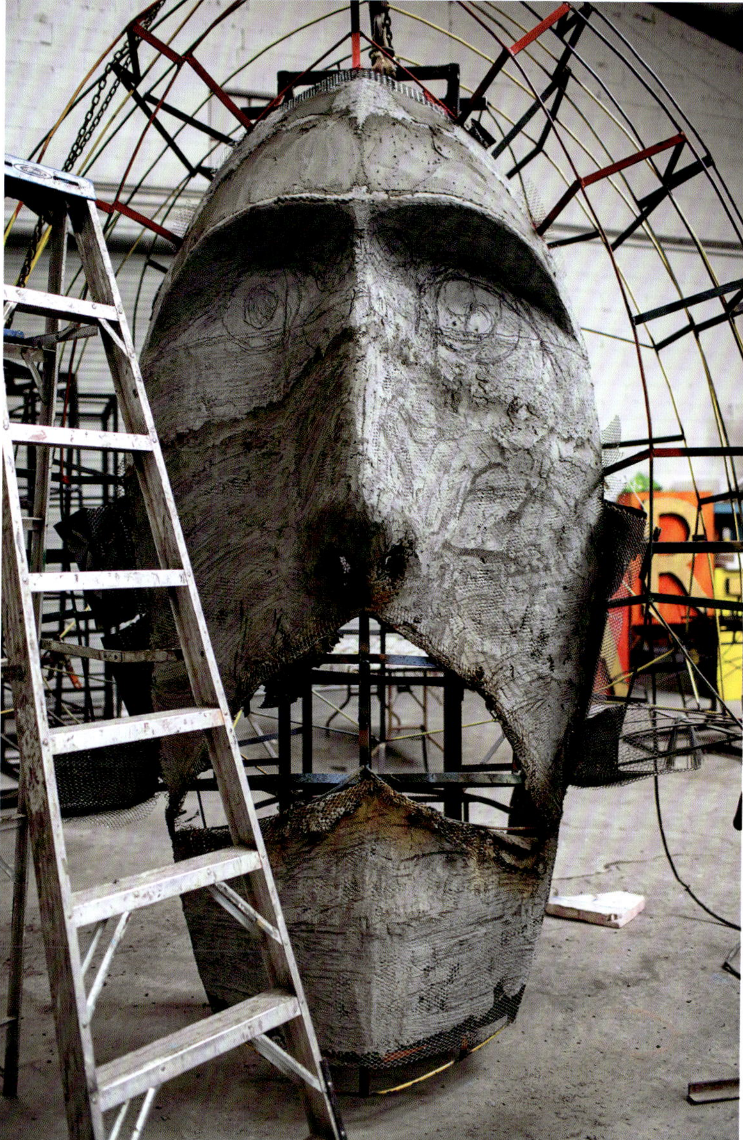

**Figures 4.72 and 4.73.** Inside the Adickes Sculpture Works Studio in Houston, Texas.

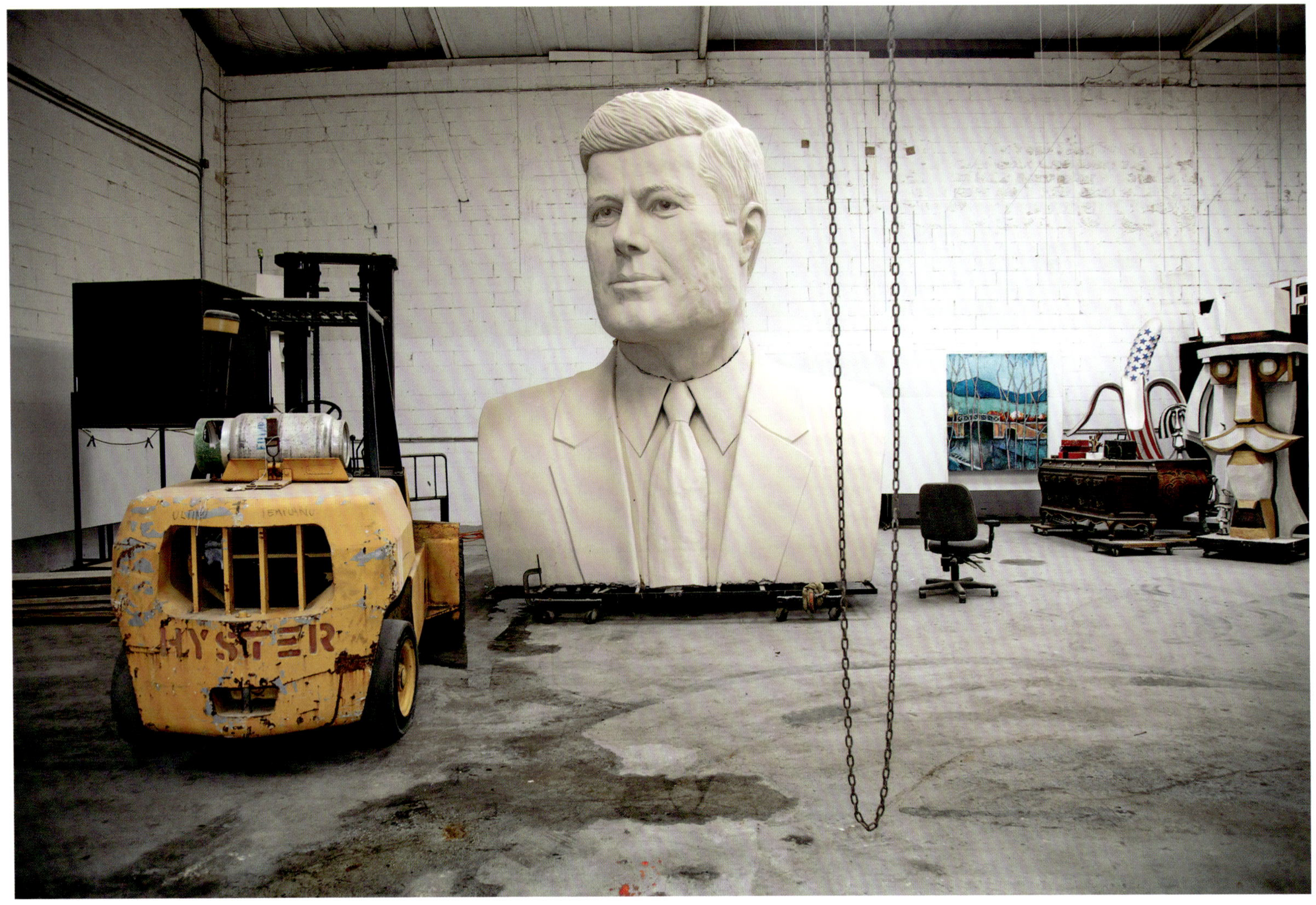


**Figure 4.74.** The head of *John F. Kennedy*, Adickes Sculpture Works Studio in Houston, Texas.

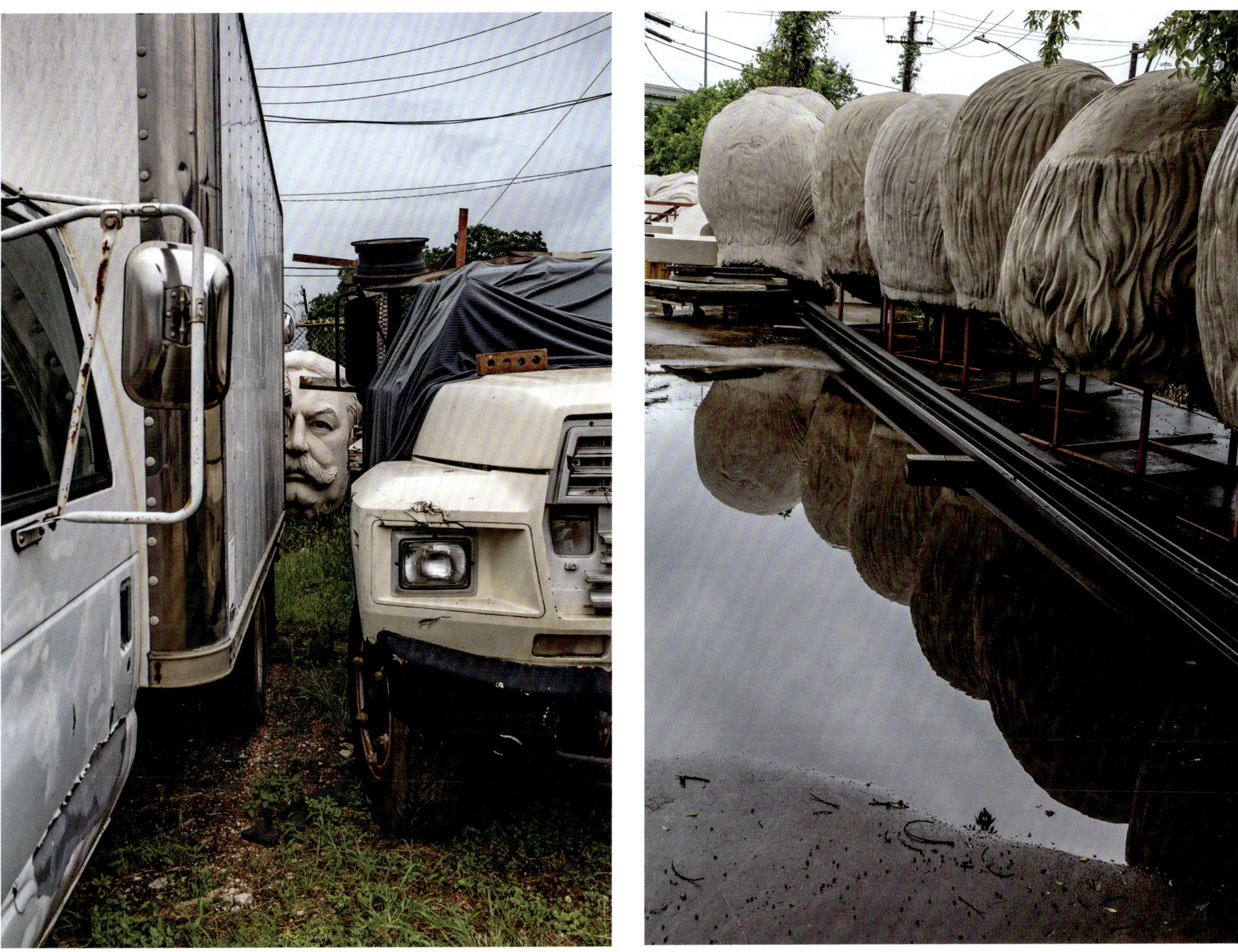

**Figures 4.75 and 4.76.** President heads, Adickes Sculpture Works Studio in Houston, Texas.

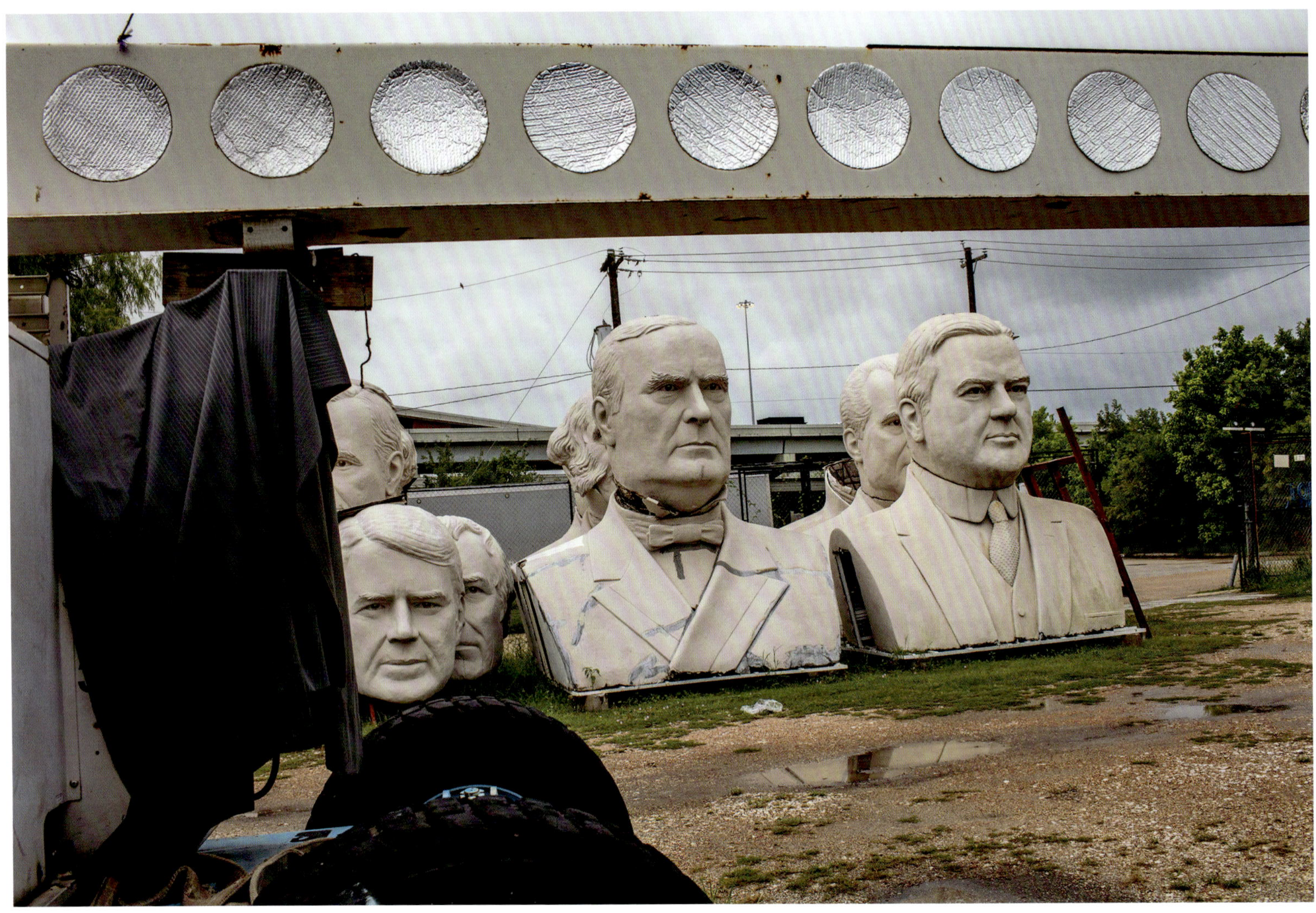

**Figure 4.77.** President heads, Adickes Sculpture Works Studio in Houston, Texas.

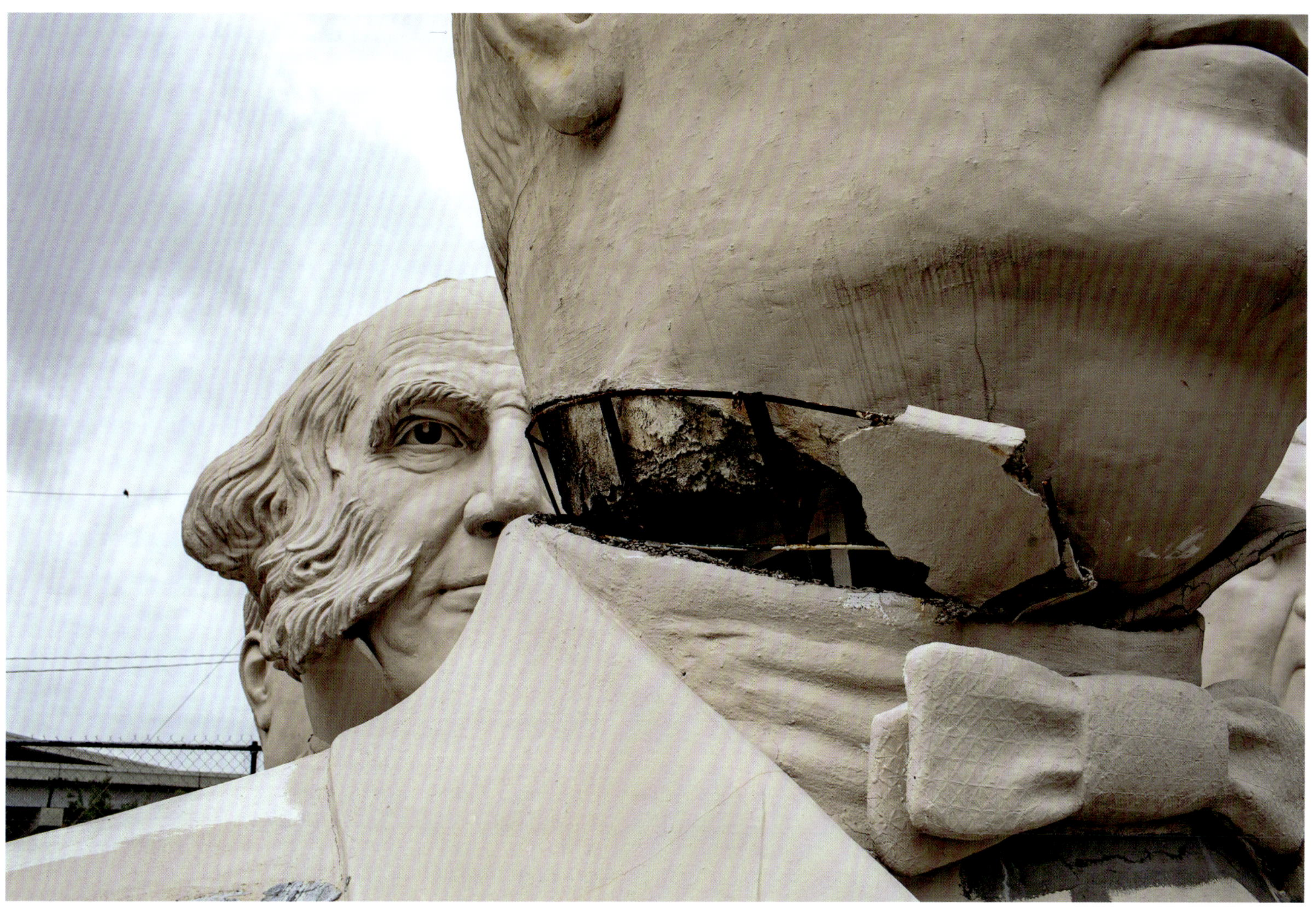

**Figure 4.78.** The eye of *George Washington*, Adickes Sculpture Works Studio in Houston, Texas.

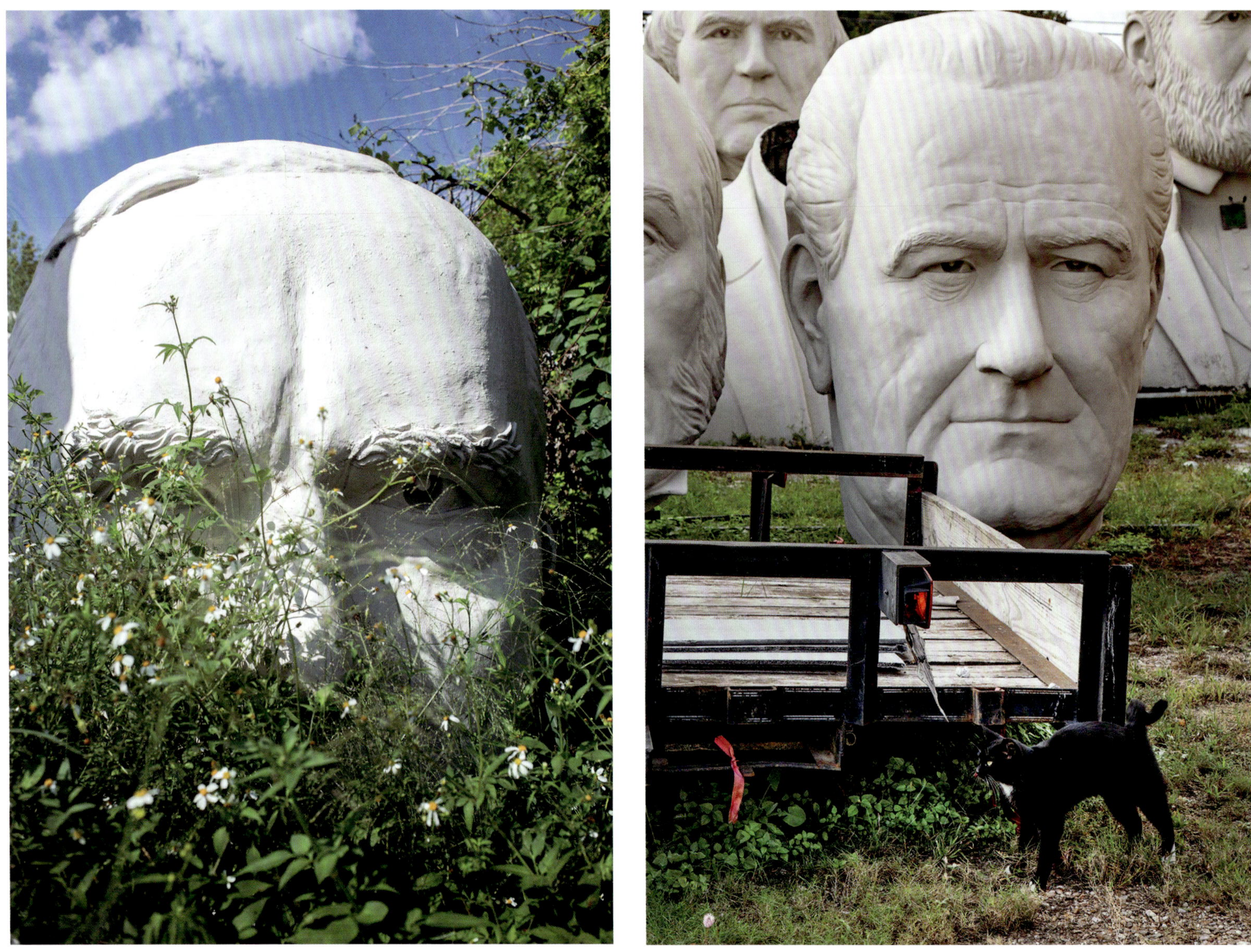

**Figures 4.79 and 4.80.** President heads, Adickes Sculpture Works Studio in Houston, Texas.

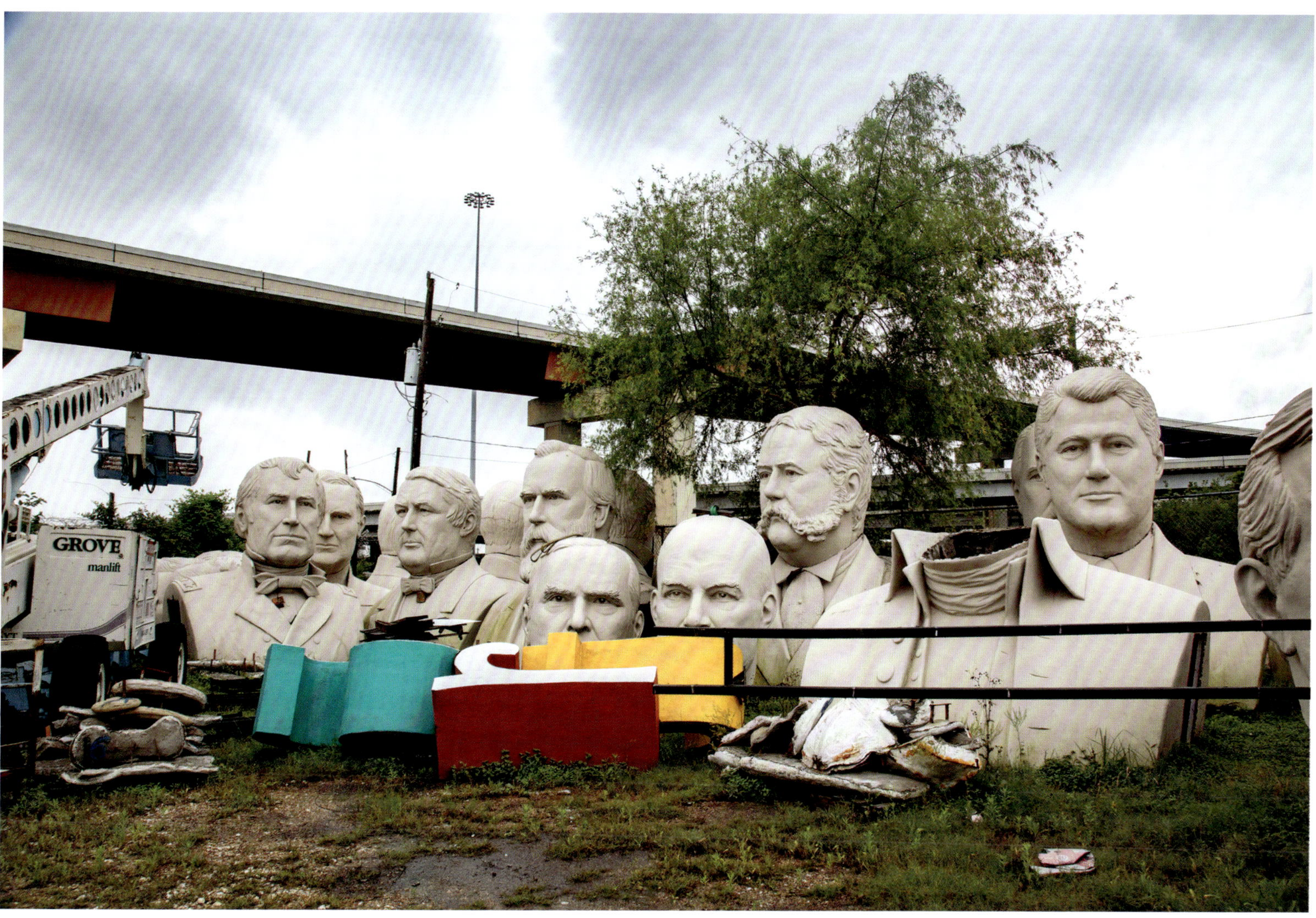


**Figure 4.81.** President heads, Adickes Sculpture Works Studio in Houston, Texas.

# Chapter 5

## In His Own Words

### *Conversations with David Adickes*

Michael H. Henderson and Melissa L. Mednicov

*David Adickes is a man of many talents and interests. A painter and sculptor with degrees in math and physics, he is also a musician and composer, a playwright, a humorist, and an entrepreneur. When not actively engaged in any of those pursuits, Adickes is a storyteller. In his ninety-four plus years on earth, he has attained a wealth of experiences that span historical periods and several continents. He loves to tell the stories of those experiences.*

*We first met with David at his sculpture studio on Nance Street in the summer of 2018. On the east side of downtown, nestled between the elevated intersection of interstates, his sculpture studio offers commuters heading south on the elevated Interstate 69 a glimpse from above of presidents' heads and giant concrete Charlie Chaplin.*

*Prior to moving to this location in 2013, David Adickes Sculpture Works was located on the opposite side of downtown Houston in an old industrial building that had previously been owned by a paint company.*

*The first presidents' heads were created in that building at 2500 Summer Street and were lined up in the parking lot. David rented out space in the building to other artists and art galleries. We were interested in knowing more about how he had developed that property into a location known for art.*

## Houston and Huntsville

**David Adickes:** There was a chain-link fence where the gate had been, knocked down by trucks that were going to U-turn in, it was a mess. There was a little sign saying for sale barely hanging on the fence. I called the guy; he says, "Raven City," and I say, "what do you got for sale? I can see the three buildings you know what I'm talking about on Summer Street . . . you know what I am talking about?" And he says, "there are six-and-a-quarter acres in the shadow of downtown. . . . the building is not in good shape."

I said, "man, whew." I went and looked at the building and while I was on that third floor—which is now very fancy and called the Astorian, they charge $10,000 for a Saturday night to have a party there—that's how things have changed.

I mean it was all . . . I put in a thousand windowpanes when I got it. It was in bad shape. So, I started fixing it up and started doing the presidents there and then putting them out in the yard, in front. There's railroad tracks, between the building and railroad tracks is where the presidents were. And people started . . . tour buses started coming by.

Morning, two buses—twice a day. People would get out for photos and selfies and all that. That changed the concept of a run-down real estate area to an art area.

Now I have 3 acres, 3.2 which is the building itself and the big lot in front of it by the railroad track so that's where I was putting all the presidents' heads. At some point, I decided to sell that and build this [The Studio on Nance Street].

Now the other big example is Huntsville, which was known as a prison town in the old days, is now a statue town. Doesn't everyone think of Huntsville, that don't know Huntsville, as where the big statue is?

They know the university's there and all the rest, but for some reason that statue, because 50,000 people see it every day, they identify it, so it reinforces or proves that art increases the value of real estate. Now that didn't mean that land in Huntsville was going to go up, but they made so much money from the hotel occupancy tax that they had a million bucks they didn't know what to do with.

## Earlier Writings about Adickes

*In 1996, Linda Wiley published* "Making It Happen: Exploring the Creative Process through the Sculptures of David Adickes." *His paintings from the 1950s and '60s are examined in* "Adickes: A Portfolio with Critique" by James A. Michener and a critique in French by Alessandra Cantey, *published in 1968 by DuBose Gallery. Adickes described how that book came to be written.*

**David Adickes:** I was living in Barcelona and one of my best friend's father was a publisher there. My friend was THE poet of Spain but couldn't publish because of Franco. . . . When Franco died, he became the poet laureate of Spain. He just died. So, I was married to a gal from Fort Worth who was just out of [Vassar].

She had just graduated from there and was smart as hell, used four-syllable words like "dichotomy," you know stuff like that.

I wanted to publish a book. We were living in Antibes and she said I'll write the book for you. So, she went back to the kitchen table, and in about three to four hours produces this incredible—it's about twenty–thirty pages. And when we got it, we translated it to French because a gal there was teaching her French. And it was so beautiful, better in French than anything I'd ever [seen] and I said Sandy, you suffer in the original, this is really great in French.

Jim Michener knew her, and knew me, I'd met him. And I asked him if he'd write a book. The first one was in '63 so in '68, six years later. He said, "I'd love to write one, but it's not going to be as good as Sandy's." And it wasn't. And when we had his translated, to French, the gal said, "this doesn't work in French." So, we published Jim Michener in the front and Sandra's original in French in the back, because in France you had to have some French.

I'll show you those two books. Those are very good. Michener—you know who Michener is. He's more of a storyteller, so he rambles around. And of course, Linda's book is all about my stuff written just before the dedication of the Sam Houston.

## After World War II—Art School and the Birth of the Houston Art Scene

*David Adickes's biography is shaped by his experience in World War II serving in the Air Force. He was fortunate to be assigned a clerical job but traveled to England and France, and after the war ended took advantage of the GI Bill to study art in France, traveled the world, and helped develop the mid-twentieth-century art scene in Houston.*

**David Adickes:** I had two years and two months on the GI Bill. I decided to spend the first two months at Kansas City Art Institute, oh and I was back in Huntsville . . . it was '47 . . . and I wanted to just get a degree . . . from Sam Houston State College, because I had so many hours from A&M. I was at LSU . . . I had a year of math from LSU.

So, I had eighty hours heading toward some degree and my older brother, who knew more about it than I did, said the nearest degree to what you've got is something in math. I signed up for a math course, I'll never forget the guy who taught it had worked in New Mexico for the atomic bomb project. Anyhow, so I got a degree from Sam Houston State University, a double major in math and physics, so I have a BS in math and physics, which I never intended to use, but it's good to know. It's really neat saying you have a mathematics degree.

So, people say, "when did art become your deal?"

In high school, I always wanted to do the posters. For theater and other people. And I always drew in the margins of my biology books. I loved to sketch; I sketched a lot. So, my mother was an artist. She painted; she was not a professional artist. She painted late in age. So, there is that in the family. My father was a civil engineer, an A&M graduate, class of 1910, who laid out Huntsville. He did all the [streets] . . . and he created some company town in Tennessee. I used to know the name of it, and I went there once. He was an engineer, so he surveyed. He knew about it. So, some of my interest in the mechanical things comes from him, but the other side, the art probably comes from my mother.

But anyhow, I decided to go to France. Get my GI Bill. Oh, two months at Kansas City Art Institute, which I loved. I loved that art school "looseness." You know, you don't have to clean up after, you know, it's pretty self-expressed.

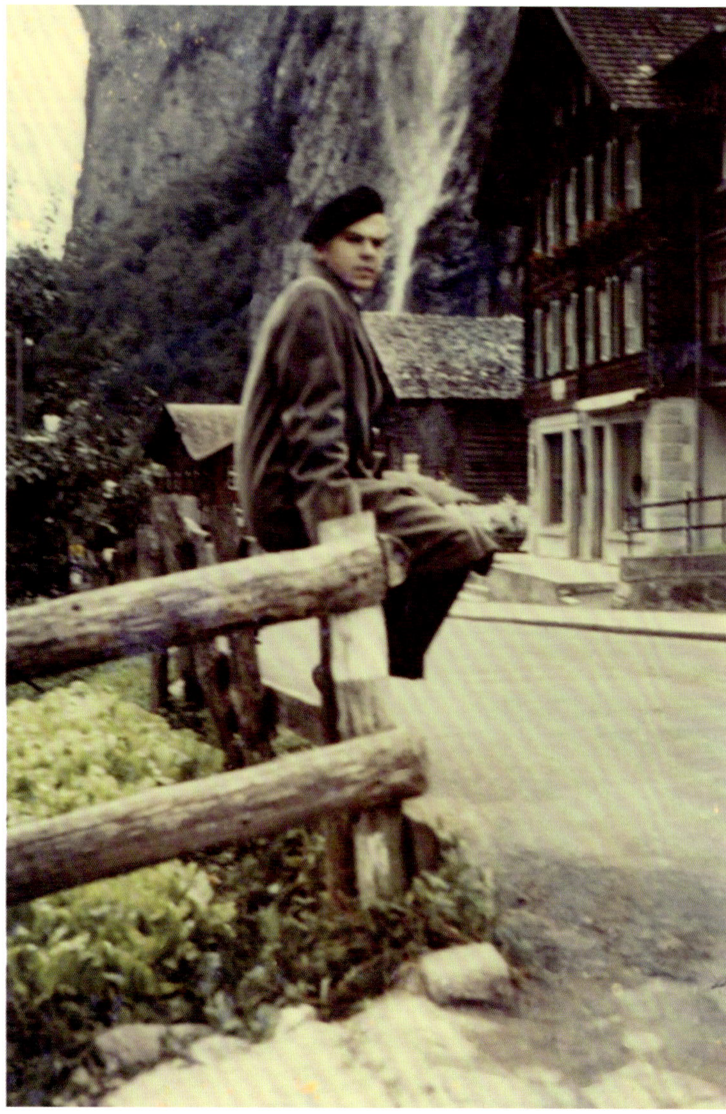

**Figure 5.1.** Only known photograph of David Adickes during his 1948–50 time in France. Photograph taken by his father during a trip to Switzerland, 1950. Collection of David Adickes.

I spent two years in France, and studied. I checked in at the Atelier Fernand Léger. Léger was one of the big names. Picasso, Matisse, Braque, Chagall, Léger, Miró, he's in there with the big ones. The reason I chose him, is because Container Corporation of America was running full-page ads on the back cover of *Fortune* magazine of different artists. And so, I was familiar with Léger's name. When they showed me all the art schools you could go to, there were the regular ones, they didn't mean anything, but "Léger" meant something, so I signed up for that school. It was up in the north part of Paris. So, I rented a room from a French student there so I could walk to my classes. Montmartre was just up the hill. I didn't learn anything from Léger. He only came in for one hour to critique what we'd done, but what I learned was from other students, just being in Paris, and going to all the museums, a gallery on every corner and a bookstore on every other.

However, there was one guy, the École des Beaux-Arts was just up the street, who had to make some money to buy his rent, so he cut out silhouettes, he had a big piece of paper, and he would fold it all up and then cut out pieces of it while you'd watch him, and then when he would unfold it, it was just a big empty square. And then he would pass his hat and people thought it was funny.

Anyhow, so spending those years hanging out, and meeting one guy in particular from New York whose name was Herbert Mears, who was five or six years older than me and had been to all the art schools in Europe and knew a hell of a lot more about art than I did, became my best friend. And so, he taught me a lot. He taught me more than I learned in school.

Then, when I moved back to Houston . . . we both came back to the states at the same time. December '50. I went to Huntsville. I moved to Houston in the spring of '51 and I called Herb Mears, and said, "Herb, I'm going to open an art school. Would you like join it? In Houston." He was on the next train.

He got a job in Queens decorating windows at a department store, and so—anything to get out of New York. So, I remember picking him up at the Union Station downtown on the train. And the only car I had was a Crosley pickup. Crosley was a company that made lawn mowers.

The engine was about that big. The back of the pickup was just big enough to hold Herb's trunk. So, I picked him up. In the meantime, I had rented a space on Truxillo Street, which is right between Main and Fannin. Cheap. You could see light through the walls. I don't mean the windows—through the walls. I'll never forget the guy that owned the place was a little Romanian and he wore spats. He said, "Get some tar paper and nail it to the outside and the wind won't come through."

Herb and I opened an art school, which promptly failed financially. Because we would charge people when they came. But we met *everybody*. The art community was very small then and everybody who cared anything about art, we knew. And then he got a job working at Houston Light and Power, and I got a job working for some company that was a competitor of Schlumberger.

Anyway, the bottom line is, coming back from Paris, I stayed with my brother who lived in New York, and took lessons in New York City in silk screen printing, which was brand new. Nobody here [Houston] ever heard of silk screen printing. Commercially, it was used on signs, but as an art medium, nobody knew it. So, the CAA was down on Dallas Street in the old days and that's when I first met the Menils. John and Dominque Menil arrived in '59 I believe it was, and started putting money into that. The first show I saw there was Van Gogh. But there was a secretary that worked there, tall, Swedish descent, pretty, blond. And when Herb went down to help me demonstrate the silk screen printing, he met Ava Jean McDaniels. Wow. Fell in love *like that*. After work he would come and pick me up, I lived on Main Street, and we'd go have dinner together and he'd say, "You've got to phone her up, you've got to phone her up," and I'd say, "I will, I will," and he'd say, "If I could just get her mother on my side."

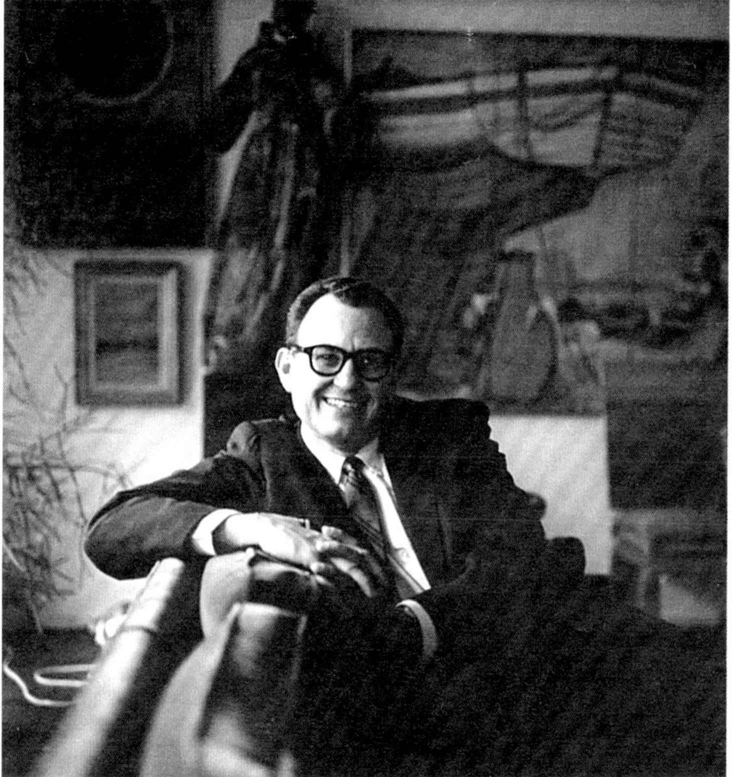

**Figure 5.2.** Photograph of Ben DuBose by David Adickes. 1968. Collection of David Adickes.

Anyhow, the bottom line, they married, and I was best man, and they had three fabulous kids, one of them is now one of the best architects in town, that helped me design this building [*the sculpture studio on Nance Street*]. Good friend, he's my godson.

Herb came, and Ava Jean married of course, and started making a career, and he made a living painting, and he died in 1999. He was the biggest influence on me in France, more than the teacher there or anything.

Then when I came back to Houston in '50, we opened the art school, which failed, but we met everybody then, Ben DuBose, the Art League had leased some space in the brand new Shamrock Hotel garage.

Anybody remember the Shamrock Hotel? It was a big thing out on Main and Holcomb. They leased the upper floor of the parking garage and gave everybody an eight-foot-square space, or something like that, for ten bucks. So, anyhow, I had my first show there. And Ben DuBose, do you know that name? Was just out of the University of Houston, I don't know what his major was, but he answered an ad from the James Bute Paint Company that had a big building downtown on Caroline and McKinney, one of the big, not a huge building, but a downtown building. They had a great big room where they sold wallpaper and paint, and in the back was a little gallery. And they advertised in the paper to have somebody to come in and close out all these prints that they had in the gallery, that were from New York, and Chinese prints. So, Ben went down there and looked at the space and said, "you ought to make a real gallery out of this, and I think I could make it go, not sell prints," so they said, "ok give it a shot." So, Ben started having shows there, one of the first shows he had was mine. We'd just met, and the first painting I ever sold was to John de Menil. For a hundred bucks. I don't know where it is now. So, I started selling paintings and making a little scrawny living, and I got this other job, which I had for a year, and I was able to make a living with painting. And then in '55, I'd won a lot of prizes by then. The first year I was here, I entered a show, the *Houston Annual* at the museum, which they don't have anymore, sorry to hear that, but that's where all the artists showed and met each other. The judge for that show that year was William Lester, who taught at the University of Texas, and he gave me the first prize. When he came back to the opening, I had been demoted to Honorable Mention, and Christine Streetman, was now first prize, and he went to the woman that ran the museum, back then it was Ruth Uhler, long before the big wing, it was the old building, and he said, "but I gave first prize to this man," and she said, "but he hadn't been in Houston for a full year." And he said, "well you should have told me that." She said, "we'll make it up to him somehow." The phone rings and she says, "How would you like to have a one man in the Museum of Fine Art?" That was the luckiest thing that ever happened to me.

So, I had a show. The back part of the museum there was a door back there, that was the entrance, on the north side by the circle. The show went up the stairs, anyway it was one of the "corridor shows." It made me known.

Then I started winning other prizes. The next year, I won the prize which is now in the collection of the museum in San Antonio. [I'd sure like to see it.] In 1955, I was invited by the University of Texas to come and teach there. And I didn't have a degree in art. But to teach art, a degree doesn't mean that much. It's your reputation, if you won a prize or not. So, I taught there for two years. Great fun, I loved every second of that. But, I thought, that's enough, I don't want to get tenure

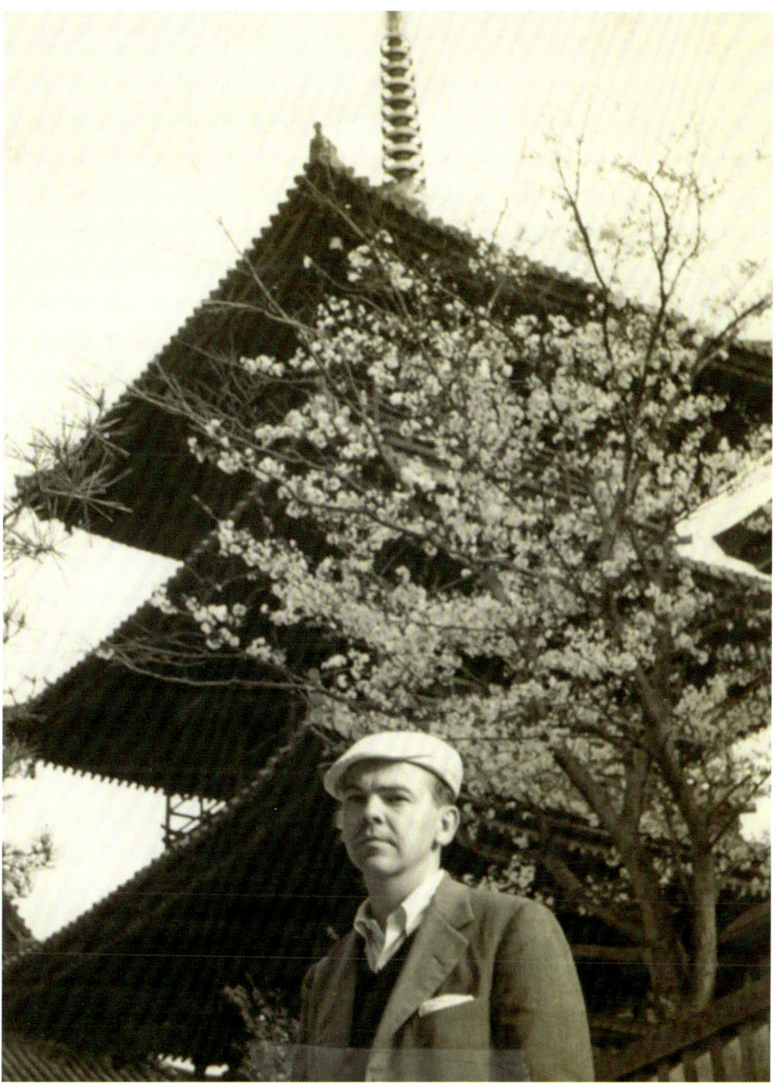

**Figure 5.3.** Photograph of David Adickes in Japan, undated. Collection of David Adickes.

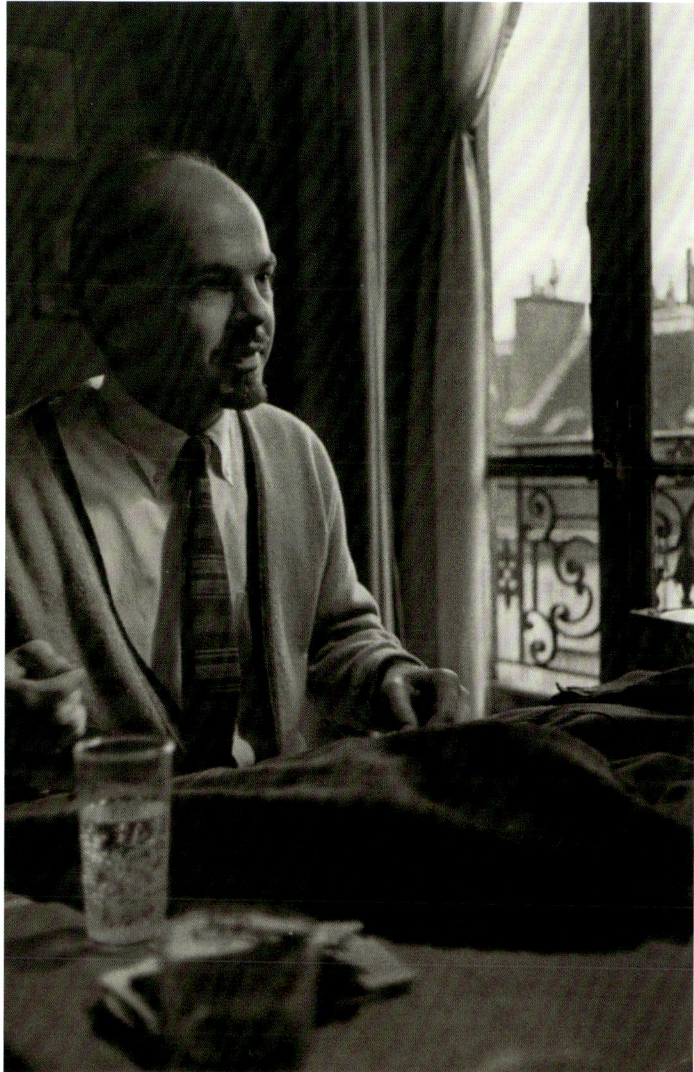

**Figure 5.4.** Photograph of David Adickes in Gilles Fern's apartment, Paris. Dated 1959 or 1960. Collection of David Adickes.

and be here forever, so I'm going to take off and go around the world, and take two years to do it. And I sort of studied every place, and a friend of mine had been to Japan and said, "Man, you really need to see Japan." So, that's where I went first. I spent the first year in Japan, and the second year for the rest of the world, ending up in Antibes, France. But that was worth it. Japan, I had a show, couple of shows, there, you may have the catalog somewhere.

That was '56, '58, or '59—going around the world. So, ending up in Antibes, which is a town where Picasso lived. I bought a studio there and went back and forth. I would come back to Houston in late November, and have a show in December at Bute Gallery, and then Christmas with family, spring here, and then be back in France about April the first, or May the first. Missing the Houston summers. Summers there, winters here.

So, I just kept showing and doing better and better in art.

## Early Life in Huntsville

**David Adickes:** My great-great-grandfather was the postmaster when General Sam Houston lived and died. And there's a story that came down through my family that my great-great-grandfather, being a staunch Methodist, would not deliver the mail on Sunday. When the old gentleman came out after his rounds, he wanted his mail on Sunday. So, there was that altercation between them. I've heard that

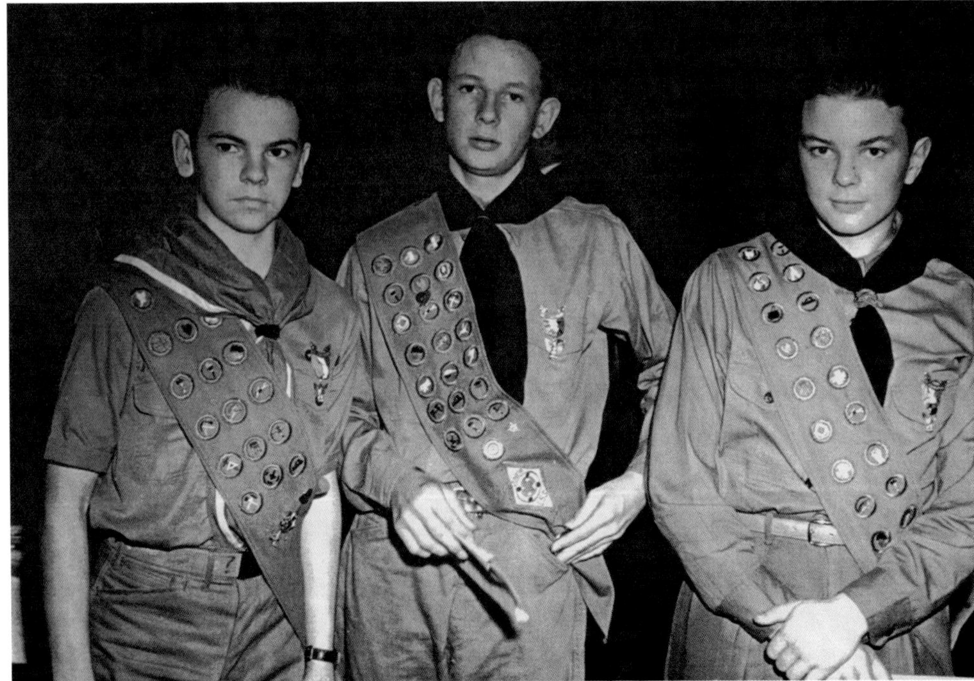

**Figure 5.5.** David Adickes with friends in the Eagle Scouts, dated December 1941. Collection of David Adickes.

all my life. When I was doing the big Sam Houston statue, I read a lot of really good biographies of Sam Houston. I was looking through them all and I click on the index and one of them said E. J. Adickes. So, there's a paragraph about my great-great-grandfather, who was the postmaster. Who was fired by Sam Houston when he was with the Congress. The first official thing he did was to fire the people that were in the wrong party. My grandpa was in the Democratic Party and Sam Houston was a part of what they call a "know nothing party" or the American party. So, it's a political thing. You're the wrong party, so you get fired. It didn't have anything to do with the mail on Sunday.

But anyhow, when I was doing the Sam Houston, north of Huntsville, on a ranch thing that the university loaned me, it was perfect. It was hot in the summer up there. I had a little house there and I had a second floor bedroom air conditioner. I would be up there reading these books in the afternoon to cool off until—my working schedule is seven to 10 a.m. And then seven to 10 p.m. In the middle of the day it was just too hot, we worked in the barn without air conditioning. And when I read about that, I'm gonna go down there and change his face to look like Stephen F. Austin, something you know, my own great-great-grandfather he fired, and then I thought, that was 200 years ago, let's let bygones be bygones. But Sam is a hero to me. I mean, I've read a lot about him, very, very interesting. Despite the fact that he fired my great-great-grandfather. So, we go back that far. That was 1856. My father was born there, I guess his father. My father was born in '81. I'm guessing his father was born there in '50 and so, his father was the postmaster. And they came from Carolina's, from North Carolina, there's an Adickes family up there that moved to Huntsville.

**Michael H. Henderson:** There are a lot of markers in the cemetery right next to Sam Houston's grave that say Adickes.

**David Adickes:** Well, right, that's my family. But right up the street where Sam Houston actually died is an addition to the old cemetery. It's called the Adickes addition, because that was owned at one point by my uncle. And Sam Houston, the steamboat house, was on that property. And Sam lived there, but then after he died, he died in that house and was in there just a half block away. And I remember that house, after Sam lived there, was moved on out of town road, you know, miles out of city, and the day it was brought to where it is now, the Sam Houston Park, was in '36, in 1936, because the Texas Centennial. The road that it was moved on was right next to our grammar school. So, we all had to go out and watch it, go by very slow, but we were all there to see it and the way they moved it is, they would put some sort of peg in the ground.

That was a rotating thing and then pull it with ropes and they'd have a horse and a donkey going around pulling this thing winding up the rope. It was very slow. And then they would go [unclear] somewhere else, so it took several days to move it across town. So, that was '36, so I was nine years old.

**Michael H. Henderson:** One of your brothers worked for Mattel? Is that right?

**David Adickes:** My younger brother was half responsible for inventing Hot Wheels. What he did with the hot wheel little cars, hot wheels were made in England, they were called matchbox cars. So, they just took those from my brother, to figure out how to make the wheels roll fast. I don't know if he put the ball bearings in them, or did something, and then he invented all that.

They would go very fast. And that's his contribution to mankind.

**Michael H. Henderson:** Was there something about your upbringing in Huntsville, or your childhood or your family that you think made you guys creative?

**David Adickes:** It had to be, you know it had to be. My mother worked in a frame shop as a young woman. In fact, I was doing some frames and she said, "let me show you how to do that." And I was surprised about certain things. My father was an engineer, a civil engineer, was a surveyor. He laid out Huntsville, the first road in Huntsville, created the square and the old main. My father was very good draftsman.

And my mother was more left brain, so I guess I am a bit of each. And my younger brother, Fred. The older two brothers were not really artistic. They were the two pilots. Yeah. My older brother, I remember, he designed an apartment house, went down and he wanted to build. But anyhow, to answer your question. I guess it comes probably from my mother.

## Art Studies

**Melissa L. Mednicov:** I wanted to ask you about your background in terms of your experiences taking classes with your main focus on math and science, but I was wondering if you saw any intersection between that training in math and science with your artwork; I was thinking possibly in your large scale of sculptures.

**David Adickes:** Well, I'm sort of right brained in that I have a feeling for physics. I was very good at it. But when you do the big sculptures you should know a little bit of math. And the rule in the big sculpture is: when in doubt, make it stout. Spend more money on steel than on . . . Building airplanes something like that would be absolutely the minimum weight equals strength, but doing some like this weight is not an issue.

**Melissa L. Mednicov:** Did you really start making art after you graduated or were you making art throughout . . .

**David Adickes:** All through school, I was sketching in margins of biology books and that kind of thing. But I was the only one in the family that sketched a lot of things, I think my little brother did. But the concept of being a professional artist was just something that never came up. Then when I finally went to art school in France, my father was pretty worried that I would be a puppet charge.

But he said, at least you could run an art store. You can sell art supplies, because he's a merchant. So, he was signing me with that. But when I first got back to Houston, and had a show, the reports were glowing. In fact, in the *Houston Chronicle*, he read it before I did. It's delivered in Huntsville, four o'clock in the afternoon. He called and says, "David, they spelled your name right."

**Michael H. Henderson:** Which is a challenge.

**David Adickes:** Yeah. He was very proud that at least I'm in the news. I'm in the paper.

Then after that, when I started doing okay, never a word after that.

## Houston and Europe

**David Adickes:** When I was a student in Paris, he [father] came over to spend a month with me in August, and we got a little car and drove all around. My mother stayed at the store when he came, then she came in next summer. So, the two of us drove all around. I bought a little used car when my dad was there. I think it was $400. And it was a Simca Fiat. Simca, a French company and Fiat, an Italian company, collaborated on cars before the war, and so this would have been a '36 or so.

It was a little thing, this big. The two people could barely get in it. It had a little convertible top, and you could just reach back and go click click. When I went back to France in '53, I bought the same little car. In Italian, they call it a *topolino*, which means a Mickey Mouse, kind of like a rabbit, you know. So, I bought a Mickey Mouse and rigged it so that I could drive to a port or something I want to paint and sit up on the back of the seat and strap a canvas on the steering with a big rubber band.

I put a canvas on the steering wheel and all my paints in the passenger seat, I got to drive up and paint the scene then drive someplace else. So, it was a mobile easel, was a great little machine. And then I started running out of money. This is in '53. And I realized that I had to move to Spain, because everybody knew it was cheaper in Spain than in France. I was in Nice, and I looked at papers and [saw] "we'll buy a car." So, I went by there, the guy had a BOF, which means Beurre Oeuf Fromage, which is a delicatessen where they sell butter, eggs, and cheese—so they always have money. And he got in the car and said, "well, we'll give the car a test, if it'll get to the top of the hill, I'll buy it."

Between Nice and Monte Carlo is the Beach Road, the middle road and mountain road. That's where Grace Kelly died, by the way. So, we get in this little car, *make it, make it, make it*, we got to the top, ok, you got it. So, we coasted all the way back down and he gave me the equivalent $400 in francs. I went to the railroad station, got a ticket to Barcelona. And with $400, I lived in Barcelona for seven months. Can you believe that? In '53. Do you know Barcelona?

There's one big square and then there's Las Ramblas going down to the port. The first street off of Las Ramblas with a view looking down on it was a top floor, sixth floor walk-up for rent called an attico. But there was a penthouse in that it had a terrace, a wall, and looked down one big room. Which was everything. And it cost $30 a month to rent. It was unfurnished, so I rented furniture, *El Greco* style Spanish furniture for seven bucks a month. So, for $37 a month, I had a furnished penthouse in the center of Barcelona. I was back there a couple of years ago, it cost $35 a night to park a car.

That's the contrast between 1953 and today, but I spent seven months in Barcelona. It was one of the greatest seven months I've ever spent. Just remember that it was fun, met crazy people, and the town itself was very interesting. There was a nightclub called the Bodega Bohemia, which was for students and all of the entertainers were clinically insane. I mean they were harmless; they were lovely people. There was one woman that thought she was Edith Piaf and she would get up and sing *La Vie en Rose*.

## Selling Shares

**David Adickes:** The way I paid for my trip to Barcelona was selling units of my next year's production for $50 a unit, which guaranteed you one painting and one print. So, I sold thirty-five units, which is 1,700 dollars. And that's the money I went to France on, bought the little car and finally got back with all of these paintings. The divvy-up day when we had the show at the old DuBose gallery down on West Gray at the time, all the paintings were there. And I had something like sixty paintings and thirty-five of them were to go to people. They drew numbers out of a hat to get their order of choice.

And one guy, who bought five units for $250, he got number one and two and seven and ten, the first choice, so I was kind of mad because I didn't like the guy anyway, but *Life Magazine* was there to cover it, took all these photographs, didn't print it something bumped it, but I still have all the photographs of that night. Other people that were there were Jane Blaffer Owen and Nina Cullinan. They were all there. I don't know if you know those names.

**Michael H. Henderson:** They had bought the units?

**David Adickes:** They had bought the units. Right. Yeah. And this doctor, an orthopedic surgeon, bought five.

And Henri Gadbois, Leila McConnell anyway, these are friends—50 bucks. But that was the money I went to Spain on.

I learned how to make copies of stuff on the printer. And so, I designed this thing, this proposal of selling my shares for 50 bucks a piece, all in hand and cut it off and sort of burned the edges so it [unclear] looked like some sort of document and then reproduce that and gave it to people and seventeen of them came forward.

**Melissa L. Mednicov:** Would you choose who you gave the document to?

**David Adickes:** Various people, just friends. My aunt bought two units, $100 worth, and when she died recently, I inherited back those pictures.

**Michael H. Henderson:** I was going to ask you if any of those existed still?

**David Adickes:** Oh, they all exist. The reason I even thought about it is there is one of them of Mary Alba, the Barcelona woman, she looked kind of like a female George Washington, but she had an interesting face. I'm sure all of those paintings are around someplace.

**Melissa L. Mednicov:** Did you ever do it again? It's kind of like . . . people do this idea now like Kickstarter and stuff. People use that as like fundraising.

**David Adickes:** Right. No, I thought of the idea. . . . Other artists maybe tried it, so I'm not, I don't know if I'm the first, but it worked.

## Paris and the de Menils

**David Adickes:** City of Paris buses had a platform on the back of the bus that you jump up onto and then pull a lever to tell the driver that you're on. I was on the back once, as it was crossing right through the Louvre, on the street next to the Louvre, and there was a black Citroën behind me that kept honking. It was John and Dominique de Menil. So, I jumped off the bus and got into their car.

They said, "what are you doing?," and I said, "I'm painting." I told them my hotel room is near here and I want to show you some new work. We went to my hotel room, right on the front end of the Île de la Cité, Notre Dame is on one end, this was on the front end. I gave them a painting of one of the still lifes I was doing.

A few days or weeks later, Dominique got in touch with me and said let's have lunch or something. She came and picked me up in the black Citroën. And we were right by the Eiffel Tower, and the car went dead—stopped. We were in the middle of the street and we had to push it to the curb. Dominique and I got out and there was a third woman with us who sat at the steering wheel and Dominique and I were pushing it, and I wished someone from Houston, Texas, had passed and seen me because they are not going to believe this story.

I dated John's niece for about a year. She had a Solex bicycle that had a little motor on the front. We went from Paris to a town on the English Channel close to their house. They had a house that was on the beach, I mean it was sand right in the front door on the beach. We pedaled up there and the tire would start losing air about every thirty minutes and we'd have to get off and pump up the tire again and get back on. And pump up the tire. I was telling Dominique this story one day just before she died. She was sitting there in the Byzantine chapel, sitting there by herself and I told her this story about *gonfler le pneu*, which means blow up the tire. *Gonfler le pneu*, then we had to stop. *Gonfler le pnue*. As I left her, she kept saying, *Gonfler le pnue, gonfler le pnue* [*whispering*], *gonfler le pnue.* She died a few days later. I never saw her again after that. She was a wonderful woman, I was crazy about them both. I saw them in France a lot more than here [Houston].

A black cat crosses in front of him. He stops and crosses the street to go another way. His friend says, "I never took you to be superstitious." He said, "Well, I am not superstitious. But why take a chance." That was John's joke.

## Picasso

**David Adickes:** I'm writing a musical about Picasso now. Anyhow there is a lot written about Barcelona in the play, Picasso lived there. That was his first place before he went to Paris. And one of the songs . . . and the thing is . . . there was a saying in Catalan, "Barcelona és bona si la bossa sona." Which means, "Barcelona is good when it first jingles [money in your pocket], but when it first doesn't jingle, Barcelona is still good." That's not true.

**Michael H. Henderson:** Was Picasso in Barcelona when you were there or was he in Paris?

**David Adickes:** He was in Paris.

I saw him four times in my life. I went to his eightieth birthday party, but 3,000 people were there. So before the Hotel

Vallauris turned out for his eightieth birthday. It was a very special deal.

**Michael H. Henderson:** I remember when that happened. I think so. I remember hearing that.

**David Adickes:** Would that be '61?

**Michael H. Henderson:** No, I don't remember about it. But I remember some of his birthdays.

**David Adickes:** Well, he had his ninetieth birthday party.

**Michael H. Henderson:** Yeah, that's probably the one I remember.

**David Adickes:** That's a big one where he wouldn't even go to visit Paris. He died at ninety-three so he was old and he didn't want to deal with that. One of his best friends was Dominguín, who was the greatest bullfighter of the day.

To honor Picasso, they built a wooden corrida one thing only for bulls. And bullfighting to kill a bull is against the law in France, they do everything but kill a bull.

Dominguín was there doing his thing. And the woman on horseback that rode around and introduced him was Françoise Gilot, who wrote a big book, who was the mother of Claude and Paloma. And I crawled under the wooden structure and Picasso was about as high as maybe the fan or about that high right there [just above David's head].

I had a Rolleiflex camera and I could see where the . . . so I clicked this picture and I'm looking right up his nose. The only picture of Picasso looking right up his nose.

**Melissa L. Mednicov:** What were the other times you saw him?

**David Adickes:** On the street, I was in Cannes and I was in an art gallery and the guy said, "There's Picasso! Don't look at him." . . . "Oh he'll come in unless he thinks that . . . " So I was careful not to look at him. But I walked fast down the sidewalk, on the other side, and crossed over so I could pass him.

And he was wearing a white shirt with his signature in green. And that was a gift. People always gave him gifts like that.

Then I saw him in Antibes. The first time I ever saw him was in Antibes in the Picasso museum. I was there visiting the museum and they were there doing a film about him and he was there. And Herb Mears was there.

Braque, I saw one time. Oh, Chagall. I went to a show of Picasso in Paris. And Picasso was in the office. You don't get to meet him unless you buy something. But right in the entrance was Chagall sitting there by himself, wishing somebody would recognize him, just a little lonely man. And Chagall was not a big household word at that time. He lived in Vence and in Vence is a very famous chapel that was decorated by Matisse.

**Melissa L. Mednicov:** So, are Picasso, Léger, and Braque your three main influences at that time?

**David Adickes:** Oh, Picasso was the main one, Braque would be next, Léger was not an influence at all. Matisse was not an influence then, but he is now. A lot of the women I do are all Matisse-ish.

Braque did still lifes that I admire so much and still do but Picasso is the only one I try to emulate. By the way, every painting I've done since June 10 [2018] is better than what Picasso did at that age because he was dead. So Picasso lived ninety-one years, 186 days. And I lived ninety-one years, 186 days on June 10. So every day after that, so I've now lived counting my years . . . I'm not counting the days anymore. But everything I do now is better than what Picasso would do.

*David's musical play about Picasso includes his wives and girlfriends, his Muse, Matisse, Braque, Léger, Gertrude Stein, and numerous other characters in scenes that depict Picasso's life as he reminisces with St. Peter at the Pearly Gates.*

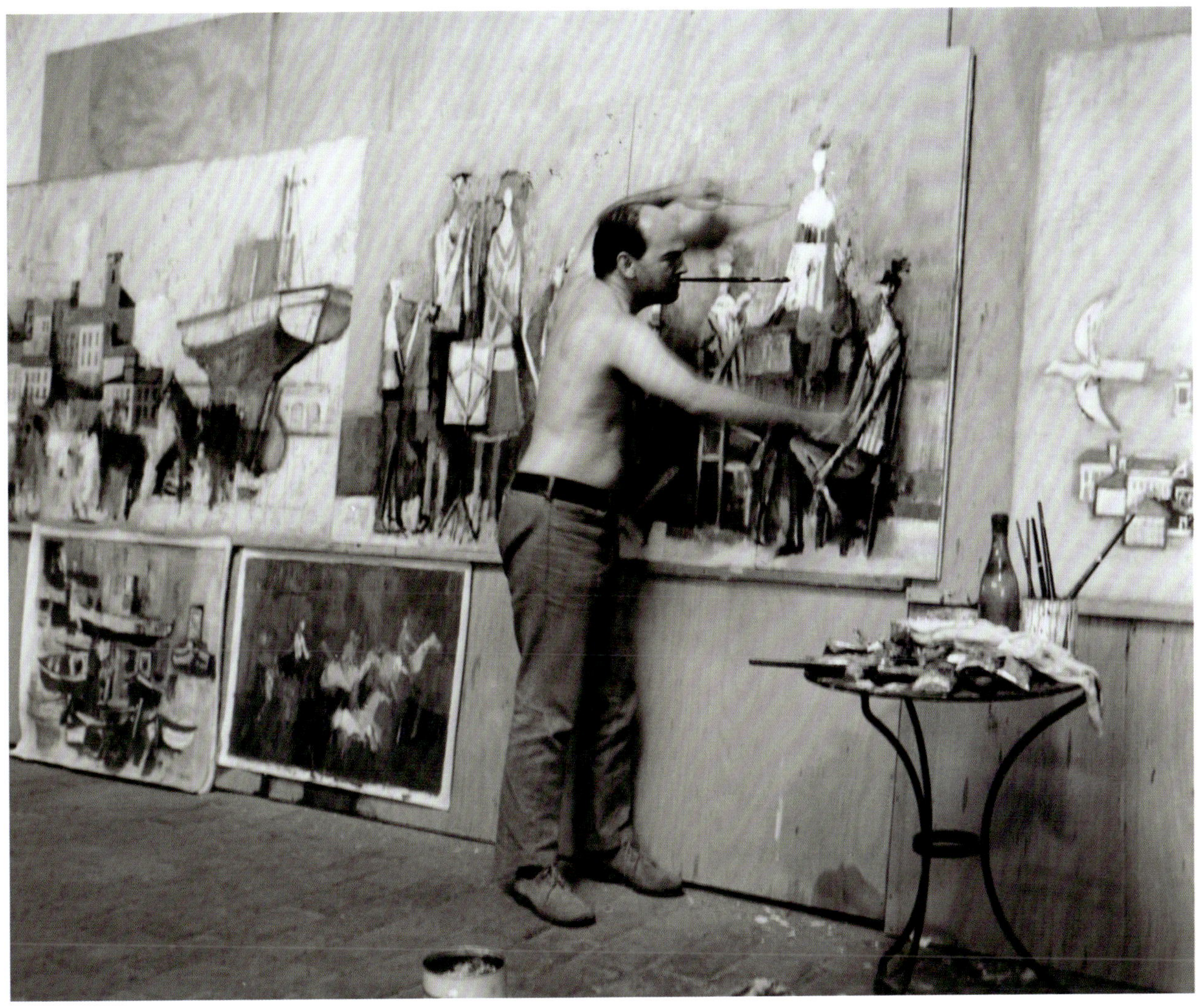

**Figure 5.6.** David Adickes painting in his Antibes studio, around 1965. Collection of David Adickes.

## From *Picasso*, a musical by David Adickes

### Scene 10

*A scrim descends in front of the bed. PICASSO and his easel are in front of the scrim. Projected video shows the couple out on the streets of Paris, in the parks, like two new lovers. They are shopping, meeting friends in cafés, walking the famous stairs of Montmartre. Light fades on PICASSO at his easel, allowing him to exit. Video shows PICASSO back in the studio painting. FERNANDE is cooking. A few weeks have passed. The scrim rises, revealing PABLO busy at another painting on the easel. The whole studio is crowded with paintings—all from the Rose Period, familiar to us all. FERNANDE is lounging in bed reading.*

FERNANDE: (*looking up from her book*) Pablo?

PICASSO: (*interrupted from his painting*) Hmm?

FERNANDE: We have so many pictures everywhere, but no furniture. Look, my clothes are still all over the floor.

PICASSO: (*not really listening*) Uh huh.

FERNANDE: Pablo, are you listening to me?

PICASSO: What? A chest of drawers? Is that what you want?

FERNANDE: Yes. And a lamp—an electric lamp. I always have to read by the window.

*PICASSO gets up, takes his palette and brush, clears a space off the wall, and paints a chest of drawers on the wall.*

PICASSO: There, you have a chest of drawers (*paints a lamp on top of the chest*) and a lamp.

FERNANDE: Ha, ha, very funny. But I can't put my clothes in that. The drawers won't open.

PICASSO: Oh, I forgot to put knobs on the drawers. (*He quickly paints drawer pulls on the drawers, opens the top one, and puts some of her clothes in the drawer. He turns to FERNANDE triumphantly.*) Voila!

FERNANDE: (*incredulous*) Beautiful! But the lamp doesn't work.

PICASSO: Oh, I forgot the pull chain. How silly of me! (*He quickly paints a pull chain, pulls it, and the lamp lights.*)

FERNANDE: (*delighted*) Simply marvelous!

*She gets out of bed, goes to PICASSO, hugs him, starts waltzing around with him, and sings:*

Life in our Chateau Bizarre
And a mouse in every drawer.
Not much to eat,
But always some wine
And the delicate smell
Of turpentine.
Life in the Bateau Lavoir.
Life in our Chateau Bizarre.
The furniture's great
For apples to crate,
But for sitting it rather leaves
Much to debate.
We live in a primitive garret
With plenty of paintings to stare at.
Character building,
All very quaint.
What we lack in furniture
Pablo will paint.
But I wouldn't trade a week at the Ritz
For a day in the Bateau Lavoir.
A day in our Chateau Bizarre.

*While FERNANDE sings, PICASSO paints a bouquet of roses on the wall. He reaches for the finished bouquet, pulls a real bouquet from the wall, and presents it to FERNANDE.*

# Chapter 6

## Conclusion

Michael H. Henderson and Melissa L. Mednicov

*Monumental: The Art of David Adickes* offers a comprehensive look at David Adickes's career, reconsidering and asserting his position within the genesis of the Houston art scene, his imprint on the Texas landscape through his monumental sculptures, and how contemporary experiences of his sculptures continue to shape the lives of many Texans and visitors to the state. Each chapter builds on the other to provide a cohesive view of Adickes's artistic career. The confluence of the chapters of this book helps reassess David Adickes's career within Texas art history.

"Adickes in Houston at Midcentury" positions Adickes at the center of the Houston art scene when the Houston galleries and museums were formed in what is now recognizable as the contemporary Houston art scene. His career in the 1950s and '60s carried many of the markers of success for a Texas artist through his participation in Texas Annuals (during which he regularly won awards), exhibitions in galleries and museums in Houston and other Texas cities, entrance into important Houston collections, and a robust travelogue. Additionally, the influence of French modernism on his paintings was typical of many successful artists during this period. His relationship with and later investment in Ben DuBose and his gallery undoubtedly places Adickes within the epicenter of Houston's gallery scene. Furthermore, Adickes's close friendship with Herb Mears, and collegial relationship with other artists, is a hallmark of the Houston art scene and its friendly atmosphere during the period.

As Adickes began to work on sculpture, "David and Goliaths: History, Monumentality, and Kitsch in the Public Art of David Adickes" examines Adickes's transition from a focus on painting to public sculpture. An analysis of influences illuminates how various sources such as Texas art history (for example, Elizabet Ney), history, popular culture, and the Texas landscape itself make his public sculptures a destination for Texans and Texas' visitors alike. Considering how the public sculptures populate social media provides one more way in which Adickes's work continues to thrive among a ready audience.

Additionally, Rebecca Finley's photographic essay, "Living among Giants: The Public Art of David Adickes," focuses on Adickes's public sculptures. Her photographs enhance the understanding of these sculptures and the many ways in which viewers interact with them daily in mundane and celebratory moments. Finley's photographs elucidate how the sculptures occupy spaces as a landmark and are unexpected monuments in mundane environments. The sculptures continue to live as destinations for celebrations such as graduation or for the Houston selfie. The sculptures also exist within a kind of ironic space, a silent trumpet that is ignored (possibly seen countless times by the passerby) or gargantuan sculptures in disrepair. Ultimately, in Finley's work, we see sculptures inherent now to the Texas landscape: where one can be assured of its existence almost to the point of taking it for granted. Through Finley's photographs and Henderson's chapter, we are able re-see these sculptures both historically and in the contemporary moment. Her photographs bring a new resonance to Adickes's sculptures, a new way of seeing how the contemporary moment may view or experience his work and how that may continue to change.

"In His Own Words" provides Adickes's recollections of his life and career. His stories tell the reader of his youth and lifelong adventures, a career and life marked by artistic endeavor and entrepreneurial spirit. His memories take us from Huntsville, Texas, to Paris, to Houston, to Spain, to Antibes, to Japan—always returning to Texas as the center of his art career. We witness an artist committed to his style and his work, continuing to work and strategize every day. We learn about how his upbringing, travels, and friendships have marked his career.

Adickes's career is remarkable in part because of his longevity. It spans movements and trends, and he has achieved pinnacles of success. He rose to prominence in the Texas art scene at a climactic moment in global modernism. His European sensibility seemed avant-garde in Texas for a time, but during a period of social and artistic transformation, it began to seem like a pastiche of a bygone era. When dismissed, ignored, and even scorned by critics and curators, Adickes persisted and was successful on his own terms. He created works that will remain in the public consciousness long after many of the artists who were favorites of his critics have been forgotten. It is likely that Adickes's work is seen by more people than any other Texas artist. Tens, if not hundreds, of thousands of people pass by his sculptures each day. He has made his work impossible to ignore, and it will not easily be forgotten.

# Appendix

## Selected Chronology

Michael H. Henderson and Melissa L. Mednicov[1]

**1927** Born in Huntsville, Texas.

**1943** Graduates from Huntsville High School.

**1943–44** Attends Texas A&M studying engineering and playing clarinet in the marching band.

**1944–45** ROTC at LSU

**1945–46** US Army Air Corps

**1948** BS Physics/Mathematics, Sam Houston State University (at the time Sam Houston State College). Takes painting class with May Schow and art classes at the college's field school in Puebla, Mexico.

**1948** Studies at the Kansas City Art Institute, Kansas City, Missouri.

**1948–50** Lives in Paris and studies at the Atelier Fernand Léger, Paris, France. Meets Herb Mears.

**1948** Robert Preusser and Frank Dolejska founded the Contemporary Arts Association; later to become the Contemporary Arts Museum, Houston.

**1951** Returns to Houston.

**1951** Houston Art League Fair (rented booth with Herb Mears), Shamrock Hilton Hotel, Houston, Texas. Adickes meets Ben DuBose at the fair.

**1951** Participates in *26th Annual Exhibition of Works by Houston Artists* at the Museum of Fine Arts, Houston (MFAH), juried by William Lester and is awarded a solo corridor exhibition of fifteen works at MFAH.

**1951** *Paintings and Drawings by David Adickes*, Museum of Fine Arts, Houston, Texas.

**1951** Herb Mears moves to Houston, Texas.

**1951** Briefly opens an art school in Houston, Texas, with Herb Mears.

**1951** *13th Annual Exhibition of Texas Painting and Sculpture*, Texas General/Annual; Cash Prize and Recommended for Purchase Prize; *Harlequins* (gouache). Exhibit traveled to MFAH, Dallas Museum of Art, and the Witte Museum (San Antonio, Texas).

**1952** *Texas Watercolor Society 3rd Annual Exhibition*, at the Witte Museum, San Antonio, Texas, Purchase Prize, *Composition*, and Cash Prize, *Still Life with Coffee Urn*.

**1952** *5th Southwestern Exhibition of Prints and Drawings*, Dallas Museum of Art, Dallas, Texas.

**1953–66** Solo and group exhibitions at James Bute Gallery with Ben DuBose.

**1953** *28th Annual Exhibition of Works by Houston Artists*, MFAH, Houston Annual Purchase Prize, *Beach Scene*, and Honorable Mention, *Fishermen on Beach*.

**1953** *Texas Watercolor Society 4th Annual Exhibition*, Witte Museum, San Antonio, Texas, Purchase Prize, *7 of the Species*, and Materials Prize, *View of the Village*. Exhibition traveled to: MFAH, Dallas Museum of Art, Texas A&M University (College Station), Texas A&M University (Kingsville), and Centennial Museum (Corpus Christi).

**1953** Texas Fine Arts Association (Spring Festival), Purchase Prize, *Harlequins*.

**1953** Texas Fine Arts Association (Fall Annual), Purchase Prize, *Three By Sea*.

**1953–54** Spends eighteen months in Spain and France, funded by sales of shares of paintings he completes while traveling.

**1954** Exhibit of works sold through shares.

**1954** *29th Annual Exhibition of Works by Houston Artists*, MFAH, Houston Annual, *Three Figures before a Black Boat* (Cash Prize).

**1954** *16th Annual Exhibition of Texas Painting and Sculpture 1954*, Texas General/Annual, *Risque-Tout*; Cash Prize. Exhibition traveled to: Dallas Museum of Art; Witte Museum; Museum of Fine Arts, Houston; and Fort Worth Art Center (Fort Worth, Texas).

**1955** (March) *30th Annual Exhibition of Works by Houston Artists*, Museum of Fine Arts, Houston, Texas, *Spanish Interior* (Purchase Prize).

**1955** (December) *31st Annual Exhibition of Houston Artists*, Museum of Fine Arts, Houston, Texas, *In Attendance* (Purchase Prize).

**1955** *17th Annual Exhibition of Texas Painting and Sculpture, 1955–1956*. Exhibition traveled to: Dallas Museum of Art, Fort Worth Art Center, Witte Museum, and Texas Fine Arts Association (Austin).

**1954–55** Instructor at the University of Texas, Austin.

**1956** Spends eight weeks of summer painting in Tahiti.

**1956** *Annual Spring Show*, Texas Fine Arts Association, First Prize, *Harlequin with Banjo*.

**1956** *6th Annual Southwestern Exhibition of Prints and Drawings,* Dallas Museum of Art (Dallas, Texas). Purchase Prize (1956), *Two Men on a Beach.* Exhibition traveled to: Centenary College (Shreveport, Louisiana); Elisabet Ney Museum (Austin, Texas); University of New Mexico (Albuquerque); Texas Tech College Museum (Lubbock, Texas); Museum of Fine Arts, Houston; University of Tulsa (Tulsa, Oklahoma); and Oklahoma A&M College (Stillwater, Oklahoma).

**1956** *Gulf-Caribbean Art Exhibition,* Museum of Fine Arts, Houston, traveled to: Dallas Museum of Art, Institute of Contemporary Art (Boston, Massachusetts), Munson-Williams-Proctor Institute (Utica, New York).

**1956** *D. D. Feldman Collection of Contemporary Art,* Museum of Fine Arts, Houston, Merit Award: *The Poets.*

**1957** *7th Annual Southwestern Exhibition of Prints and Drawings,* Dallas Museum of Art, Dallas, Texas.

**1957** Solo exhibition at Witte Museum, San Antonio, Texas.

**1957** Group exhibition, *Recent Contemporary Acquisitions—Houston,* Contemporary Arts Museum, Houston, Texas.

**1957** Solo exhibition, Laguna Gloria Gallery, Austin, Texas.

**1957** *32nd Annual Houston Artists Exhibition,* Museum of Fine Arts, Houston, Texas.

**1957** *David Pryor Adickes,* Dallas Museum of Art, Dallas, Texas.

**1957** *Survey of Painting in Texas,* Dallas Museum of Art, Dallas, Texas, circulated by American Federation of Arts.

**1957–58** Spends one year in Tokyo and Kyoto, Japan. Solo exhibitions at Formes Gallery, Tokyo and Osaka, Japan. Meets James Michener in Tokyo.

**1959–64** Acquires studio in Antibes, France, and spends one year there and then divides time between Houston and Antibes. Exhibits in Houston at DuBose Gallery, New York, California, and throughout Texas.

**1959** *60 Prints by 60 Artists from Local Collections: Post-War Prints, 1946–1959,* Dallas Museum of Art, Dallas, Texas.

**1959** *34th Annual Houston Artists Exhibition,* Museum of Fine Arts, Houston, Texas.

**1959** *Made in Texas by Texans,* Dallas Museum of Contemporary Art, Sheraton-Dallas Hotel, Dallas, Texas.

**1959** Solo exhibition at Janet Nessler Gallery, New York, New York.

**1959** *21st Annual Texas Painting and Sculpture Exhibition, 1959–1960,* travels to Dallas Museum of Art; Witte Museum, San Antonio; Beaumont Museum; Museum, Texas Tech, Lubbock; and Museum of Fine Arts, Houston.

**1961** Solo exhibition, Galerie de la Vieille Échoppe, St. Paul-de-Vence, France.

**1961–62** Solo exhibition, Haydon Calhoun Gallery, Dallas, Texas.

**1962** Solo exhibition, Fifth Ave. Gallery, Fort Worth, Texas.

**1962** *24th Annual Texas Painting and Sculpture Exhibition, 1962–1963*, travels to Witte Museum, San Antonio; Centennial Art Museum, Corpus Christi; Beaumont Art Museum, Beaumont; and Dallas Museum of Art, Dallas, Texas.

**1962** Solo exhibition, Steward-Ricard Gallery, San Antonio, Texas.

**1963** *34th Annual Dallas County Exhibition: Painting, Drawing, Sculpture*, Dallas Museum of Art, Dallas, Texas.

**1963** *25th Annual Texas Painting and Sculpture Exhibition, 1963–1964*, traveled to Dallas Museum of Art, Dallas; Centennial Art Museum, Corpus Christi; Beaumont Art Museum, Beaumont; El Paso Museum of Art, El Paso; Witte Museum of Art, San Antonio; and University of Texas at Austin.

**1963** *University of Texas Art Faculty—Past and Present*, Museum of Fine Arts, Houston, Texas.

**1966** Ben DuBose opens the Ben DuBose Gallery at 2950 Kirby, Houston, Texas (May). Adickes regularly exhibits at the gallery.

**1966** Begins working with tapestries.

**1967** Opens Love Street Light Circus and Feel Good Machine in Houston, Texas. Adickes ends his involvement the following year.

**1970** Solo and group exhibitions Wally Findlay Galleries, New York and Palm Beach, Florida.

**1973** *The Michener Collection: American Paintings from the Twentieth Century*, in the Michener Galleries at the University of Texas, Austin.

**1983** *Virtuoso*, Lyric Center, Houston, Texas.

**1984** *Stone Trumpet*, Louisiana World Exposition, New Orleans, Louisiana, *Big Alex*, Montrose, Houston, Texas.

**1987** *Stone Trumpet* installed on The Strand, Galveston, Texas.

**1990** *Winds of Change*, Bush Intercontinental Airport, Houston, Texas.

**1994** *A Tribute to Courage*, Interstate 45, Huntsville, Texas.

**1994** Visits Mount Rushmore.

**1996** Establishes Sculpture Works Studio, 2500 Summer Street in Houston, Texas. Begins work on President Heads.

**2003–10** *Presidents Park*, Lead, South Dakota. First set of presidential busts.

**2004–10** *Presidents Park*, Williamsburg, Virginia. Second set of presidential busts.

**2006** *Stephen F. Austin*, Angleton, Texas. *Denton Cooley*, Texas Heart Institute, Houston, Texas.

**2007** *The Beatles*, 8th Wonder Brewery, Houston, Texas.

**2008** *Founders of Houston Art: Thirty Artists Who Led the Way*, William Reaves Fine Art, Houston, Texas.

**2009** Purchases Huntsville High School building in Huntsville, Texas. Exhibits paintings in renovated auditorium and gymnasium galleries until 2019 when he sells building to Sam Houston State University.

**2011** *Standing Tall with Charlie Wilson*, Charles Wilson VA Hospital, Lufkin, Texas.

**2012** *American Statesmanship Park* (a.k.a. *Mount Rush Hour*) Interstate 10, Houston, Texas.

**2013** *Pat Summitt Statue*, Knoxville, Tennessee. Moves Sculpture Works Studio to 2401 Nance Street in Houston, Texas.

**2018** *Onward*, Baytown, Texas.

**2021** *Three Colorful Friendly Trees*, installed on Heights Boulevard in "True North 2021," Houston, Texas.

**2022** Solo exhibitions, Reeves Art + Design Gallery, Houston, Texas.

**2023** "David Adickes: Bronzes from the Past," Redbud Arts Center, Houston, Texas.

**2023** *John F. Kennedy,* installed on JFK Boulevard near the entrance to Houston Intercontinental Airport, Aldine, Texas.

**2024** David Adickes continues to work in his painting and sculpture studios and exhibit new work.

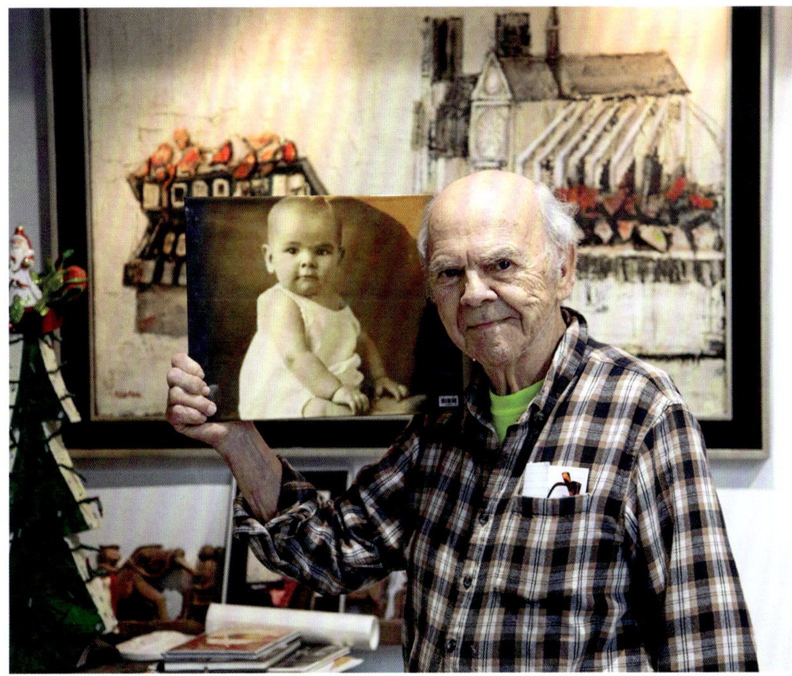

**Figure 7.1.** Photograph of David Adickes, 2021, by Rebecca Finley.

# Notes

## Chapter 1

1. Madge Thornall Roberts, *The Personal Correspondence of Sam Houston: Volume IV 1852–1863* (Denton: University of North Texas Press, 2001), 267.

2. Tori Brooks, "Hot Wheels Co-creator, 80, dies in Huntsville," *Huntsville Item,* August 9, 2011.

3. Katie Robinson Edwards, *Midcentury Modern Art in Texas* (Austin: University of Texas Press, 2014), 184–85.

4. Edwards, *Midcentury Modern Art in Texas,* 1.

5. Edwards, 169.

6. Edwards, 169. Additionally, Sarah C. Reynolds cites 1950 as the beginning of a surge of change in Houston: "From 1950 to 1975, Houston underwent explosive change, growing from an incubator of yet-to-be-realized dreams into a renowned metropolis—a center not only of commerce and political power but also of the arts." Sarah C. Reynolds, *Houston Reflections: Art in the City, 1950s, 60s, 70s* (Houston: Rice University Press, 2008), xi.

7. Edwards, *Midcentury Modern Art in Texas,* 327n44.

## Chapter 2

1. Interview with David Adickes, November 16, 2020. The artist was unable to specifically date the work and noted this was the only time the James Bute Gallery had an artist paint a holiday work. The artist estimates the date as 1952–53. The work remains in Adickes's collection. The work is titled *Three Wise Men* and dated to 1954 by William E. Reaves in William Reaves, "Traveling with David Adickes: The Zestful Journey of a Texas Artiste," in *Adickes . . . Early: Fifty Paintings from the Formative Period* (Houston: William Reaves Fine Art, 2009), 5–6. Exhibition October 9–24, 2009.

2. Katie Robinson Edwards, *Midcentury Modern Art in Texas* (Austin: University of Texas Press, 2015), 176. The Contemporary Arts Association became the Contemporary Arts Museum (CAM, now Contemporary Arts Museum Houston [CAMH]) in 1949. See also Katie Robinson Edwards, Jim Edwards, and Mark L. Smith's *Texas Modern: The Rediscovery of Early Texas Abstraction (1935–1965)* (Waco, TX: Martin Museum of Art Baylor University, 2007) for a brief overview of Texas modernism.

3. Carolyn Lanchner, "Fernand Léger: American Connections," in *Fernand Léger* (New York: Museum of Modern Art, 1998), 58.

4. Lanchner, "Fernand Léger: American Connections," 58.

5. Nancy Stone, "David Adickes: Archetypes of a Changing Scene," *Southwest Art* (July 1980): 100.

6. Lanchner, "Fernand Léger: American Connections," 59.

7. Edwards, *Midcentury Modern Art in Texas,* 5.

8. Edwards, 169.

9. Edwards, 169.

10. Edwards, 185.

11. Edwards, 184–85. Edwards includes some of the biographical information summarized. Also, see "In His Own Words."

12. Richard Stout quoted in Pete Gershon, *Collision: The Contemporary Art Scene in Houston, 1972–1985* (College Station: Texas A&M University Press, 2018), 45.

13. Gershon, *Collision*, 45.

14. Edwards, *Midcentury Modern Art in Texas*, 185.

15. See "In His Own Words."

16. Gershon, *Collision*, 193. Gershon includes Richard Stout, Dick Wray, Jim Love, and Jack Boynton with Adickes.

17. Edwards, *Midcentury Modern Art in Texas*, 185. Also, see "In His Own Words."

18. Reaves, "Traveling with David Adickes," 3.

19. Sarah C. Reynolds, ed., "David Pryor Adickes," in *Houston Reflections: Art in the City, 1950s, 60s, and 70s* (Houston: Rice University Press, 2008), 3.

20. Edwards, *Midcentury Modern Art in Texas*, 184.

21. Reynolds, "David Pryor Adickes," 3.

22. Reynolds, 3.

23. For a thorough double biography of John and Dominique de Menil, see William Middleton's *Double Vision: The Unerring Eye of Art World Avatars Dominique and John de Menil* (New York: Knopf, 2018).

24. A. Cantey, *Adickes: A Monograph* (Houston: James Bute Gallery, 1962), n.p.

25. Cantey, *Adickes: A Monograph*.

26. Cantey.

27. Edwards, *Midcentury Modern Art in Texas*, 185.

28. Katie Robinson Edwards, "Liberty and Lone Star Modernism," in *The Art of Texas: 250 Years*, ed. Ron Tyler (Fort Worth: Center for Texas Studies at TCU and Texas Christian University Press, 2019), 372.

29. Edwards, "Liberty and Lone Star Modernism," 373.

30. Edwards, *Midcentury Modern Art in Texas*, 44n327.

31. Ann Holmes, "Houston: New Interests," in *Art in America* 51 (January 1963): 136–38 at 138.

32. Interview with Leila McConnell, December 17, 2020.

33. Interview with William E. and Linda J. Reaves, December 15, 2020.

34. Interview with William E. and Linda J. Reaves, December 15, 2020.

35. Edwards, *Midcentury Modern Art in Texas*, 62. The annual event (by that time called the "Annual Exhibitions of Houston Artists") ended in 1961 when James Johnson Sweeney became director of the MFAH, replaced by a national juried show (201). By the 1950s, the museum only received Texas art into its collection via donation and the annual purchase prize. Greene, Alison de Lima. *Texas: 150 Works from the Museum of Fine Arts, Houston*. (Houston: Museum of Fine Arts, Houston, distributed by Harry N. Abrams, 2000), 18.

36. Greene, *Texas: 150 Works from the Museum of Fine Arts, Houston*, 264.

37. "David Pryor Adickes," *Houston Reflections: Art in the City, 1950s, 60s and 70s*, 4.

38. "David Pryor Adickes," *Houston Reflections: Art in the City, 1950s, 60s and 70s*, 4. See also "In His Own Words."

39. Reaves, "Traveling with Adickes," 5. For the Houston Annual, Adickes was awarded the Purchase Prize in 1953, 1955 (March and December), Cash Prize in 1954, and an Honorable Mention in 1953. For the Texas General/Annual, he was recommended for the Purchase Prize in 1951 and the Cash Prize in 1951 and 1954. For the Texas Watercolor Society, he was awarded the Purchase Prize in 1952 and 1953, the Cash Prize in 1952, and the Materials Prize in 1953. For the Texas Fine Arts Association, he was awarded the Purchase Prize in spring and fall 1953 and First Prize in 1956. Prize and placements information provided by Sarah Foltz and the Foltz Fine Art Gallery archives. Accessed on December 21, 2020.

40. Greene, *Texas: 150 Works from the Museum of Fine Arts, Houston*, 21.

41. Greene, 22. She reframes these events as a somewhat positive legacy for Texas art in that Sweeney created new expectations for Texas artists. Greene, 22. The MFAH "renewed" its commitment to showing Texas artists in the 1980s, beginning with Barbara Rose and Susie Kalil's *Fresh Paint: The Houston School* exhibition in 1985. Greene, 25–27.

42. Interview with Leila McConnell, December 17, 2020.

43. Greene, *Texas: 150 Works from the Museum of Fine Arts, Houston*, 22.

44. Alison de Lima Greene, "Modernism in Houston" *Art Lies* 41 (Winter 2003): 19–23; at 23. https://texashistory.unt.edu/ark:/67531/metapth228006/, accessed November 28, 2020, University of North

Texas Libraries, The Portal to Texas History, https://texashistory.unt.edu.

45. Much of this analysis is informed by Randy Tibbits; I am grateful for his analysis and sharing of Houston's art history. Interview with Randy Tibbits, December 17, 2020.

46. Ben DuBose, *New Paintings by David Adickes* (Houston: James Bute River Oaks Gallery, 1962). Exhibition December 14–31.

47. Susie Kalil, "Dynamic Pioneers: A Brief History of Painting in Houston," in Barbara Rose and Susie Kalil, eds., *Fresh Paint: The Houston School*, Museum of Fine Arts, Houston (Austin: Museum of Fine Arts, Houston, and Texas Monthly Press, 1985), 25.

48. Interview with Adickes, November 16, 2020.

49. Kalil, "Dynamic Pioneers: A Brief History of Painting in Houston," 25–26.

50. Kalil, 26–27.

51. Kalil, 27.

52. Kalil, 26.

53. Susie Kalil, *The Color of Being/El Color del Ser: Dorothy Hood, 1918–2000* (College Station: Texas A&M University Press, 2016), 70.

54. "David Pryor Adickes," *Houston Reflections*, 3.

55. "David Pryor Adickes," *Houston Reflections*, 5.

56. Gershon, *Collision*, 47.

57. Interview with David Adickes, November 16, 2020. Gershon, *Collision*, 47.

58. "David Pryor Adickes," *Houston Reflections*, 4.

59. "David Pryor Adickes," *Houston Reflections*, 4.

60. Interview with William E. and Linda J. Reaves, December 17, 2020. Interview with Randy Tibbits, December 18, 2020.

61. Interview with Kirby Mears, January 4, 2021.

62. "Herb Mears," *Houston Reflections*, 79.

63. "Herbert Richard Mears (1923–1999)," Foltz Fine Art artist page: https://foltzgallery.com/artist/herb-mears. Website accessed by the author on November 28, 2020.

64. Campbell Geeslin, *Adickes: A Monograph*, compiled for the James Bute Company's River Oaks Gallery by Ben J. DuBose, Houston, 1957, exhibition catalog, unpaginated.

65. Geeslin, *Adickes: A Monograph*.

66. See "In His Own Words."

67. "Herb Mears," *Houston Reflections*, 80.

68. "Herb Mears," *Houston Reflections*, 81.

69. "Herb Mears," *Houston Reflections*, 81.

70. Interview with Kirby Mears, January 4, 2021. The Mears family spent 1967–68 in Antibes, France, staying in Adickes's apartment. Mears describes a visit from David Adickes during that period, watching his father and Adickes paint side by side in the studio and observing their friendship.

71. Edwards, *Midcentury Modern Art in Houston*, 185.

72. Edwards, 186.

73. "Leila McConnell (b. 1923)," Foltz Fine Art artist page: https://foltzgallery.com/artist/leila-mcconnell. Website accessed by the author on November 28, 2020. She joined the Ben DuBose Gallery when he opened his own space. Interview with Leila McConnell, December 17, 2020.

74. "Leila McConnell," *Houston Reflections*, 78.

75. Interview with Leila McConnell, December 17, 2020.

76. Interview with Leila McConnell, December 17, 2020.

77. Interview with Leila McConnell, December 17, 2020.

78. "Henri Gadbois (1930–2018)," Foltz Fine Art artist page: https://foltzgallery.com/artist/henri-gadbois. Website accessed by the author on November 28, 2020.

79. "Henri Gadbois," *Houston Reflections*, 47.

80. "Henri Gadbois," *Houston Reflections*, 47.

81. "Henri Gadbois," *Houston Reflections*, 47–48.

82. "David Pryor Adickes," *Houston Reflections*, 5.

83. Interview with Larry Martin, December 17, 2020.

84. Interview with Leila McConnell, December 17, 2020.

85. "Kermit Oliver," *Houston Reflections*, 100.

86. Interview with Kirby Mears, January 4, 2021.

87. Eleanor Freed, "Texas Round Up," *Art in America* 56 (1968): 102–5; at 102.

88. Freed, "Texas Round Up," 102.

89. Freed, 102.

90. Freed, 102.

91. Freed, 102.

92. Scott Grant Barker, "An Unconventional Vision: Remembering the Fort Worth Circle," in Scott Grant Barker and Jane Myers, *Intimate Modernism: Fort Worth Circle Artists in the 1940s* (Fort Worth: Amon Carter Museum, 2008), 11.

93. Edwards, *Midcentury Modern Art in Texas*, 1.

94. Susan J. Baker and Randy Tibbits, "Bayou Bohemia: Early Modernism in Houston," *Art Inquiries* 18, no. 3 (2018): 284.

95. Baker and Tibbits, "Bayou Bohemia," 289.

96. Baker and Tibbits, 290.

97. Baker and Tibbits, 290.

98. Edwards, *Midcentury Modern Art in Texas*, 180. Preusser left Texas to work at the Massachusetts Institute of Technology in 1954. Edwards, 202.

99. Edwards, 61.

100. Edwards, 61.

101. Edwards, 171–72. Additionally, Alison de Lima Greene states the AFA Convention "marked a turning point in Houston's involvement in contemporary art." Greene, *Texas: 150 Works from the Museum of Fine Arts, Houston*, 129.

102. Edwards, *Midcentury Modern Art in Texas*, 174–75.

103. Greene, *Texas: 150 Works from the Museum of Fine Arts, Houston*, 130.

104. *Adickes: A Portfolio with Critique by James Michener and a Critique in French by Alessandra Cantey* (Houston: Dubose Gallery, 1968), unpaginated.

105. *Adickes: A Portfolio*.

106. Upon Michener's death, he donated $10 million for the establishment of the University of Texas, Austin, art museum, A UTNEWS article published on October 17, 1997: https://news.utexas.edu/1997/10/17/university-of-texas-at-austin-loses-great-friend-in-death-of-james-michener/. Website accessed by author on July 16, 2020.

107. Honolulu Museum of Art website: https://honolulumuseum.org/stories/2019/05/asian-art-2/talking-story-across-the-us-about-homas-japanese-print-collection/. Accessed by author on February 3, 2021.

108. James A. Michener, "The Collector: An Informal Memoir," in *The James A. Michener Collection: Twentieth Century American Painting* (Austin: University Art Museum: The University of Texas, Austin, 1977), viiii.

109. A. N. "David Adickes," in *The James A. Michener Collection*, 4.

110. A. N. "David Adickes," in *The James A. Michener Collection*, 4. Quote reflects A. N.'s spelling of Hawai'i.

111. A. N. "David Adickes," in *The James A. Michener Collection*, 3–4.

112. A. N. "David Adickes," in *The James A. Michener Collection*.

113. Eleanor Freed, "Windfall for Texas" *Art in America* 57 (1969): 78–85; at 78.

114. Louise Siddons, *Centering Modernism: J. Jay McVicker and Postwar American Art* (Norman: University of Oklahoma Press, 2018), 30.

115. Siddons, *Centering Modernism*, 5. Siddons's use of italics.

116. Siddons, *Centering Modernism*, 30.

117. "David Pryor Adickes," *Houston Reflections*, 6.

118. "David Pryor Adickes," *Houston Reflections*, 6.

119. Vicki Welch Ayo, *Boys from Houston* (CreateSpace Independent Publishing Platform, 2013), 332.

120. Sara Gredler, "Love Street Light Circus Feel Good Machine," *Handbook of Texas Online*, accessed December 14, 2020, www.tshaonline.org/handbook/entries/love-street-light-circus-feel-good-machine. Published by the Texas State Historical Association.

121. "David Pryor Adickes," *Houston Reflections*, 6.

## Chapter 3

1. J. G., "David Adickes [Wally F]," *ArtNews* (November 1970): 17.

2. W. D. A., "Adickes at Wally F," *Arts Magazine* (September/October 1970): 61.

3. Thomas McEvilly, "Double Vision in Space City: 'The Houston School' of Barbara Rose and Susie Kalil; William Camfield's Houston Artists," *ArtForum* (April 1985): 52–56.

4. Susie Kalil, "Dynamic Pioneers: A Brief History of Painting in Houston," in Barbara Rose and Susie Kalil, eds., *Fresh Paint: The Houston School* (Houston: Museum of Fine Arts, Houston; Austin: Texas Monthly Press, 1985), 25.

5. Linda Wiley, *Making It Happen: Exploring the Creative Process through the Sculptures of David Adickes* (Austin: My Own Backyard Press, 1996), 146.

6. Hubley worked at UPA—the United Productions of America —an animation production company that pioneered the modern style of cartoons.

7. Amid Amidi, *Cartoon Modern: Style and Design in Fifties Animation* (San Francisco: Chronicle Books, 2006), 7.

8. Clement Greenberg, "Avant Garde and Kitsch," in *Art and Culture* (Boston: Beacon Press, 1961), 10.

9. Wiley, *Making It Happen*, 9.

10. Wiley, 10.

11. Wiley, 23–24.

12. See the introduction herein.

13. Wiley, *Making It Happen*, 41.

14. Unattributed, "Adickes Talks About Creating Summitt Statue," first published on November 21, 2013, University of Tennessee Athletics website: https://utsports.com/news/2013/11/21/Adickes_Talks_About_Creating_Summitt_Statue.aspx. Accessed by author on July 5, 2021.

15. Wiley, *Making It Happen*, 74–75.

16. Wiley, 107.

17. Interview with David Adickes, June 7, 2021.

18. Wiley, *Making It Happen*, 98.

19. Emily Fourmy Cutrer, *The Art of the Woman: The Life and Work of Elisabet Ney* (College Station: Texas A&M University Press, 2016), 1. Ebook accessed July 3, 2021.

20. Cutrer, *Art of the Woman*, xi.

21. Cutrer, 124.

22. Curter cites Thomas J. Hurley's letter to a Travis County judge. Cutrer, *Art of the Woman*, 124.

23. Patricia D. Hendricks and Becky Duval Reese, *A Century of Sculpture in Texas, 1889–1989* (Austin: University of Texas Press, 1989; Archer M. Huntington Art Gallery), 10.

24. Hendricks and Reese, *A Century of Sculpture in Texas*, 10.

25. Cutrer, *Art of the Woman*, 126.

26. Cutrer, 133.

27. Cutrer, 134.

28. Wiley, *Making It Happen*, 81.

29. Wiley, 80.

30. Cutrer, *Art of the Woman*, 139.

31. Cutrer, 139.

32. Alan Turner, "State Father's Tribute Will Be Larger Than Life," first published on December 14, 2004, *Houston Chronicle*: www.chron.com/news/houston-texas/article/State-father-s-tribute-will-be-larger-than-life-1985073.php, accessed by author on July 5, 2021.

33. It cannot be ignored that Adickes's two largest sculptures are of white men who were slave owners. Popular versions of Texas history pay little attention to this and the fact that Texas sought independence from Mexico in order to keep slavery legal and attract white immigrants. Adickes and Ney created the statues of Austin and Houston to celebrate Texas history. Like some versions of Texas history, they mythologize politicians as "founding fathers" and unassailable heroes. The statues of Houston and Austin support this mythology. Stephen F. Austin's promotion of slavery is well documented and remains attached to him. Sam Houston refused to lead Texas in the Confederacy, was removed as governor, and was ostracized for his support of the Union. He was also known to have close relationships with Native Americans and supported them in his government positions. Adickes emphasizes Houston's stand against slavery in *A Tribute to Courage.*

34. Susan Warren, "Concrete Cowboy: Sculptor of Tall Art Sets Sights Higher," first published on January 18, 2006, *Wall Street Journal*: www.wsj.com/articles/SB113755479869549378, accessed by author on July 5, 2021.

35. John T. Paoletti and Rolf Bagemihl, *Michelangelo's David: Florentine History and Civic Identity* (Cambridge: Cambridge University Press, 2015), 54. E-Book accessed July 4, 2021.

36. Paoletti and Bagemihl, *Michelangelo's David.*

37. Paoletti and Bagemihl.

38. See "In His Own Words."

39. Erin McCann, "There's a Failed Mount Rushmore in the Middle of Virginia," from Ranker.com, published on May 8, 2019. Date accessed by author: July 5, 2021, www.ranker.com/list/story-of-virginias-presidents-park/erin-mccann.

40. Photographs by Hannah Price and text by Mark Leibovich, "Heads of State," the Voyages Issue, Photographic Dispatches from the Extremities of the Earth, the *New York Times Magazine,* September 24, 2019. Date accessed by author: July 5, 2021, www.nytimes.com/interactive/2019/09/24/magazine/presidents-park-photos.html.

41. Josh Reyes, "Giant Set of Presidential Busts Get[s] Second Life as an Attraction, Still Await[s] Permanent Future," *Daily Press,* August 21, 2019, date accessed by author: July 5, 2019. www.dailypress.com/entertainment/dp-nw-president-heads-williamsburg-new-life-20190829-jwpoigj6nze7vcfoenibvg4q6a-story.html.

42. Dane Schiller, "Heady Art in Plain Sight: American Statesmanship Park," *Houston Chronicle,* September 5, 2013, date accessed by author: July 5, 2021, www.houstonchronicle.com/news/houston-texas/houston/article/Heady-art-in-plain-sight-American-Statesmanship-4791003.php#photo-5144433.

43. Unattributed, "We Love Houston: The History of EADO's Beloved Attraction," *EaDo,* May 16, 2019, accessed by author July 5, 2021, https://eadohouston.com/news/we-love-houston-the-history-of-eados-beloved-attraction/, May 16, 2019.

44. Unattributed, "We Love Houston."

45. See "In His Own Words."

46. Unattributed, "David Adickes Adds "ART" to the Silos at Sawyer Yards," *Houston Chronicle,* November 2, 2015, accessed by the author July 5, 2021, www.chron.com/culture/main/article/David-Adickes-adds-ART-to-the-scene-6606250.php.

47. Craig Hlavaty, "Tall Texas Sam Houston to Tower Over Baytown, Created by artist David Adickes," *Houston Chronicle,* October 30, 2018, accessed by the author July 5, 2021, www.chron.com/neighborhood/baytown-news/article/Tall-Texan-Sam-Houston-to-tower-over-Baytown-13347864.php.

48. Norman Rockwell Museum, "Illustration History: Iwao Takamoto," www.illustrationhistory.org/artists/iwao-takamoto, accessed by author July 5, 2021.

## Appendix

1. The authors express gratitude to Sarah Foltz for the use of her artist files and artist chronologies which form the basis of and create the foundation and structure for this chronology. We also are grateful to the materials gathered by William E. Reaves's exhibition records and gallery publications. Chronology includes selected exhibitions.

# Selected Bibliography


*Adickes: A Portfolio with Critique by James A. Michener and a Critique in French by Alessandra Cantey*. Houston: Dubose Gallery, 1968.

Amidi, Amid. *Cartoon Modern: Style and Design in Fifties Animation*. San Francisco: Chronicle Books, 2006.

Baker, Susan J., and Randy Tibbits. "Bayou Bohemia: Early Modernism in Houston." *Art Inquiries* 18, no. 3 (2018): 278–93.

Barker, Scott Grant, and Jane Myers. *Intimate Modernism: Fort Worth Circle Artists in the 1940s*. Fort Worth: Amon Carter Museum, 2008.

Cantey, A. *Adickes: A Monograph*. Houston: James Bute Gallery, 1962.

Cutrer, Emily Fourmy. *The Art of the Woman: The Life and Work of Elisabet Ney*. College Station: Texas A&M University Press, 2016.

DuBose, Ben. *New Paintings by David Adickes*. Houston: James Bute River Oaks Gallery, 1962 (exhibition December 14–31).

Edwards, Katie Robinson. *Midcentury Modern Art in Texas*. Austin: University of Texas Press, 2015.

Edwards, Katie Robinson, Jim Edwards, and Mark L. Smith. *Texas Modern: The Rediscovery of Early Texas Abstraction (1935–1965)*. Waco, TX: Martin Museum of Art, Baylor University, 2007.

Freed, Eleanor. "Texas Round Up." *Art in America* 56 (1968): 102–5.

Geeslin, Campbell. *Adickes: A Monograph*. Compiled for the James Bute Company's River Oaks Gallery by Ben J. Dubose, Houston, 1957.

Gershon, Pete. *Collision: The Contemporary Art Scene in Houston, 1972–1985*. College Station: Texas A&M University Press, 2018.

Greenberg, Clement. "Avant Garde and Kitsch." In *Art and Culture*. Boston: Beacon Press, 1961.

Greene, Alison de Lima. "Modernism in Houston." *Art Lies* 41 (Winter 2003): 19–23. *Art Lies* edited by John Bryant. (https://texashistory.unt.edu/ark:/67531/metapth228006/: accessed May 16, 2024), University of North Texas Libraries, The Portal to Texas History, https://texashistory.unt.edu.

———. *Texas: 150 Works from the Museum of Fine Arts, Houston*. Houston: Museum of Fine Arts, Houston, distributed by Harry N. Abrams, 2000.

Hendricks, Patricia D., and Becky Duval Reese. *A Century of Sculpture in Texas, 1889–1989*. Archer M. Huntington Art Gallery. Austin: University of Texas Press, 1989.

Holmes, Ann. "Houston: New Interests." *Art in America*, 51 (1963): 136–38.

*The James A. Michener Collection: Twentieth Century American Painting*. Austin: University Art Museum, University of Texas, 1977.

Kalil, Susie. *The Color of Being/El Color del Ser: Dorothy Hood, 1918–2000*. College Station: Texas A&M University Press, 2016.

———. "Dynamic Pioneers: A Brief History of Painting in Houston." In *Fresh Paint: The Houston School*, edited by Barbara Rose and Susie Kalil, 11–46. Austin: Texas Monthly Press, 1985.

Lanchner, Carolyn, ed. *Fernand Léger*. New York: Museum of Modern Art, 1998.

McEvilly, Thomas. "Double Vision in Space City: 'The Houston School' of Barbara Rose and Susie Kalil: William Camfield's Houston Artists." *ArtForum* 23, no. 8 (April 1985): 52–56.

Middleton, William. *Double Vision: The Unerring Eye of Art World Avatars Dominique and John de Menil*. New York: Knopf, 2018.

Paoletti, John T., and Rolf Bagemihl. *Michelangelo's David: Florentine History and Civic Identity*. Cambridge: Cambridge University Press, 2015.

Reaves, William. *Adickes . . . Early: Fifty Paintings from the Formative Period*. Houston: William Reaves Fine Art, 2009.

Reynolds, Sarah C., ed. *Houston Reflections: Art in the City, 1950s, 60s and 70s*. Houston: Rice University Press, 2008.

Siddons, Louise. *Centering Modernism: J. Jay McVicker and Postwar American Art*. Norman: University of Oklahoma Press, 2018.

Stone, Nancy. "David Adickes: Archetypes of a Changing Scene." *Southwest Art* (July 1980): 99–105.

Tyler, Ron, ed. *The Art of Texas: 250 Years*. Fort Worth: Center for Texas Studies at TCU and TCU Press, 2019.

Wiley, Linda. *Making It Happen: Exploring the Creative Process through the Sculptures of David Adickes*. Austin: My Own Backyard Press, 1996.

# Index

Page numbers in italics refer to illustrations; boldface indicates artwork.